Tipton
COUNTY   TENNESSEE

Tipton
COUNTY TENNESSEE

Gaylon Neil Beasley

Charleston · London
History PRESS

Published by The History Press
Charleston, SC 29403
www.historypress.net

Copyright © 2007 by Gaylon Neil Beasley
All rights reserved

First published 1981 by the Tipton County Historical Society
The History Press edition 2007

Manufactured in the United Kingdom

ISBN 978.1.59629.413.4

Library of Congress CIP data applied for.

Notice: The information in this book is true and complete to the best of our knowledge. It is offered without guarantee on the part of the author or The History Press. The author and The History Press disclaim all liability in connection with the use of this book.

All rights reserved. No part of this book may be reproduced or transmitted in any form whatsoever without prior written permission from the publisher except in the case of brief quotations embodied in critical articles and reviews.

*Dedicated to those citizens of Tipton County who helped
make this book a reality.*

Contents

Preface	9
Acknowledgements	11
The Early Years	13
Communications	21
The Mexican Foe	29
The Civil War	39
Days of Desperate Men	81
Reunion and Dedication	95
Amusements	111
The Courthouse and the Courts	127
The World Wars	137
Disaster Years	159
Tipton County's Own	173
Appendix A Terrific Storm	201
Appendix B Tipton County Men Who Died While in Service	205
Chronology	209
Notes	249
About the Author	255

Preface

As the title implies, this book is a collection of stories about Tipton County and some of her people from early times to the present. It is not, nor is it intended to be, a history of the county *per se*. Instead, an attempt has been made to highlight interesting people and events that have moved across the pages of the county's history. Special care has been taken to bring from the shadows little-known stories rather than to rehash those that have appeared time and again over the years.

To be sure, not every interesting personality or event is included. To have done so would have probably necessitated the printing of a second volume. The stories selected for publication were chosen on the basis of historical importance, available information and/or possible interest to the reader.

In addition to the stories, a chronology has been provided that serves a two-fold purpose. It gives the reader a brief outline of Tipton County history and at the same time places each story of the text into its proper time frame, thus showing how each relates to the rest of the county's history.

In short, this volume represents the efforts of the writer to squeeze as much history as possible into a two-hundred-page book. The result is a potpourri of stories, biographies and pictures, which run the gamut of Tipton County history from early settlement to the present day—from the ring of the pioneer's ax to the soul music of Isaac Hayes.

Acknowledgements

It is impossible for the author to express his gratitude to all who aided in this endeavor. This is especially true in the case of those, too numerous to mention here, who so graciously loaned the use of their photographs. Their contribution to a book of this nature is readily apparent.

It would be remiss, however, not to mention some to whom particular thanks are due. My most special note of gratitude goes to my sister, Mrs. Pat Boswell, who spent countless hours proofreading and typing the manuscript. Special thanks also go to Rhonda Cross and Mrs. Lana Cross Andrews for typing my notes, and to Mrs. Gloria Van Huss for typing the index.

A large measure of gratitude is also owed my fellow board members of the Tipton County Historical Society, not only for their guidance and cooperation but most especially for their confidence in me as a writer. The following is a list of members, both past and present, who have served with me on the board of directors during the course of this project: Professor P.B. Brown, Mrs. Durward Dickey, Floyd Franklin, Mrs. Edith Jones Fyfe, Morgan Fyfe, Peter Fyfe, Mrs. B.S. Jamieson, Albert Kelley, Mrs. Frank McBride Sr., Dr. Rosella McClain, Dr. Bill McCullough, Mrs. T.H. Price, Dr. J.S. Ruffin, Paul Shoaf, Tim Sloan, James A. Smith, Judge Mark A. Walker and Mrs. A.S. Witherington Sr.

Not as evident but of utmost importance was the quiet support and strength maintained throughout by my wife, Claudette. But for her patience and understanding, I would never have been able to write this book.

The Early Years

Mystery of the Bricks

Joseph Williams, in his book *Old Times in West Tennessee*, tells of an early settler finding "a fragment of a well burnt brick" in the vicinity of some ancient mounds on the Hatchie River near Millstone Mountain. The fragment had the well-defined footprint of a goat on it. "To suppose about it," wrote Williams, "would be that the goat left his footprint upon the brick while lying upon the yard, and before it was put into the kiln to be burnt."

The origin of the brick is just as big a mystery today as it was the day it was found. Neither the pre-Columbian race that built the mounds nor their successors in the area, the Chickasaws, are known to have made bricks or to have kept goats. The earliest settlers did not move into what is now Tipton County until after the Chickasaw Treaty of 1818.

A hint that the brick might have been of European origin can be found in the story of the finding of another brick in 1827. In November of that year, Felix D. Robertson was hunting about a mile and a half east of Covington on a ridge running east and west and leading back toward that town. "I found," he wrote, "on the north side a gully washed about 6 ft. deep in which I found a whole brick in the side about 3 feet from [the] surface, and several pieces of less size scattered down the gutter."[1] He described the brick as being "very hard burnt and of the usual size."[2]

Robertson also found what he described as "some other European articles" in the gully but failed to mention what they were.[3] Since it was cold and he was chasing an old buck at the time, he postponed further search and never returned to the spot.

It was Robertson's belief that the location was the site of a camp of the Spanish explorer Hernando De Soto. The depth of the brick indicates that

Millstone Mountain. During the winter, when the foliage is off the trees, the Hatchie River can be seen from its summit.

it certainly could have dated back to that time, but most historians agree that De Soto approached the Mississippi River farther to the south.

Robertson went into great detail in describing the location of his find. He related that it was near several springs: that Daniel Dunham lived farther to the east on the opposite side of the ridge; and that Peter Cheatam lived about a mile to the east. Yet, he wrote not a word of description about the European articles he found. If he had, perhaps the riddle of the bricks could have been solved. As it stands, one can only surmise as to their origin. The mystery probably will forever remain just that.

THE BLACK PATRIARCH

No one really knew how old Shirley Fisher was when he died of a stroke at his home in Covington in June 1898. He was one of the oldest, if not the oldest, man in Tipton County. As nearly as could be figured by descendants of his former master, he was ninety-seven at the time of his death. Some believed, however, that he had reached the century mark or was even older than that. He had come to Tipton County from Nashville in 1823 as the slave of Daniel A. Dunham, and it was known that he was then a grown man.

During his early years Fisher experienced or became familiar with enough interesting incidents to fill a good-sized book. He was personally acquainted with the famous pioneer David Crockett, and before leaving

The Early Years

Nashville, he knew and worked for Andrew Jackson, or "Old Hickory," as he preferred to call him. Sometime in the early 1830s he was stolen by the gang of the infamous John A. Murrell, which intended to sell him in New Orleans. At some point in Mississippi he escaped and returned to his old master in Tipton County.

Fisher cleared the ground for the pitching of a tent from which the first merchandise in Covington was sold. (This was also the site of the first store building in the town.) He also helped to clear the ground for the building of Tipton County's first courthouse and also dug the first grave in Munford Cemetery. He often told of killing many deer in the timber, which then stood around Town Spring.

Sometime in the 1820s Shirley passed into the possession of Dr. Charles G. Fisher, the son-in-law of Daniel Dunham. He was devoted to Dr. Fisher and to his descendants, and the Emancipation Proclamation did nothing to abate his love and devotion to them.

Shirley Fisher was described as straightforward, upright and honest. He was a man of quickness of perception, fine common sense and a rare sense of the ridiculous. Above all he was an excellent Christian man. He was a lifelong member of and a power in the Methodist Church.

The black people regarded Fisher as a patriarch and looked up to him as a man possessing supernatural powers. By the white people he was universally held in the very highest esteem. When he was laid to rest in Hall Cemetery near Covington, his burial was attended by a large number of people of his own race, as well as by several white descendants of his former master in slavery days.

The Big Hatchie Turnpike and Bridge Company

In 1832 certain farsighted citizens of Randolph and Covington organized the Big Hatchie Turnpike and Bridge Company for the purpose of constructing a turnpike from Haywood County to the Hatchie River, with a bridge crossing the river in the vicinity of a place later known as Indian Bluff. Though Randolph was in her heyday as a flourishing river port, her citizens, as well as those of Covington, realized the importance of good roads into the interior country. Likewise the interior towns were interested in an outlet to the Mississippi River for their products.

In the beginning, the company was in essence a private subscription stock company. This being long before the time of liberal state and federal aid for bridges and highways, such improvements depended entirely upon private enterprise.

The original board of directors was composed of John T. Brown, Edmund Booker, Daniel A. Dunham, Nathaniel Potter, Charles G. Fisher, William Harper, Marquis Calmes, George W. Hockley and Dan Vaught, all of Randolph and Covington. Robert W. Sanford and Jacob Tipton were added to the board in 1833 and 1834 respectively.

After organization, the directors began letting contracts for the construction of the turnpike and bridge. Most of the work was done by slaves whose monthly salary of $10 was paid to their owners. Sawyers received monthly wages of $13, while an overseer made $50.

By October 1833 the bridge and a portion of the turnpike were completed and a toll collector was appointed. His job was to collect a specified toll from everyone who passed over the pike and bridge. Toll was charged for those on foot as well as for horseback riders, vehicles and livestock. Some examples follow: man and horse, twelve and a half cents each; loose horses, six and a half cents; hogs and sheep, one cent; cattle, three cents; carry-all wagons, fifty cents; two-wheel carriages, fifty cents; four-wheel phaeton carriages, $1. The only ones exempt from paying the toll were members of the board of directors and ministers known to the toll collector.

Between April and August 1834 the toll gatherer, who had difficulty in collecting tolls, succeeded in collecting only $90. The directors also had the problem of securing a toll gatherer honest enough to turn in all monies collected.

When the turnpike had not been completed by December 1835, the *Randolph Recorder* asked:

> *Can anyone tell us what has become of this Turnpike and Bridge Company, or what is most likely to become of it: Who has the management of it, disposal, &C. and whether there is any probability of its ever being resuscitated? We are astonished that no efforts are apparently made to renew this undertaking and secure the great trade and business that must otherwise shortly find a market through some other channel than Tipton and Randolph. The work is partly complete, and only needs enterprise to complete it. The citizens of Brownsville are determined shortly to have a road to the Mississippi elsewhere, if they can find none safe by way of the Hatchie bottom.*[4]

By the year 1836 it was discovered that the bridge was becoming impassable due to faulty construction. Directors Harper, Fisher, Dunham, Hockley and Calmes, all of Covington, had signed the bridge contractor's security bond guaranteeing the satisfactory completion of the bridge. Thus discredited by other stockholders, the Covington directors soon found

The Early Years

themselves outnumbered on the board by Randolph men. The latter not only changed the place of meeting to Randolph but also began proceedings to compel the Covington guarantors to repair the bridge. The books were also reopened in 1836 for new stock subscriptions at various Tipton County locations and at Brownsville.

The *Recorder* now rejoiced:

> It affords us unusual pleasure to announce that the Hatchie turnpike and Bridge Company is at length attacked with the premonitory symptoms of convalescence. The physicians now managing its case, Messrs. Booker, Vaught and Potter, are not quacks, and will doubtless pursue an energetic and altogether different course with their heretofore abused and neglected patient. It needs much purgative and tonic medicines, as it has had the shakes for the past two or three years.
>
> This object is one of immense importance to our county and Randolph, and its friends should rejoice that such gentlemen as are now advertised as the acting Commissioners are individuals that will act, and we doubt not most efficiently.[5]

No meetings were held by the board in 1837 and apparently no work was done on either the turnpike or the bridge. Financial problems continued to plague the company with directors having trouble collecting money from stockholders who were slow in making payments for subscribed stock. Finally the board negotiated a loan of $1,800 through the Jackson branch of the Bank of Tennessee, but this sum still proved inadequate to meet the company's expenses.

In 1839 the state, now under the control of the Whigs, came to the aid of the company. Governor James K. Polk selected the following men as state directors: J.T. Collier, Robert B. Clarkson, John Postlewaite, Frederick R. Smith, Nathaniel Potter and W.C. Hazen. In addition to these, the board contained directors selected by the stockholders: James Sweeney, Samuel T. Bates, Peyton Smith, R.P. Mitchell, Henry Cotton and William McGuire. Covington was again fixed as the meeting place and specific plans were formulated to complete the turnpike.

The state subscribed to one-half of the stock issued by the company, or $8,000 worth. A provision of the loan stipulated that state money was to be spent only in equal amounts with money collected from delinquent stockholders. Such a small sum was collected, however, that the directors spent the state money despite the provision.

By this time the bridge had been swept away by high water and was abandoned. In its place a ferry was installed with a ferryman hired to

Deputy Sheriff James R. McCall. His efforts resulted in the reestablishment of the old turnpike between Covington and Brownsville.

collect toll. After the state money had been spent, the directors found it even more difficult to collect enough money to meet the necessary expenses. The turnpike fell into such bad repair that few people used it. In fact the ferryman was not able to collect enough toll to pay his $20 per month salary. In 1849, the last year of the company's existence, his books showed that the company owed him $187.54.

   The ferry was soon discontinued and moved a short distance up the river where an important landing was established with a large shed for receiving and storing cotton for shipment. The warehouse was also used as a depot for merchandise and wares. Captain Flem Chaney was the merchant, warehouseman and ferryman.

The Early Years

Through the ensuing years, the familiar scenes of the old turnpike disappeared. Rows of dense forest trees gave way to small plots and patches until the land adjoining the abandoned road was largely under cultivation.

During the summer of 1927, a scouting party headed by Deputy Sheriff James R. McCall made a trip up the old thoroughfare. Though obstructed by treetops, briers, bushes and even medium size trees, the original levee, from three to five feet high, was clearly visible at the edge of the overflow lands. Across the river the levee was again visible, and a short distance from the river was found the remains of the old well at Chaney's landing. It was still about twelve feet deep with a large sweet gum tree growing out of it.

Through the efforts of McCall and the property owners of the section a great road working program was undertaken to reestablish the old turnpike. The road would provide a direct route from Covington to Brownsville, cutting by one-third the distance being traveled by highway between the two county seats. Plans called for the reestablishment of a ferry at the old landing site.

In March 1928, when Judge C.B. McClelland and R.W. Sanford conferred in Nashville with the state highway commissioner, Colonel Harry S. Berry, on the status of proposed state roads in Tipton County, they were informed that the state would maintain the proposed road from Covington to Brownsville if the counties would do the dirt work. The state would immediately assume maintenance of the road once the dirt work had been completed. It was also promised that the state would pave the road at some future date.

The old turnpike was, at last, transformed into the important road envisioned nearly one hundred years before by the members of the Big Hatchie Turnpike and Bridge Company. The new thoroughfare was designated State Highway 54.

Communications

Early Newspapers

Newspapers usually followed close behind settlement. This was due primarily to the low cost of the hand press, a common fixture of the pioneer community. A small printer had little difficulty in acquiring the necessary capital to enter the publishing business and even less difficulty in finding a suitable location for his press. Such a printer was F.S. Latham, who located his press at Randolph in 1834 and established the *Randolph Recorder*, Tipton County's first newspaper.

Latham, a twenty-six-year-old native of New York City, chose Randolph because he thought its position on the Mississippi presented "greater facilities for commercial and other news than any other point or place in the country."[6] He believed that Randolph, not Memphis, would become the principal city of West Tennessee.

Up to this time, the people of Tipton had had to depend on the papers of towns in nearby counties to meet their newspaper needs. Jackson, Paris, Memphis and Bolivar had been the only towns with newspaper facilities in the Western District.

The first edition of the *Recorder* appeared on June 21, 1834, and in it young Latham promised to, each week, give news of local, general and political interest. But it, like most newspapers of the time, gave more space to state and national than to local affairs. Most of the news was gathered from other journals subscribed to by the editor, and because of his dependence upon them, wet or late mail more than once forced him to suspend publication for periods of two weeks or longer.

Politically, the *Recorder* was anti-Jackson, which meant support of Hugh L. White in the presidential campaign of 1836. The paper also supported the anti-Jackson Democrat Davy Crockett for Congress.

The *Recorder* served the people of Tipton County until September 23, 1836, when Latham announced that he had sold the business. Convinced that Memphis had a brighter future than Randolph, he went into the newspaper business there. The *Recorder*'s new owner, Allen M. Scott, soon moved that paper's press to Brownsville.

Fifteen months later, on January 6, 1838, the first number of the *Randolph Whig* was issued by David M. McPherson, who had his office in a room over the Randolph Post Office. He adopted the title *Whig* "more on account of its brevity than anything else," but it was an appropriate title; like its predecessor, the *Recorder*, it was Whig in character and supported the policies and candidates of that party.[7] In giving the paper's political views, McPherson wrote:

> *It is true that we have taken a stand in politics—the position of*
> *"The man who glides*
> *Between both sides,*
> *And thus escapes a jam."*
> *Will not answer in these times—a neutral course is impossible, in fact out*
> *of the question—consequently we feel an unwillingness to attempt it.*[8]

Described as a splendid and newsy paper, the *Whig* offered its readers news, current prices, agricultural information, literature and science until May 1841, when it failed. McPherson gave hard times as the reason for its demise.

Tipton County's next newspaper was the Covington *Weekly Spy* founded in 1860 by R.C. Russ. Locating his printing office on the second floor of the Masonic hall, west of the public square, Russ filled the pages of his weekly with editorials, letters and poems in praise of the Southern Cause and in defiance of abolitionists. The paper was put out of business in 1862, when Federal troops, on one of their first visits to Covington, destroyed Russ's equipment and threw it down a nearby well.

In August 1867 two young Confederate veterans, William Sanford and Morrison Munford, founded the *Tipton Weekly Record* at Covington. Unlike its predecessors, the *Record* was successful and destined for a long life. One reason for its initial prosperity was its ability to attract advertisers. A look at one of the first copies of the paper shows not only a host of local advertisers but some from as far away as St. Louis and Louisville. Even during the hard times caused by the drought of 1874, when advertising dropped off considerably, the *Record* was able to hold its own.

This, however, was not true in the case of the *West Tennessee Clarion*, founded that year by M. Wood and George Hunt. After almost a year of

Communications

The *Weekly Spy* of May 18, 1861, the only issue of the paper known to have survived, provides a glimpse of what Covington and Tipton County were like at the beginning of the Civil War.

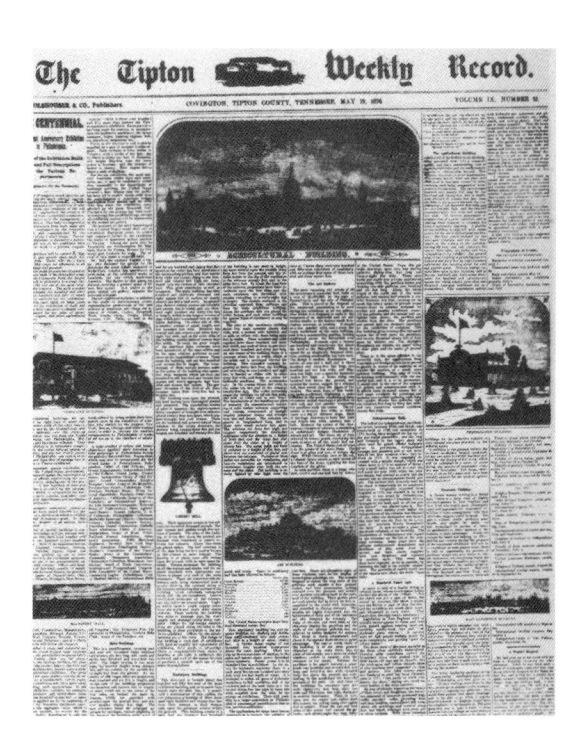

Special centennial edition of the *Tipton Weekly Record*.

struggle, it succumbed in 1875, despite praiseworthy perseverance and energy on the part of its founders. The *Record*, which bought the *Clarion*, gave the following explanation for that paper's failure:

> *Covington is so near Memphis that most of her inhabitants take papers published in that city, and the advertising done by Covington merchants, taken collectively, would scarcely purchase sufficient salt to pickle a jay bird. Divide this by two and the result is—a "bust."*[9]

Mason entered the county newspaper picture in 1879 with the establishment of the *Mason Call* by L.D. Hamner. Though this was his first experience in the newspaper business, Hamner soon gained the reputation of being one of the best all-around country newspapermen in Tennessee.

In November 1881 Hamner moved his operation to Covington and continued the paper's publication under the name of the *Covington Call*. At the same time he sold a half interest in the paper to Joseph Townsend, and early the next year Charles R. Shelton was admitted as an equal partner.

The *Covington Call* was absorbed in 1884 by the *Tipton Record*. Shelton accepted a job with the Government Printing Office in Washington, and Townsend became a member of the book and job printing firm of Rowe, Townsend & Creighton in Memphis. Hamner temporarily retired from the publishing business but returned in October 1886 to found the *Covington Leader*.

In 1888, Hamner took Sam A. Montgomery in as a partner, but later that same year, he again retired from active newspaper management. He was never again the editor of a Covington paper, but later served on the staff of the *Record*. In the interim, he started the *True Light* in Mason in 1892, again retiring from editorship after a short period of time.

The *Leader* purchased the *Tipton Record* in 1917 when that paper's owner, R.H. Green, was appointed Covington postmaster. "The many and exacting duties of the work of postmaster," explained Green, "make it impossible for me to do the work of the post office and also give that time necessary to the successful publication of a newspaper."[10]

At the time of the sale, the *Record* was one of the oldest newspapers in the state. It had been brilliantly edited by a number of men during its fifty-year existence. Besides those already mentioned, the editors included such able gentlemen as Charles B. Simonton, J.C. Boals, Townes Boyd, L.E. Gwinn, J.J. Green, John Green Hall and Samuel P. Rose.

Ownership of the *Leader* remained in local hands until 1965, when it was sold to a new corporation, the Covington Publishing Co., whose stockholders are from various Tennessee cities. As of this writing (1981) the *Leader*, at ninety-five, is the oldest business in Tipton County.

Communications

The *Covington Leader* office as it appeared around 1900.

COMMUNICATION WITH THE WORLD

If a stranger to Tipton County had visited the homes and offices of telephone subscribers in Covington and the immediate vicinity during the middle of March 1939, he would have observed something very curious: side by side on tables and desks throughout the area sat not one but two telephones—the familiar old manual instrument and the latest model in compactness and efficiency, the dial phone. Had he inquired about the situation, he would have been told that the new phones had just been installed and awaited only the throwing of a switch to become operable. Once this had been done, the old magneto instruments would be taken out.

Installation of Covington's dial telephone system began in July 1938, but concentrated efforts were not initiated until September of that year. A new brick building to house the exchange was constructed on Washington Avenue by R.A. Baxter & Son at a cost of $4,000. Equipment for the new central office, which cost the Southern Bell Company $49,576, was installed by workmen from Western Electric, the company that manufactured the new apparatus.

Much of the cable outside the central office had to be replaced to accommodate the new system. All homes, offices and stores with telephone service were rewired to make certain that the dials worked perfectly.

Batteries became a thing of the past under the new system. A unit housed in the central office produced the current for the entire exchange, removing the necessity of changing batteries in homes and offices and ensuring more efficient service by eliminating the possibility of weakened individual battery units. With the absence of the batteries and with the bell situated in the base of the instrument, only one piece of equipment was necessary at each station.

The new system was inaugurated in simple ceremonies on March 18, 1939. At 11:00 p.m. Reverend Paul E. Sloan, pastor of St. Matthew's Episcopal Church, pulled the switch in the new brick office, which started the system on its way. The first call was placed by Mayor H.M. Fleming, who dialed C.Y. Walker, Tipton County court clerk and president of the Lions Club. Miss Madie Fyfe, the reigning Miss Covington, had the honor of making the first long-distance call.

There was no interruption of service. Persons making calls before 11:00 p.m. used the old manual phones, while calls placed after the hour were made on the dial machines.

One of the most important features of the dial system inaugurated in Covington in 1939 was the great improvement of rural service. New lines were built to Solo, Gift, Detroit and Gilt Edge by way of Garland, out the Holly Grove Road and out the Mason Road to Dennis's Store. Lines maintained by the farmers themselves, toward Brighton and Mt. Carmel, were all rebuilt to improve service.

A total of 600 subscribers were served by the new exchange, 70 of whom were new patrons in rural areas. By 1945 the total number of subscribers increased to 853, and by 1952 there were 2,032 telephones in service at the Covington exchange.

Having been developed in 1896, the dial telephone was about as slow making its appearance in Tipton County as had been the first form of instant communication—the telegraph. Though the telegraph had been in use since 1844, it was not until the Chesapeake, Ohio & Southwestern Railroad was at work completing its track from Covington to Paducah, Kentucky, that thoughts were given to running a telegraph line from Memphis to Covington.

By the middle of November 1881 all necessary instruments, wire and batteries for building the line had been received in Memphis, and all the telegraph poles had been contracted for and were being delivered. During the last week in December, poles were distributed along the line of the railroad, and a large force of men began digging the holes for them. The party worked as far as Covington digging holes, then back to Memphis erecting poles. From Memphis they returned, putting up the wire.

Work on the line between Memphis and Covington was finished by March 31, 1882, except for two short breaks at the crossings of the Loosahatchie

Communications

C.Y. Walker taking the first call on Covington's new dial telephone system.

and Wolf Rivers. High water at these points forced a short delay in completion. A week later the announcement was made that Covington, at last, had telegraphic communication with the world.

The telegraph station remained Covington's only direct communication outlet for but a short period of time. The first telephone in Tipton County was soon installed in McFadden and Son's Livery Stable just off the square on West Liberty Avenue. Located in the stable office, it was a long-distance instrument connected to Memphis (one ring) and Dyersburg (three rings), which served the whole town.

Because of its location, the phone was used almost exclusively by men. The livery stable, located across the street from the Last Chance Saloon, was not considered a place for nice ladies to be around.

Local cotton buyers, making several business calls a day, were the phone's biggest users. Since a messenger's fee of ten cents was charged to anyone who had to be called to the phone, a considerable sum was collected during the busy cotton season.

In 1894, James E. Caldwell of Nashville, president of the Cumberland Telephone Company, appointed Cecil McFadden manager of the county's

McFadden and Shelton livery stable as it appeared after the county's first telephone was installed. Note the telephone sign hanging between the arched doors.

first telephone exchange. McFadden had the exchange installed in his home directly behind the livery stable. His wife, Julia, and her sister, Miss Pet May, were the first operators.

The number of the exchange's first subscribers is not known, but one of the first directories listed forty-five phones in the town. The directory offered the subscriber instructions on "how to turn the crank and lift the receiver" and cautioned that obscene language and talking to the operator were strictly forbidden. It also warned that connections would not be made after 10:00 p.m. except for emergencies.

By 1896, business had picked up to such an extent that Miss Bessie Owen was employed as night operator. She worked from nine in the evening to six the next morning and was paid the sum of $15 a month. With her bed near the switchboard, she often had her rest disturbed by people calling for a doctor.

In 1906 a telephone exchange was started in Munford by a group of that town's progressive citizens. It was first operated by Roxie Norris, who was followed in succession by Miss Odell Moore, A.H. Yarbro, Mack Pope, Misses Ruth and Pearl Moore and Andrew Greene. An exchange was also installed at Brighton sometime during the early part of the century.

The Mason Telephone Exchange began operation in November 1914, with G.W. Marsh, the former postmaster, in charge. Fifty businesses and residences in and around Mason were connected with the new exchange. Both the Mason and Munford exchanges were eventually purchased by the Millington exchange.

The Mexican Foe

THE BLACK BEAN INCIDENT

Robert Holmes Dunham is one of the most revered of Texas heroes, yet very little is known about him. The scant information available indicates that Robert was a young boy when his father, Daniel A. Dunham, moved with his family to Tipton County from Nashville in 1823. The trip was made in a flatboat, the party landing at a point on the Hatchie River later known as Piljerk. Since most of the country was then a wilderness, a roadway had to be cut through the virgin forest from that point to a spot about two miles east of the present site of Covington, where the family settled.

Robert received his early education at the Mountain Academy under Dr. James Holmes, and as a young man he joined the Baptist Church at Covington, then under the Reverend Peyton Smith. He, with Joe Borum, organized the first union Sunday school in town in which, according to one of his pupils, John Uriah Green, Dunham "showed his faith by his work."[11]

In about 1836 Dunham moved with his father's family to Texas. From January 10 to December 8, 1837, he served in the Texas army.

On October 1, 1842, Dunham joined, as a lieutenant, the 750-man volunteer force of General Alexander Somervell, who was under orders from President Houston to avenge attacks made by Mexican General Woll on San Antonio in March and September of that year. When Somervell picked his staff, he chose Dunham as his brigade inspector and promoted him to the rank of major.

The command began its march from the Medina River on November 25 and reached Laredo on December 8 after a tiring trek over boggy flatland.

Moving down the Rio Grande, they began bickering and quarreling among themselves, and two hundred of their number resigned and marched home. The rest crossed over and captured the little town of Guerrero without opposition, but when Somervell received information that a large force of Mexicans was in the area, he decided to call off the expedition.

Some of the soldiers made loud and earnest protests against disbanding. At length, three hundred men seceded, without opposition from Somervell, from the main command. Robert Dunham was among this determined band, which elected William Fisher colonel then turned inland toward the small town of Mier.

On the afternoon of Christmas Day, the Texans attacked a strong force of three thousand Mexicans camped there under General Pedro de Ampudia. The fighting commenced in earnest and lasted through the dark and drizzly night. After seventeen continuous hours of battle, Fisher, with supplies running low, surrendered to the Mexicans.

Dunham and his comrades soon found themselves on a weary journey to Mexico City as prisoners of war. Marching between two columns of vigilant Mexican soldiers, they trudged the two hundred miles from Mier to Matamoras. Here, Dunham wrote a letter to Bailey Peyton, a distinguished Tennessean and a kinsman of the Dunham family.

Matamoras, January 11, 1843

Bailey Peyton:

Dear Sir—Although our acquaintance has been very limited, still the friendship you have ever expressed for the family, and the ties of blood, together with my present situation, embolden me to address you.

I am now a prisoner of war in this place together with some two hundred others. The particulars of the battle and the surrender you will learn through the Mexican papers. My motive in addressing you is to request you to write to my mother and inform her of my situation. We are destitute of clothing, and without means of obtaining any. The length of our term of stay here is very uncertain, but it is thought by many that we will start for the City of Mexico in a few days. I think it more than probable that we will remain here for a month at least.

Any assistance you may render will be thankfully received and ever remembered with gratitude by

Robert Holmes Dunham[12]

The Mexican Foe

This view of Texans on their way to Mier was drawn by Charles M'Laughlin, a member of the expedition.

From Matamoras, the prisoners were marched to Monterrey and then on to Saltillo. At Hacienda Salado, a hundred miles south of Buena Vista, the Texans made a surprise attack on their guards while they were eating breakfast. They quickly overpowered and disarmed the astonished sentinels, taking whatever weapons they could find. After a brief, sharp conflict in which five of the Texans were killed, the prisoners were free once more.

They headed for home much divided over what would be their safest route. Eighty miles from Salado along the route to Moncova, they made the mistake of taking to the dry, rugged mountains. The band soon grew hungry, thirsty, tired and bewildered. Several fell in their futile wanderings and died. On the fifth day of their wretched ordeal the survivors were surrounded by a band of Mexican soldiers and were made prisoners once more.

All 176 captives were bound and made to lie in rows. With the arrival of a new escort on March 21, the march back into the interior was begun. By March 25 the Texans were again at Hacienda Salado.

Santa Anna had issued orders for all those captured to be shot, but Francisco Mexia, the Mexican governor, refused to obey the order. His action, however, only delayed the punishment as the Texans were lined up to hear a new edict. Though many expected clemency, it did not come. Instead Santa Anna ordered immediate death for one-tenth of the prisoners. The order explained that all of the escapees had originally been sentenced to die, but that the government, with a change of heart, had decided to reduce the figure to seventeen. Thus began the famous "Black Bean Incident" or "Lottery of Death."

When the reading of the cruel order was finished, an officer appeared holding an earthen jar in his hand. In the jar were 176 beans—159 were white and 17 black. Each prisoner was to draw a bean from the jar. The black beans meant death.

Beginning with Ewen Cameron, the leader of the ill-fated escape attempt, each man stepped bravely forward as his name was called and drew from the container. Not one step faltered; not one hand trembled. They had been face to face with death too often to fear it now.

Robert Dunham was one of those who drew a black bean. When he saw its color, he turned to his comrades and bravely said, "I am prepared to die and would to God I had the chance to do the same thing over again."[13]

The unfortunate seventeen who had drawn black beans were marched away from the scene of the lottery and told to prepare for death. Their irons were knocked off, and they were furnished with pen and paper with which to write letters of goodbye to their loved ones back home. Dunham hurriedly scratched off a letter to his mother and gave it to a friend, A.D. Hadenburg, for delivery.

A Catholic priest was present to offer absolution to those who repented, but only two or three took advantage of his services. When Dunham was asked by the priest to confess and receive the sacrament according to the laws of the Catholic Church, he replied, "I confess not to man but my God."[14] He then began a feeling prayer with all of the condemned, a prayer that was interrupted and disallowed by the priest himself.

Dinner was served, and some of the condemned ate as though nothing out of the ordinary was about to happen to them. At twilight they were tied, blindfolded and lined up against a wall. The death march was mournfully played on fife and drum and the signal given to fire. Again and again gunshots rang out, and then all was silent. The awful deed was done.

One of the seventeen, James L. Shepherd, suffered only a scalp wound but fell with the others. The Mexicans discovered his body missing the following morning—he had escaped during the night. Some weeks later his good fortune ended when he was recaptured near the Rio Grande and promptly shot.

Abraham Hadenburg kept the letter entrusted to him by Dunham and carried it home to Texas when he finally obtained his release with the rest of the Mier prisoners in September 1844. He tried in vain to locate Dunham's mother and was equally unsuccessful in his attempts to locate any of his

The Mexican Foe

M'Laughlin drawing depicting the "Lottery of Death" at Hacienda Salado.

executed comrades' kin. Eventually he decided to try to reach Dunham's mother through the regular mail and turned the fatal missive over to the officials of the post office at Waco, Texas. They continued the search for a while, but in time gave up themselves. The letter was soon forgotten and then lost.

When the old post office was torn down years later, a laborer found the long lost letter and, not knowing exactly what to do with it, forwarded it to Sam Houston. After Houston's death the letter was found among his collection of historical papers and given to the ladies who had custody of the Alamo. Today the remnants of Dunham's farewell message can be seen in the museum at the Alamo in San Antonio.

Mexico

Dear Mother

I write to you under the most awful feelings that a son ever addressed a mother for in half an hour my doom will be finished here on earth for I am doomed to die by the hands of the Mexicans for our late attempt to escape the…by Santa Anna that every tenth man should be shot we drew lots I was one of the unfortunate I can not say anything more I die I hope with firmness farewell may god bless you and may he in this my last hour forgive and pardon all my sins A. D. Hadenburge will…should he be…all to inform you farewell

Your affectionate sone [sic]
R.H. Dunham
March 25th 1843

The bodies of the sixteen men executed at Hacienda Salado remained buried there until the Mexican-American War. On May 3, 1847, Captain John E. Dusenberry led a group of soldiers into the place and had the bodies exhumed and carried back to Texas. Captain Dusenberry was one of those who had drawn a white bean on that blistering March afternoon four years before.

The remains were reburied at La Grange, Texas, where a state park was established to honor their memory. A beautiful monument marks the last resting place of the Black Bean heroes. Since Dunham was a mason, Dunham Lodge in Covington was named in his honor.

The Mier Expedition: A Postscript

Robert H. Dunham was not the only ex–Tipton Countian on the ill-fated Mier Expedition. At least two others, T.A. Thompson and William A. Clopton, were numbered among that reckless devil-may-care band captured at Mier. Both survived nearly two years of hopeless bondage and unmerited suffering in a Mexican prison.

Little is known of Thompson other than the fact that he enlisted on October 17, 1842, as a private in Company D, 2nd Regiment, 1st Brigade of Somervell's command.

Clopton, a 1st lieutenant in Company B of Colonel James R. Cook's regiment, was born in Tennessee in 1815. After living for a time in Tipton County, he moved to Bastrop, Texas, in 1837.

On the day that most of the men who had broken free at Hacienda Salado were recaptured, William Clopton and a few others separated from the main body to try to find water. It was understood that whoever found it would build a fire—rising smoke would call the fellow sufferers together.

Wandering alone and lost for two days, Clopton was almost delirious with thirst when he spotted smoke curling skyward. Determined to reach the water promised by the signal, he turned with sore feet and aching body in that direction. He had not had a drop of water in days.

Exhaustion made his efforts painful. He would walk a few steps, fall, then rise and struggle diligently onward.

When Clopton finally reached his destination, someone handed him a gourd of water, and he drank. Only then did he realize that his benefactors were Mexican soldiers and that he was once again their prisoner. Around the waterhole he recognized his pale, haggard, fellow prisoners who, once strong and handsome, now resembled walking skeletons.

Clopton escaped the fate of Dunham by drawing a white bean in the death lottery at Salado. He was marched with the surviving Texans to Mexico City, where they were put in chains and forced to work on roads and other public projects.

On September 20, the prisoners were transferred to the Castle of Perote, a massive fortress midway between Mexico City and Veracruz. Here, the life of burden and insult imposed upon them at Mexico City was continued. They were forced to carry heavy sacks of sand on their backs and were paired off like horses to pull rock-laden carts. Adding even more to their misery was an outbreak of typhus fever, which struck all but seven of the prisoners and claimed many lives.

In the midst of all their suffering, the prisoners explored many possible means of escape. When one of Clopton's fellow townsmen, a gunsmith by trade, was put to work in the armory at Perote, he made small files and saws with which the prisoners often cut their chains. One night during the usual inspection, Clopton's chains were found to be loose. The inspecting officer hit him several times across the head with a sword, inflicting severe wounds. He was removed to a hospital where he was confined, still in chains, for four days.

The Mier prisoners remained captive until September 16, 1844, when Santa Anna, mourning his wife's death, granted a general amnesty. Destitute, the Texans returned home with bitterness in their hearts. There they discovered with grim joy that relations between the United States and Mexico were strained near the breaking point.

The Mexican War

When war was declared with Mexico in May 1846, Tennesseans hurried to volunteer with the same patriotic zeal that their fathers had exhibited in 1812. Almost immediately more than thirty thousand offered their services to fight in a war they believed would be brief against an enemy whom they had learned to hate since the Texas Revolution. Most, however, had their hopes dashed when they learned that the War Department wanted the mobilization of only two regiments of infantry and one regiment of cavalry from Tennessee—in all about twenty-five hundred men.

Among the disappointed companies not selected for duty was one organized in Tipton County by Captain Jonas Seaman. So determined were he and eight of his men to see action in Mexico that they went to Fayette County and joined a cavalry company that, having qualified under the strictest of requirements, had been selected for service. Besides Seaman, the group included Benjamin J. Sanford, Nat Tipton, J.H. Cockrill, Richard O'Marrell, Thomas S. Lauderdale, Sam Glass, Rufus Glass and W.C. Wood.

In late May 1846 Captain Joseph Lenow, commander of the "Fayette Cavalry," received orders to report by June 15 to Memphis, the point of assembly for all cavalry troops recruited in the state. When the company reached that place on June 10, they were greeted by thunderous cheers from citizens who lined the streets all along the route of march to their quarters at Camp Carroll, two miles east of the city. No doubt much of this enthusiasm was due to the fact that Lenow's was the first cavalry contingent from the state to arrive.

At Camp Carroll the "Fayette Cavalry" was mustered into service as Company A, First Tennessee Cavalry Regiment. Jonas E. Thomas was elected colonel of the regiment, and Robert D. Allison was elected lieutenant colonel.

On July 27, Colonel Thomas issued orders for the long overland march on the military road through Arkansas to San Antonio, Texas—a distance of 822 miles. A prearranged schedule called for the troopers to cover about 15 miles per day with the tentative date of arrival being about September 1.

The march was a particularly tough one due mainly to a lack of good drinking water. Twenty-five men of the regiment were left in Little Rock suffering from chills and fever, and thirty-eight more were hospitalized in Washington, Arkansas. Seventy-five men were eventually recorded on the sick list, but most improved rapidly and were able to rejoin their command. Three men died on the long journey, and only one was discharged because of an inability to keep up the march.

Captain Lenow wrote of the march in a letter published by the Memphis *Appeal* on September 18:

> *We have been on the road for 50 days and have marched 650 miles—an average of 13 miles a day. That looks like slow traveling, but it's the best we can do. The health of the Tennessee Regiment has not been very good. The surgeon, Dr. Roberts, informs me that there have been many cases of sickness among the men…The horses look well, however, and everyone is in fine spirits.*

The Mexican Foe

On September 20, when the regiment was nearly to the seat of war, the *Appeal* again published correspondence from Captain Lenow.

> *All the way the men have behaved in an exemplary fashion. Col. J.E. Thomas is an excellent commander, universally loved by the men and officers. It may be thought vanity in me when I report that the Fayette County boys have shown a better spirit and finer discipline than any company in the regiment.*

The regiment crossed the Rio Grande at Matamoras, Mexico. When it reached Tampico, the men took passage by boat to Veracruz. There the long march was taken up through the wilds of Mexico, the First Tennessee being engaged in many skirmishes and minor engagements before joining the American army under General Scott at Cerro Gordo the day after the battle at that place.

One of the Tipton volunteers later related that General Scott told Captain Lenow that if the Tennessee cavalry had arrived in time for the battle, General Santa Anna would probably have been captured, as the cavalry horses of the regiments that participated in the battle came principally from the Northern part of the United States and so were not acclimated to the extent that the Southern horses were. Hence, the pursuit of the retreating Mexicans had to be abandoned temporarily because of the lack of endurance of the U.S. mounts.

Company A remained with General Scott's command, taking part in a number of battles, until the army reached Jalapa, where they were scheduled to remain as garrison troops. However, as their term of enlistment was nearly up and their clothing and barest comforts were almost completely exhausted, the men were ordered on May 5, 1847, to embark for New Orleans. Upon their arrival they were to be mustered out, paid and sent home. At New Orleans the government took over their horses, for which it paid the soldiers the market price.

The Tipton contingent of Company A took passage on a steamboat for home, landing at Randolph in July 1847. The men had seen plenty of action, and not being career soldiers they were glad to be home, being well qualified to give firsthand accounts of the war and their part in it. Some of their stories included the fact that each man of the company was armed with two horse pistols and a carbine; that rations consisted of coffee, bacon and bread; and that the pay was $8.00 a month, which was paid to them in gold and silver whenever the army paymaster happened to reach camp.

Under the War Department's second call for volunteers, Company G of the 4th Tennessee Infantry Regiment was organized at Covington in 1847.

The company was made up of an equal number of men from Tipton and Lauderdale Counties. Among the Tipton volunteers were Captain Henry Travis, the company commander, Second Lieutenant Thomas Epperson, D.J. Wood, William Wood, J.C. Wright, A. Perrett, J. Adams and J. Witherington. Company G remained in service until the war ended in May 1848.

One of the most interesting of Tipton's Mexican War veterans was Thomas Lauderdale, the grandson of Colonel James Lauderdale for whom Lauderdale County was named. Born near Covington in 1828, young Lauderdale enlisted at the age of eighteen. After a year's service with the First Tennessee Cavalry, he retuned home and soon began what was to become a long and distinguished career of public service. In 1854 he became the first clerk and master of the newly created chancery court of Tipton County—a position he held until the Civil War. Following that conflict, he served most creditably in various other public offices.

Lauderdale outlived all of his comrades in arms to become the county's last surviving Mexican War veteran. He died in December 1917 at the age of eighty-nine.

The Civil War

A Call to Arms

Shortly after South Carolina seceded from the Union, Tennesseans were asked to vote on a proposal to call a secession convention. At that time most Tennesseans looked with reluctance at the idea of separation from the Union and rejected the proposal.

Pro-Southern sentiment, however, grew rapidly with the help of fire-eating orators and newspapers clamoring for secession. The Covington *Weekly Spy*, with pages full of editorials and poems in support of the secessionist cause, was as belligerent in its pro-Southern expressions as any newspaper in the state. To leave little doubt as to its sentiments, the *Spy* carried an engraving of the Confederate flag beneath its masthead.

Matters were finally culminated in April 1861 when, following the fall of Fort Sumter, Lincoln issued a proclamation calling for seventy-five thousand volunteers. Governor Isham G. Harris answered Lincoln with an emphatic refusal.

The governor's bold stand was cheered and supported by most of the state's populace, and on May 6, the legislature directed that the electorate be presented with an ordinance dissolving the union between Tennessee and the United States. The ordinance was not brought to a vote until June 10, 1861, when it passed by 108,511 to 47,338.

Of this referendum, a Covington resident later wrote:

> So soon as it was found that a resort to arms was inevitable, her people (Tipton's) turned out and voluntarily espoused the southern cause, in defense of their rights, home and property with a zeal, determination and unanimity unparalleled by any county in the state.[15]

Tipton County cast 943 votes for secession and only 16 against. All 16 anti-secession votes came from the village of Portersville where a few native Northerners resided.

During the period between the vote on the secession convention and the vote on secession itself, volunteer military units had sprung up throughout Tennessee. By the end of May 1861, three companies of volunteers had been organized in Tipton County. "So anxious was I to get to enlist," wrote a young Haywood Countian, "that we joined a company in Tipton County as there was not at that time a company forming in our part of the county."[16]

This eagerness to be off to war was displayed by many men throughout Tipton. They were motivated for many different reasons—for some it was hatred of the North, and for others a desire for adventure. Once in training, however, almost all shared in the prevailing desire to fight Yankees. Because most felt that the war would be short-lived, they wished to hurry into action for fear of missing out altogether. "We, poor silly souls, thought the war would be over before we could have a chance to be in a battle," confessed one anxious volunteer.[17]

All of these early recruits had a long wait, however, before they experienced the thrill of combat. There was usually a period of several weeks between the time they enlisted and the time they were finally mustered in by the Confederate government. They spent this time setting up camp and learning the rudiments of drill.

One soldier called it "a sort of picnic time," when home folks furnished choice rations and young ladies visited the camp almost daily, cheering the men with their presence.

At some early stage in its organization a company elected officers. Generally, the office of captain was voted to the man who had been most instrumental in raising the company. Consequently, John B. Turner became captain of the "Tipton Rifles," the first company raised in Tipton County. Other officers included Lieutenants John McKenzie, H.W.B. Jones and John T. Barrett.

Organized at Covington in April 1861, the infantry company went into camp and began training at the old fairgrounds. "I heard," recalled a young visitor to the camp, "the gallant McKenzie's shrill voice uttering strange commands which, to my schoolboy ears, were very unlike the drillings in Latin and Greek, or mathematics to which I had been used, as he took the Tipton Rifles through their first evolutions."[18]

The company of ninety-three men remained encamped at Covington until the morning of May 14, when it left for Germantown. Upon its arrival there the next day, it was mustered into service as Company I, 4th Tennessee Infantry.

The Civil War

With the departure of the "Tipton Rifles," Covington took on the look of a town gone to war, with only a few people passing along its streets. The *Weekly Spy* of May 18 reported, "Everyone and his family has left for the wars," and it lamented, "Our Barber has left—there's no one left to shave us now—there's no one left to regret."[19]

The town's silversmith, S.T. Lane, was another who had left. He had closed his shop on the northeast corner of the square to join the "Southern Confederates," the second company to be enlisted in Tipton County.

The "Southern Confederates" were organized at Clopton Campground on April 22, by David J. Wood and James I. Hall. It is doubtful whether a better location could have been found anywhere in the county. Campground shelters, an excellent spot for drilling and a convenient nearby spring all combined to make it an excellent training site.

When the election of officers was held, Wood, a Mexican War veteran, was voted captain. Hall, C.B. Simonton and R.W. Lemmon were elected lieutenants. No doubt many newly elected officers shared the feelings later expressed by Simonton:

> *I did not know the simplest military maneuvers or word of command even and I guess it occurred to me just then that an officer was expected to lead the men always in the face of danger, and if need be, to teach them by example how to die, and these reflections made me modest. I really wanted to avoid that post of distinction and—danger.*[20]

The men who enlisted in the "Southern Confederates" came from Covington, Portersville, the Mountain, Randolph, Mt. Zion, Mason and Stanton. They were farmers, schoolteachers, shopkeepers, ministers and college students. At least one-third of the total command of 106 was either college graduates or had come directly from college to enlist. One proud member described it as "one of the grandest companies in the Confederate Army."[21]

On the morning of May 21, 1861, the "Southern Confederates" boarded a train at Mason bound for Jackson. When they arrived there the next day, they were organized into the 9th Tennessee Infantry, becoming Company C of that regiment.

Two more infantry companies were organized at Clopton in the fall of 1861 by B.M. Browder and Edward D. Shelton. Both units were mustered into the 51st Tennessee Infantry in November with Browder's becoming Company G. Another company, organized at Clopton and commanded by S.E. Sherrill, joined the regiment in March 1862, as Company K.

Tipton County's first cavalry unit was organized by Charles H. Hill at Mason's Depot on May 31, 1861. It consisted of men from Tipton,

This prewar photograph shows Major Charles H. Hill in an early militia uniform.

Haywood and Fayette Counties. Following its organization, "Hill's Cavalry," as it came to be known, marched to Clopton Campground, where it remained encamped and drilling until late in the summer. It was then ordered to Columbus, Kentucky, where it was transferred to Confederate service as Company C of Logwood's 6th Tennessee Cavalry Battalion. At this time Captain Hill was promoted to the rank of major, and Lieutenant J.U. Green took Hill's place as captain of Company C.

On March 7, 1862, Major Hill became commander of the 6th Tennessee Cavalry battalion. In April the battalion was merged into the 7th Tennessee Cavalry with Hill's old company becoming Company B of that regiment.

A second cavalry company was raised in Tipton County in February 1862. Captained by Lafayette Hill, a Covington physician, it became Company I of the 7th regiment on March 15.

On March 18, Company K was mustered into the 7th Regiment with Samuel Taylor as captain. Composed of horsemen from Tipton, Fayette and Shelby Counties, it began service with a total of only seventy-eight men. Casualties and discharges soon depleted the unit to such an extent that by

L.P. Marshall, a young and well-armed member of the 12th Tennessee Cavalry.

September 1862 it was declared too small to function as a company and was disbanded, the men being transferred to other companies in the regiment.

J.U. Green, who had been promoted to captain of the county's first cavalry company in late 1861, lost that position in the spring of 1862 and returned to Tipton County to form another command. In October 1862, he organized a unit that eventually became Company C of the 12th Tennessee Cavalry. When this regiment was organized, Green was elected colonel, and John L. Payne became captain of Company C. R.A. Field, who had been an officer with Green in the first cavalry company, raised what became Company G of the 12th Regiment in February 1863.

The county's first artillery company was organized at Covington on January 27, 1862, by H.J. Maley. It took its place as Company C of the 1st Tennessee Heavy Artillery Regiment.

Another artillery company, the "Reneau Battery," was organized within Federal lines by Baylor Palmer and was mustered into service on June 1, 1863. Composed of men from Tipton and Fayette Counties, it was the twelfth and last company that Tipton County helped furnish for the Confederacy.

It was said that the county furnished more men in proportion to its size than any other county in the South. At one time during the war there were some eleven hundred men from Tipton County actively engaged. This number was almost equal to that of registered voters and was more than had ever voted in the county before.

Miss Molly and the Flag

As the time drew near for the "Southern Confederates" to leave Clopton for the seat of war, they became a part of a ceremony like none ever witnessed before in Tipton County. This was a flag presentation similar in almost every detail to the many being held throughout Dixie in 1861.

The ladies of the county made a beautiful Confederate flag for the company from material purchased at a cost of forty dollars. When the banner was completed, the ladies asked that a suitable date be set for its presentation.

It was determined that the flag would be presented at a dress parade on May 20, the eve of the company's departure. A beautiful belle named Mollie Thompson, a teacher at the Female Seminary, was selected by the ladies to make the presentation. Knowing of her grace, patriotism and skill in composition, Captain Wood "was more troubled about his reply than he would have been about arranging the details of a battle."[22] He obtained a copy of Miss Thompson's speech in advance and asked two capable young men of his command to compose for him a fitting response. When completed, their work was accepted graciously, but the captain ultimately decided to be himself and deliver his reply in his own way.

The morning of May 20 saw a great crowd gathered at Camp Clopton. Proud but sorrowful parents were in attendance, as were all the old gentlemen who had taken an interest in the organization of the company.

Activities began with the company displaying its newly acquired marching skills. The men looked smart in their hickory shirts and yellow-trimmed gray uniforms as they drilled to a monotone "hep," "hep," "hep," around the parade grounds. Their new uniforms had been made up by the patriotic ladies of the county from material financed by public subscription.

At 11:00 a.m. the company marched before the speaker's stand erected especially for the occasion. Miss Thompson stood before them "with her lovely animated face lifted" as she delivered the presentation address.[23] In a tender but firm voice, she expressed sentiments that drew loud applause from the audience. Near the conclusion of her speech she offered the colors with these remarks:

The Civil War

Judge Mark Walker, *right*, with assistance from Larry Whitley, proudly displays the silk flag presented to the "Southern Confederates" at Clopton. Judge Walker's grandfather, Charles Bryson Simonton, served first as lieutenant, then as captain of the company.

> *And now, Captain Wood, permit me, in behalf of the rest of my sex, to present you and your gallant band this flag, as a testimonial of our admiration, heart-felt gratitude and entire confidence in your undertaking. May it never be trailed in the dust, but be borne triumphantly in every battle. Unfurl it to the breeze, and may it inspire you with fresh courage, and incite others to join you in this holy cause…And when at last this flag has been shredded by the stormy elements, may your names be handed down through future generations as your country's honor and your nation's glory.*[24]

Captain Wood accepted the flag and made a fitting response. He then turned to Ensign William Young and said, "I now place it in the hands of our noble and heroic color bearer."[25] Handing Young the banner, he continued, "Take this standard and protect and defend it as you would your life; unfurl it to the breeze, and may it wave on forever until nations shall learn war no more."[26]

Ensign Young, taking Captain Wood quite literally, unfurled the flag and waved it then and there, bringing cheers from the throng. "I think," wrote one envious soldier, "I never saw a man look so brave as Ensign Bill Young did just then. There were no Yankees near and there were any number of beautiful and admiring women looking proudly at him."[27]

Young's action proved a fitting climax to a ceremony that thrilled the hearts of everyone present. The cheers soon gave way to the clash of cymbals and the roll of drums as the company did some quick step marching beneath its new banner. Shortly, the command to break ranks was given, affording the soldiers an opportunity to eat their last dinner at Clopton and to say goodbye.

Many of the hopes that had been expressed by Miss Thompson and Captain Wood were never realized. But that beautiful silk flag, which served as the regimental standard of the 9th Tennessee Infantry regiment at Shiloh and Perryville, was always guarded and never "trailed in the dust." The bravery with which it and the principles for which it stood were defended is exhibited by the fact that only 13 of the original 106 members of the company were present at the final roll call in April 1865. Most of the rest had been disabled or had filled unmarked graves.

THE BURNING OF RANDOLPH

Tipton County was probably as little disturbed by big troop movements during the Civil War as any county in West Tennessee. "We were but little raided upon by large bodies of either army," recalled one resident.[28] This was due primarily to Tipton's location and the fact that no major thoroughfares passed through her territory. Troops could travel faster and with greater ease along the Mississippi and Hatchie Rivers, which bound the county on the west and north.

The incursions that were made into the county were carried out by small detachments of Federal troops that came from posts in neighboring counties. Following the fall of Memphis in June 1862, Federal troops were stationed there, at Fort Pillow in Lauderdale County and at such points along the Memphis and Charleston Railroad as Collierville, La Grange and Grand Junction.

Some of these raids were for the purpose of breaking up small bands of Confederate partisans operating behind Federal lines. Others were for foraging for whatever property suited their fancy, particularly livestock. But the first big raid was for neither of these reasons; it was a reprisal for a rash act perpetrated by a few irregular Confederates or guerrillas at Randolph.

On September 23, 1862, the packet *Eugene* from St. Louis landed at Randolph and was fired upon by a small band of some twenty-five to fifty men. The act enraged General W.T. Sherman, who was commander of the district with headquarters in Memphis. "That boat," he reported, "was laden with stores for the very benefit of families some of whose members are in

Colonel Charles C. Walcutt, commander of the Federal troops that burned Randolph. *Generals in Blue.*

arms against us, and it was an outrage of the greatest magnitude that people there or in connivance with them should fire on an unarmed boat."[29]

Referring to the incident again, Sherman wrote, "Acts of this kind must be promptly punished and it is almost impossible to reach the actors, for they come from the interior and depart as soon as the mischief is done. But the interest and wellbeing of the country demands that all such attacks should be followed by a punishment that will tend to prevent a repetition."[30]

The punishment that Sherman chose was the destruction of Randolph. For the task he picked Colonel Charles C. Walcutt and his 46th Ohio Volunteer Infantry Regiment. His written orders to Walcutt read in part:

> *Sir: The object of the expedition you have been detailed for is to visit the town of Randolph where yesterday the packet* Eugene *was fired upon by a party of guerrillas…*

Colonel Walcutt, under orders from Sherman to leave one house to mark the site of Randolph, chose the home of J.H. Barton, pictured here in 1937.

>...I think the attack on the *Eugene* was by a small force of guerrillas from Loosahatchie, who by this time have gone back, and therefore that you will find no one at Randolph: in which case you will destroy the place. Let the people know and feel that we deeply deplore the necessity of such destruction, but we must protect ourselves and the boats which are really carrying stores and merchandise for the benefit of secession families, whose fathers and brothers are in arms against us...
>
>...Keep your men in the reach of your voice, and do your work systematically. Let your quartermaster take a minute account of every house or piece of property destroyed under this order, with the names of owners if possible. If all is clear, you can send parties inland toward Covington, but not over 5 miles.
>
>...If you find men whom you suspect of guilt bring them in, but no women and children. Also you may capture any slaves, horses, or mules belonging to known rebels.[31]

Colonel Walcutt had two boats placed at his disposal, the *Eugene* and another chartered especially for the expedition. On the afternoon of September 24, he placed two companies on the *Eugene* and the remainder of his regiment and a section of rifled artillery on the other boat and headed upstream toward Randolph. Arriving early the next morning and meeting no opposition, the 46th Ohio set about its task of destroying all that was left of a once proud and flourishing town.

The residents of each house were given a certain amount of time to remove their belongings; then the torch was applied. Guards were stationed to see that none of the fires were extinguished.

Some of the soldiers used the pretext of helping residents carry out household furnishings in order to steal anything of value that they could find. In one case they carried a woman who was sick and alone out into the yard on her bed and set fire to her house.

In little more than an hour Randolph lay in smoldering ashes except for the one house spared on Sherman's orders. This was the residence of J.H. Barton. According to tradition Barton managed to save his dwelling because he was a member of the same lodge as Colonel Walcutt.

When the Yankees finally departed, they left some twenty families homeless on the bluff. The next day General Sherman reported, "The regiment has returned and Randolph is gone."[32]

Campfires and Creek Bottoms

On September 6, 1862, Colonel R.V. Richardson received authorization from his superiors to organize a regiment of Confederate partisans in West Tennessee. He immediately moved into that area, setting up a camp and rendezvous in Fayette County and Galloway's Switch. At the time, his field of operations for recruiting purposes was surrounded by a cordon of enemy military posts. Federal attempts to break up his activities behind their lines would result in numerous skirmishes in West Tennessee with some occurring in Tipton County.

Colonel Benjamin H. Grierson, commander of the First Cavalry Brigade, Sixteenth Army Corps, was Richardson's chief adversary. On October 23, 1862, he attacked and routed the outnumbered Partisans at Galloway's Switch. He then turned northeast, crossed Beaver Creek in Tipton County and surprised a detachment of Richardson's men who had bivouacked for the night. Proceeding on the Somerville-Randolph Road, he encamped two miles east of Portersville.

At daybreak the next morning Grierson dashed into Portersville fully expecting to find a company of rebels there. After a thorough search of the town and its environs proved fruitless, he moved on to Randolph, where he embarked on a steamer for Memphis.

Richardson ultimately moved his principal camp to the neighborhood of Bloomington in Tipton County. It was from his headquarters there on January 25, 1863, that he issued a proclamation in reply to one issued by Colonel J.K. Mizner, commander of Federal forces at Brownsville. Mizner's proclamation was addressed to fourteen prominent men of Tipton and Haywood Counties whom he claimed would be held responsible in case of the molestation by Confederate sympathizers of the person or property of citizens loyal to the U.S. government living in the military district of Jackson, Tennessee. Richardson's response read in part:

> *Now therefore in reply to this paper bullet fired across the Hatchie River by the brave Colonel Mizner at unoffending non-combatants be it known that for each man named and every other good and loyal citizen of the confederate States living in Haywood and Tipton counties, Tenn., who may be arrested under the aforesaid proclamation I will have shot twice the number of Yankee soldiers taken in battle or on duty, and for each dollar's worth of property taken under said proclamation I will take or destroy twice the amount from the United States, their soldiers and Union men.*[33]

On February 14, Richardson completed the organization of his regiment by holding an election for the offices of lieutenant colonel and major. John U. Green of Tipton County was elected to the former and Berry B. Benson to the latter. The regiment now consisted of ten companies organized and five others in the process of organization. "I claim," wrote Richardson, "to be the First Tennessee Regiment of Partisan Rangers, C.S. Army."[34]

At daybreak on February 27, Richardson's camp at Bloomington was attacked by two hundred mounted men of the 2nd Illinois Cavalry from Fort Pillow. Luckily, however, Richardson had moved out the previous day, leaving only eight men to collect conscripts and guard the camp. The guard and everything in their charge—twenty-seven mules and horses, wagons and commissary stores—were taken. The camp itself with its numerous large buildings and comfortable quarters was completely destroyed.

Richardson, continuing to recruit and organize, set up his next camp near Somerville. This camp was the destination of Colonel Grierson when on March 8 he left La Grange with nine hundred troopers of the 6th and 7th Illinois Cavalry and a six-gun battery. When within a few miles of Somerville, the Federal advance came upon a small party of Confederates, who immediately fled. Here Grierson received information that Richardson was no longer in the area, a fact confirmed by scouts who the Union colonel had earlier sent out to go into the Confederate camp.

At 3:00 a.m. the next morning, Grierson proceeded with his command to the northwest, covering by forced march some thirty miles in nine hours over roads made almost impassable by recent heavy rains. At noon, the 6th Illinois, which was in advance of the brigade, discovered the First Tennessee Partisans drawn up in line of battle in the Lemmon Woods near Covington.

This photograph of Grierson's cavalry troopers was taken less than a month after the Lemmon Woods fight. *Photographic History of the Civil War.*

The position, a densely wooded area in a swampy creek bottom, was three miles southeast of Covington, according to Grierson, and only two as reported by Richardson.

The Federals made a vigorous attack, the men "not only risking the balls of the enemy, but…leaping fences, ditches, logs, and swamps of all depths of mud and water."[35] The outnumbered Confederates were driven steadily backward for five or six miles when, finding themselves about to be outflanked, they retired from the field. According to Richardson, his men engaged in the two-hour fight did not exceed 150.

The 7th Illinois having marched in the rear of the 6th participated but little in the engagement. Company H of that regiment was given the task of destroying the camp and equipage of Colonel Richardson, which consisted in part of the train, commissary and quartermaster's stores, tents and records. Among the latter were found the paroles for over two hundred Federal soldiers, all of Richardson's muster-rolls, lists of conscripts, maps, letters, receipts, etc. In reporting the loss of his regimental property, which he valued at about $4,000, Richardson would write: "We are consoled…by the reflection that we had taken it in former conflicts from him."[36]

Having scoured the country in the vicinity of Covington and the Hatchie River, Grierson marched southeast to Mason's Depot on March 10. Here he met a detachment of three hundred men from the Seventh Kansas and

Fourth Illinois Cavalries, which had marched up from Collierville under the command of Lieutenant-Colonel Martin Wallace.

With orders from Grierson to do what he thought proper, Wallace proceeded west on the Randolph Road, and just as he entered East Beaver Dam Creek bottom, he ran into Richardson's command. The Federal advance drove the outnumbered Confederates rapidly along the road until they reached the edge of the bottom. At that point Richardson left the road and turned south into the bottom's swamp. Wallace soon lost track of the Partisans, and after becoming satisfied that they were well scattered, he gave up the chase and marched back to Collierville.

Thus ended two days of skirmishes, which saw light casualties on both sides. Considering the magnitude of many of the war's battles, the actions of March 9 and 10 were insignificant indeed, but they proved to be the only engagements of any size in Tipton County during the war.

A Rebel Demand

At 6:00 p.m. on October 27, 1864, the steamer *Belle Saint Louis*, captained by Alexander Zeigler, left Memphis destined for Saint Louis. Onboard were a large number of passengers, including about fifty furloughed and discharged soldiers and several officers. Among the latter were six paymasters who had just completed payment of Federal troops in the field in and around Memphis.

At midnight, the boat reached Randolph and landed to take on eight bales of cotton under a permit from the military authorities in Memphis. The cotton belonged to a man named Harris who, once the staging had been run out, was the first to leave the boat.

As the deckhands made their way ashore to load the cotton, Harris was seen to hasten to the top of the bluff. Immediately, a force of about forty Confederates appeared and charged down toward the boat with guns blazing.

Captain Zeigler instantly called for the *Belle* to be backed away from the bank. The obeying of the order left the deckhands stranded on shore. Before this was accomplished, however, six rebels managed to get on board.

The Confederates quickly made their way to the engine room and ordered the two engineers to land the boat again. Colonel Loren Kent of the 29th Illinois Infantry, the senior officer on board, had given orders a short time before for the steamer not to be landed again under any circumstances, feeling that once under way the rebels on the boat could be overcome by superior numbers. By their coolness and knowledge of their duties, the engineers only complied in part with the rebel demand and managed to keep the boat sufficiently far from the shore to prevent other rebels from coming aboard.

By now the passengers were thoroughly aroused, and most were panic-stricken. A feeling that they were beyond help was brought on partially by the fact that the only firearms onboard the boat were revolvers belonging to the officers. In several cases these were either in the officers' baggage in their rooms or were in unserviceable condition.

Having been thwarted in their efforts to get the engineers to land the boat, the rebels attempted to reach the pilot to compel him to carry out the orders previously given to the engineers. Two of the paymasters, Majors D.C. Smith and A. Beeler, secured their revolvers and moved to the forward part of the steamer just as two rebels were ascending to the pilot house. Shots were exchanged, and Major Smith fell mortally wounded with a bullet in the chest. Major Beeler immediately fired upon and wounded the man who had shot Major Smith and then directed his attention toward the other rebel. Both men fired simultaneously with deadly accuracy, the rebel being killed instantly and Major Beeler receiving a wound from which he would die the next day.

At this point, as the bow of the boat neared the bank again, the engineers began backing the craft with the full power of its engine. The Confederates, seeing that they had failed in their attempt to capture the boat and becoming aware of their own dangerous situation, escaped by jumping overboard amid volleys of musketry from the shore. The boat was soon backed out of musket range to a place of safety.

None of the boat's crew or passengers, except Harris, was suspected of collusion with the rebels. A government aide on board had seen the permit for the *Belle* to land and had given his consent for the cotton to be taken aboard.

Credit for saving the boat was shared by a number of people. The two Federal majors gave their lives in preventing the Confederates from reaching the pilot house; the pilot and his assistants stood unflinchingly by the wheel though heavy fire was repeatedly directed at them from the shore; the chief engineer and his two assistants, though their lives were threatened, never left their posts.

The attack on the *Belle* resulted in but few casualties. Besides those already mentioned, three people on the boat were seriously, but not fatally wounded. They were a paymaster's clerk, an engineer sick in his berth and a black crew member.

The wounded rebel, who identified himself as Willis Jones, was removed from the boat at Cairo and placed in a hospital. He confided that General

Forrest was at Jackson, Tennessee, and was going to make a raid into Kentucky. He explained that the force that attacked the *Belle Saint Louis* was under the command of William Forrest. This force, along with another of equal size under a Captain Ford, was sent out as flankers to guard the Mississippi River from the mouth of the Wolf to Randolph. They were to report to Forrest the landing of any Federal infantry sent out to cut him off.

Forrest's objective was not Kentucky, however, but Johnsonville on the Tennessee. On November 4, he destroyed this important transfer and storage point along Sherman's line of communication.

A hint as to the reason for the Confederate attack on the *Belle Saint Louis* can probably be found in a message sent by Forrest to his superior General Richard Taylor prior to the Johnsonville expedition. "The amount of supplies reported as being in West Tennessee has been greatly exaggerated," he wrote. "Our currency (Confederate) cannot be used in that region."[37]

Since the Confederates went to so much trouble to lure the boat to the landing at Randolph, they might possibly have known of the paymasters' presence aboard and the fact that they had about $40,000 in Federal currency in their possession. Though the rebels had orders to destroy Federal property, their primary purpose for the attack was obviously to secure much needed money and supplies.

It is ironic that this last action of the war in Tipton County involving regular troops of both sides should be so similar to the county's first action—the firing upon the packet *Eugene* at Randolph in 1862. It could be said that the war in Tipton County began and ended at that historic old town.

Tipton's Men in Gray

The typical volunteer who marched out of Tipton County to fight in the Civil War was a non-slaveholding, middle-class individual who possessed certain distinctive qualities that contributed to his being among the best fighting men produced by the war.

One of the most conspicuous of these qualities, devotion to duty, was vividly reflected by the actions of W.M. Carnes, a member of Company C, 9th Tennessee Infantry, who was discharged from service in 1862, just prior to Bragg's invasion of Kentucky. Refusing to go home, he made the campaign at his own expense, and following the battle of Perryville, he was found severely wounded, his discharge still in his pocket. He eventually recovered, rejoined his unit and fought bravely through the rest of the war.

The Civil War

A strikingly similar but more tragic case two years later involved another member of that same company. Robert W. Lemmon, a frail, boyish-looking young man, was given a medical discharge but refused to be released from duty. He was killed in the Atlanta campaign at New Hope Church.

Another private who exhibited a deep devotion to cause and country was Ebenezer Daniel, better known as "Hurricane Horse." Daniel joined the "Tipton Rifles" on its organization at Covington in May 1861 but was soon discharged because of a heart condition. Undaunted, he returned to Covington and joined H.J. Maley's heavy artillery company, which was being organized there in January 1862. Although physical examinations were required for induction, they were often cursory, and Daniel's big raw-boned appearance belied his true condition. This time he saw plenty of action until his capture at Vicksburg in July 1863. He was then exchanged and again discharged because of his old ailment, thus finally ending his short but intrepid army career.

Another quality demonstrated by Tipton Rebs was raw courage. Some of the most consistent acts of courage were performed by the standard bearers—those entrusted with carrying and guarding the colors. Men vied for the honor of holding the standard high in the thickest of the battle, even though it meant drawing unusually heavy fire upon themselves.

Three examples, all involving men of Company C, 9th Tennessee Infantry, will serve to illustrate the gallantry shown by some of Tipton's noble men. During the second day's fighting at Shiloh, Corporal Newt McMullen had the flag knocked from his hands by a shell while retreating with his comrades from an advanced position that they had occupied. The shell shattered the staff to pieces and wrapped the banner around a bush. With the enemy pressing hard upon him, McMullen stopped, untangled the flag, placed it inside his coat and carried it safely from the field.

In the thick of the same battle, John Meux charged, unarmed, with his comrades and captured the flag of a Minnesota battery. As a reward for his bravery, Meux was ordered to Richmond to present the banner to President Davis.

Robert Gibbs applied for and was appointed standard-bearer of his regiment during the reorganization of the army at Corinth in 1862. At the battle of Perryville later that year, his regiment was ordered to charge up a steep hill to silence a battery of Napoleon guns that was creating havoc in their ranks. Gibbs was killed in the charge but not before he had placed the regimental colors on one of the guns of the enemy battery. His brave action inspired one of his comrades to call him the "most heroic soul that ever died on any battlefield."[38]

Ensign Robert H. Gibbs, Company C, 9th Tennessee Infantry. *Military Annals of Tennessee.*

Still another trait shown by Tipton's men in gray was their ability to withstand extreme hardship. They were often required to go for days with little more to eat than a few grains of parched corn and to suffer through harsh winter weather due to a lack of adequate blankets and clothing.

During Hood's retreat through the sleet and snow following the battle of Nashville, many Tipton Countians were involved in protecting the rear of the army. "Our shoes were worn out," related T.J. Walker of the 9th Tennessee Infantry, "and our feet sore and bleeding…I have actually seen blood on the snow from the bleeding feet of those poor barefoot soldiers."[39]

Capture and imprisonment by Federals brought little relief from the suffering. James Alexander Moore of Company G, 51st Tennessee Infantry later wrote of such suffering brought on after he and a number of other Tipton County members of his regiment were captured at Fort Donelson and subsequently confined at Camp Butler near Springfield, Illinois. "We remained there about Six months," he wrote, "where we had Some miserable treatment quite a good deal of Sickness, and Several deaths in our Squad."[40]

Love of home and family was one of the most worthy attributes shared by men whose family ties had been severed by the war. Letters written to loved ones back home vividly reflected the soldiers' concern for their families' well-being and their own desire to be home again. One such letter was written by Lieutenant William P. Malone of Company I, 7th Tennessee Cavalry, to his brother Robert from "Camp Starvation" in northern Mississippi in early 1862. In it William expressed concern that he had the family mule with him, and it was needed by Robert for spring plowing. "He is now with the wagon train," wrote William, "but I have sent for him and when he comes I will send him."[41] He closed the letter by telling his brother: "I have heard some of the boys say that as soon as they get home they never intend going outside of their plantations again as long as they live. I am agreed of their notion. I think if I can get back home again in peace I will be willing to stay at home satisfied for the balance of my days."[42]

THE LIGHTER SIDE

Their humor was a trait that Tipton Confederates had in common with the soldiers of both armies. Spontaneous gaiety gave them an escape from the worries and hardships of soldiering and made the war a little more tolerable.

Humor was manifested in the soldiers' letters home and in remarks made in the field. Just as often it was found in camps in the form of pranks and horseplay. A good example of this type of mirth making is found in "Reminiscences of the Civil War," a manuscript written in 1905 by T.J. Walker, a volunteer in a Tipton company during the war. In the following excerpt, Walker is the victim of horseplay perpetrated by his messmates just prior to the Battle of Chickamauga.

> *By some means or other, our mess had procured an old rooster, and the day before the battle, we had put him on to boil. Before he had sufficiently cooked, we were all sitting around like half starved wild animals eagerly*

eyeing the boiling pot as the delicious aroma arose and was wafted to our highly sensitive olfactory nerves. Our minds and almost famished stomachs were wrought up to the highest pitch of excitement and expectancy when we contemplated what intense joy and satisfaction those fragrant morsels would create when safely deposited within our half starved stomachs. Just at this time, the bugle sounded! A detail was called for to go on picket duty. As no delay was possible, the rest of my mess was selected for the picket posts, I was at that time excused from picket duty, so I was left sole custodian of the thoroughly cooked and fragrant rooster! When the five stalwart fellows left…the leader of the mess turned to me and said, "Look here, Walker, you take one-sixth of that rooster and put the rest away for us. If you eat any more than your share, it won't be good for you when we come off picket duty." I said, "All right, boys." Well, after the boys had departed, I put the rooster on a board and carved him up into six equal shares and fell to eating. When I had finished my allotted portion, my appetite was keener then ever! So craving was my appetite and longing for a few more morsels that I thought I would just take a small portion from each share. The more I ate, the more my stomach called for that rooster until—I am ashamed to say it—I ate the whole rooster! I ate not only the meat but sopped up the gravy in the pot and like a wild animal of the forest, after my appetite was satiated, I lay down and went to sleep. How long I slept, I could never tell. I know in the contented condition of a full stomach, I was dreaming of home and loved ones. After a while, I dreamed that I was in the presence of the loved one of my dreams and that she had clasped her tender sweet arms around my neck and the sensation was so thrilling that I awoke! But, alas! Instead of my dreams being a reality, when I fully came to myself, I was in the grasp of those five half-starved boys just off of picket duty. Four of them had hold of each one of my limbs and the fifth was slipping a large piece of wood between my teeth. Struggling and unable to articulate on account of the piece of wood that by this time had gotten between my teeth and prized my mouth open, I said, "What does this mean?" The big fellow that was looking after my head said, "Be quiet, my boy, we will show you in a few minutes." He took from out his shirt pocket a long rubber tube about six or seven feet long about the size of my finger. It had a bulb in the center with a funnel at the end! Will you believe it, without lubricating it, he rammed half that tube down my throat and commenced pouring into that funnel by the quart! He would pour in water and then start the pump. Chicken and bread galore would come pouring out like a never ceasing fountain until the last vestige of that rooster was out of my stomach! Then he said, "I will pour in a half gallon for good measure for fear that some of the gravy might be left." As they let me up after having removed the gag from between my teeth, the spokesman said, "Now, damn you, we determined if our stomachs couldn't get part of that chick, yours shouldn't either!"

You may imagine what rage I was in! The whole squad broke and ran the minute they released me. I looked for my gun, but it was gone. They had taken it out of the tent before the operation commenced. Raging like a maniac and threatening dire vengeance on the whole set I dashed after them. Just then, the bugle sounded. Orders were heard far and wide. Fall in ranks! Boys, the enemy is advancing! All hatred and dire vengeance were gone. Every man to his place! The word of command was given! Forward march! Double quick! The Chickamauga Creek was crossed and the Battle of Chickamauga was on!

The McDills of Portersville

Family life in Tipton County during the Civil War is no better exemplified than in a manuscript written by Harriet McDill McLaughlin sometime prior to her death in 1937. Titled *Some Reminiscences of My Father and Mother Robert and Nancy Wilson McDill*, the work covers the twenty-eight-year period between the marriage of Harriet's parents in 1837 and the end of the War Between the States. The bulk of it, however, deals with the experiences of the McDill family through four turbulent years of war.

The following portion of her manuscript mirrors the struggles, the sacrifices and the sorrows that were shared by many families of that period.

I was brought up when children were to be seen, not heard, yet listening was not forbidden. The table-talk consisted in discussing the latest news from the North, and "if so and so happened" there would be war and war meant the dissolution of the Union. Father argued against this. He thought a compromise better if it could be brought about. He knew that the North had many advantages over the South and felt that it would mean defeat for the South. Even after war was declared he told our boys what a terrible thing war between the states would mean; the great financial losses it would bring as well as the loss of life and the hardships on the all classes. He said "Dont [sic] be too hasty to rush into it." However, when troops were called for, the boys felt that it would be a disgrace not to respond to their country's call and three of them volunteered to go.

For a while the business [Mr. McDill owned what today would be called a department store] *was continued but it soon became* difficult to keep up the stock as father was prevented from going to the North by the river blockage. He made a few trips to Cincinnati but it was dangerous and his last purchases were in St. Louis.

Father visited the camps where the boys were in training. He seemed so proud of them and came home full of enthusiasm. It was not long until they were called into active service. Skirmishes soon became battles and almost every day the ranks grew on both sides.

Many fine letters were written home by my brothers and the neighbor boys and we were kept in touch with what was transpiring at the front.

A fine young man Dumpy Daniels, was the letter carrier and brought them to my mother. She kept the letters in two large bags that were fastened on each side of a strong hoop skirt that she wore. When it was safe to send them to anxiously waiting mothers, sisters and sweethearts, I was called and told to dress for I must go on an errand. Mother tied my bonnet or hood under my chin and put the letters in my cloak pockets. Sometimes the journey was rather long for a child of my age (eight years) to walk and I remained over night. On one occasion I had to stay in the country all night at my Uncle Gladney McCreight's place. It was Grandfather's old home, a large plantation. There were many negro slaves but only my three aunts were there as my uncles were in the army.

We had all retired, and were fast asleep when we were awakened by the sound of many footsteps on the porch, the clank of spurs and the rattle of sabers, frightening me almost to death; then orders to "open the door and be d— quick about it" or it would be kicked open. "Get up and prepare breakfast for my men!"

My oldest aunt who was manager and house keeper replied "When we are all dressed I will open the doors but not before." It was about three o'clock in the morning.

Aunt Margaret called Sara the house-maid and together they awakened the cooks and the boys to make the fires, and soon the cooking began. Trips had to be made to the smoke-house to get hams; biscuits were made, ham sliced and fried and eggs too were cooked. Great pots of coffee were prepared.

By this time the men were swarming all over the house and the food was eaten as soon as it could be taken off the fire. I noticed that the men became more quiet after they were fed and warmed by the big wood fire.

After daylight they began to inspect the premises to see what they could take away or destroy. They brought out most of the horses and mules. Just as they were about the start with them, Aunt Margaret walked out and called for the Captain. A rather weak looking and shame faced fellow was pointed out and she addressed him and said: "Captain you have seen how many souls on this plantation must be fed and clothed, and it will require every horse and mule I have to make the crop or they will starve, and I am responsible for them."

After some consultation among the officers, they left a few of their own broken down and blind animals and took with them all our good ones.

As they rode away we were grateful that our lives had been spared from such a mob.

The first heart-breaking news that we had from the line of battle where our boys were stationed, was that brother Scott had been killed in a battle that took place near Chickamuaga Tenn. He was struck by shrapnel from an exploding shell as he was in front of his company when they rushed over the breast-works. I remember that I was told about the place and the meaning of the word. It is an Indian word meaning "the stream of death."

Mother was prostrated and it was the first time I ever saw father shed tears. He was so young and a great favorite with everyone. In school one day my teacher was talking to the rhetoric class. He was speaking of the emotions when he mentioned bravery and said: "If Miss Harriet will pardon me I will tell you about the bravest thing I ever witnessed and the effect it had upon me and all who saw it;" and he gave a graphic account of how brother Scott looked as he waved his hat and bade the boys follow him as he mounted the breastworks.

The next shock was that George had been desperately wounded in a battle at Perryville Kentucky. He was left to die on the field but later some of his comrades ran back and found him sitting against a tree with the blood pouring from a bullet hole in his lung. Going through his body the bullet had cut its way out by the seam of his coat (a grey jacket). An ambulance was called and tender hands carried him in on a stretcher. Later he with other wounded companions was placed in a private home that had been turned into a hospital. Mr. James Holmes of Covington Tenn. was one of the boys. Their wounds were almost identical, one shot in the right lung and the other in the left.

Weeks and days of anxiety followed. We hardly dared hope for his recovery. Then in the providence of God something happened. The Reverend David H. Cummins was a brother-in-law of James Holmes and the pastor of our church. He was born and educated in New Jersey but his sympathies were with the South. He knew conditions for he came in contact with all classes in his religious work. He was a striking character, tall and straight as a silver pine, his bright eyes sparkling. His strong personality impressed everyone. He was truly a man of God and wielded great power for good wherever he went.

He came to father one day and said "Captain McDill, I am going to Kentucky to see our boys and if possible I am going to bring them home." Father told him that if any man could bring them through the lines, he was the man. He went—for with him to decide was the act.

In about a week or ten days, one morning a buggy drove up to our gate and Holmes Cummins a son of David H. got out and began to assist George out from under the many blankets wrapped around him to keep him warm and pillows to prop him up. Only his pale smiling face was visible. The family all rushed out to assist but he could not stand any hearty embraces. The greeting had to be expressed in smiles and tears. He was soon in a big rocking chair before a big wood fire in the living room. Truly a miracle had been wrought.

Mr. Cummins said that when he reached Kentucky, none of the boys had been able to sit up a minute, so he began to prop them up with pillows. Their wounds drained, there was no fever and the hope of getting home helped them to gain strength and he found it safe to start.

The news soon spread and friends and neighbors came bringing many good things to eat, but his diet had to be very limited for awhile. He almost lived on cod liver jelly. "Scott's Emulsion" was not known then.

Recovery was slow but his strength grew a little every day and when spring came he was able to walk about the place and entertain his friends by telling them about his experiences.

The poet of the family, Aunt Mary McDill, wrote a very touching poem about our hero. I can recall only a few lines of it for it has been so long since I read it.

"On the battlefield near Perryville in eighteen-sixty-two
A gallant Tennessean fell,
pierced by a bullet through.
He fell but did not sink in
death upon the battlefield
For his heavenly Father's
sheltering arm
Was there it's [sic] power to
yield."

In October his condition was so much improved that he began to ride about the neighborhood and visit some of the relatives and friends. One afternoon he dressed and put a fine new saddle on his riding horse. Just as he was about to mount, he called mother and said "I heard that the enemy had spies posted about, so I am going to ride around and perhaps I can find out something."

The Civil War

He got his information but in a way he did not Expect, for when he came to the cross roads he was arrested and made prisoner and we never saw him again until after the war was over! He was taken to Memphis and placed in the Irving Block, a temporary jail. This house and property belonged to a Mr. Norton who recovered damages from the Government many years after the war. His son was our neighbor here in Little Rock for a time.

Father went to Memphis to beg for his release, thinking that his physical condition would make it easier, but they were determined to send him to a Northern prison.

Father reached home in a very depressed condition and was scarcely able to stand the terrible change that had taken place in his absence.

A company of four hundred mounted men came down upon us late one afternoon. The advance guard first inspected the barns and shouted "Captain, there is enough provender for every horse and food for all the men! Let us camp here for the night."

You can imagine how we felt when we heard this. By morning the corn, fodder and hay had all been consumed, the hams eaten and most of the chickens roasted. I dont [sic] think Peter could have heard a cock crow but once that night!

In the morning they demanded the key to the store and took everything they could use, and packed great bundles to carry with them. When they came to the millinery rooms they decided to stage a flower parade. They took great bunches of French flowers and tied them to each ear of their horses; then the ribbons and laces were twined about their bridles. The plumes were used on their own hats and what was left of the stock was so trampled and torn by their spurs that it was useless.

There was one thing mother was always grateful for. We should always be willing to give justice and honor where it belongs.

There was not a man on the place that night. My brother was about twelve years old. Sam the negro servant was there, but he seemed dazed and kept himself aloof from the family. The Captain came to the door and asked to speak to mother. He said, "Madame, I see that you and your daughters are alone, and if you will permit me I will bring my blankets and lie right here in your room and assure you and your family protection." Mother thanked him, and we all went upstairs and felt safe in his keeping.

After all this was over Father spent little time in grieving over what had been done. He said that it was now a time for action. He saw the need of a home guard or militia. He called a meeting and helped organize one at once. He was asked to drill the company. The question of equipment was a serious one. There were only a few old shot guns and muskets in the country. Father fitted up the old shop and told the men to bring what they had and he would put them in condition. He had some shot and lead bars from the store and almost every man had bullet moulds for rifle balls.

Then he made swords, or a kind of long knife from carriage springs. Here I did my part to help along. I turned the grindstone many a weary hour while they were being sharpened. The training and drilling began.

On drill days the large woods lot near town was thronged with people who came to encourage and cheer the old men.

In the meantime father fitted up another shop with tools and a turning lathe, where he made spinning wheels and reels. My grandmother had brought her's [sic] from South Carolina, and my aunts had it brought out and set up. Soon everything was humming. Thread was spun and some beautiful cloth was woven.

Aunt Emma wove enough to make herself and sister Mary a dress. When the Yankees saw Aunt's dress hanging in the closet, one of them said "I will take that and send it to my girl in the North to show what a home spun dress looks like."

Our girls wore them with much pride, and a song was written about them. The chorus ended with the lines "Hurrah for the homespun dress that Southern ladies wear!"

Father was so pleased with the grey jeans that they wove, that he cut himself a suit of clothes from a bolt of it. He was a rather large man and it took several yards for a frock tailed coat.

Mother had to make it as Osborn the tailor had gone North some time ago. She had no machine of course. She worked all the week basting and stitching the long seams. There was much pressing and fitting the notched pieces together.

Late Saturday afternoon the last stitch was taken and the basting removed. Mother drew a sigh of relief. Sunday morning when father went into his room to dress for church, he found the suit all neatly laid out on the bed. Mother waited anxiously for him to appear. Presently the door burst open and he came out and in a very angry voice he said "Nancy! You have ruined my suit! I wont [sic] wear it. I had every notch marked and you did not pay attention to them." He stood up and the front coat tails touched the floor! He jerked it off.

Mother who was always so patient in all circumstances, was almost in tears. Father said, "You sewed the bias seam of tail to the front!" "Well," said mother, "we have found out what is the matter with the coat Robert and I will rip it up and make it all right." And then we all roared with laughter for it was excruciatingly funny.

The Civil War

When mother had spent a few more days on the coat, it was all right, and father seemed so proud of it that he had his picture taken in it.

You may ask what became of the McDill Band. True a number of the boys were in the army, but others took their places. In war nothing appeals to patriotism like martial music. Now the marches were not so quick and lively. Sometimes they were almost as slow and solemn as the "Dead March" from the oratorio "Saul," as it led the funeral cortege of some victim of camp fever or of one who had been killed in battle and whose body was brought home by some relative or friend.

Things moved on as usual. It was work, work until late into the night.

One day a letter came from George who had suffered the terrors of prison life and had at last been exchanged and finally gotten back to his old regiment and what was left of his company.

When the roll was called so many were absent that it made him very sad. For them taps had long been sounded. On Nov. 30th 1864 the bloody battle of Franklin was fought. It had been called the bloodiest battle and the greatest blunder of the war. George said, "It was the greatest trial of my life. Uncle John McCreight, my brother William and many of my best friends were killed. I shed tears and wished that I might have died with them. I realized that the cause for which they died and I had suffered, was lost and that the last drama would soon be enacted."

Lee had already surrendered and Johnston's army of which George's regiment was a unit, was camped at Greensboro, N.C. The scene was most pathetic. Gen. Johnston talked to the boys and thanked them for their loyalty and support, then ordered them to stack arms, and as they went back to their homes he said, "Take this thought with you. You have fought for a cause you felt was right and just (states' rights)—for home and loved ones. You have won honor for your bravery and great sacrifices that war demands." They stacked their guns around a tall pine tree. George reached up and cut a twig as a memento and put it into his knap sack.

His home coming was a mingling of joy and of sorrow for those left in their "silent tents whose doors have no outward swing."

I will not dwell on the "Reconstruction Period" that followed. No true history can ever be written of those dark days of humiliation in the dear old South.

I cannot recall ever seeing my father in the kitchen. It was detached from the other building as was the custom in the South. One morning my sister Annie and I were busy cooking or washing the dishes when father came to the door and asked for a pan or bucket. Annie picked up a large tin pan and he said "I guess this will do," and disappeared. In perhaps half an hour he returned with the pan filled with dirt and silver money that he had buried in the old shop. It took several washings to clean it. I don't remember how much it was. It consisted of dollars, halves and quarters, many dimes and five cent pieces. We came to the bottom of the pan and were reminded of the Arabian Nights story of the "Forty Thieves" for the print of the money was there just as it was in the measure that was lent to measure their money.

With this money father managed to get a few goods together and opened the store again. My brother Shannon was old enough to assist him. George could not stand confinement and went back to work on the farm.

As things became more normal social activities took on new life. There were barbecues, picnics, public celebrations of various kinds. The Band was again organized and added much to the pleasure of the occasions. They would often play a medley of Old Southern airs such as "Listen to the Mocking bird," "Nellie Gray," "My Old Kentucky Home," but "Dixie" was always the favorite as it is today.

Father seemed still to get great pleasure out of his music. Sometimes as we sat on the porch in the moonlight, he would bring out his violin, prop his chair against one of the columns and play until late into the night. We were all very quiet and I think the mocking birds were listening too, for no other sound was heard. The air was fragrant with the odor of roses and star Jessamine and all the old fashioned flowers. I am glad that all our people seemed to have the garden spirit and in their own simple way made the world a wee bit sweeter and better for having lived in it. For all these things, and what they have done, I am glad and count it a heritage.

"Deep in my grateful heart
there lies
A memory that never
Dies"—

"Not Unpleasant Memories"

A most succinct but graphic description of the tragic Civil War years can be found in the court records of Tipton County. Following the December term of 1861, clerk John T. Douglas wrote:

> The end of an evil year in the history of America—what another year will bring forth remained to be seen—perhaps and most likely the bloodiest war ever known in America. God forbid![43]

The Civil War

Richard S. Barrett, clerk in 1865, penned the following on the same page:

> *Another and another and another—each worse than its predecessor have followed. How well that the future could not be penetrated. 1865.*[44]

The war meant different things to different people, but few were able to escape the cataclysmic effects only intimated at by Douglas and Barrett. Yet, despite the devastation, hardship and grief brought on by the war, many Tipton Countians were able to gain some measure of happiness. This was particularly true of the children who possessed an exhilaration and vigor, which served to shield them from the troubles of the times.

Some youngsters actually derived great pleasure from privation. One of these was W.V. Byars, who, as a boy under ten, lived in Covington during the war. His "not unpleasant memories" help provide a glimpse of how county residents coped with one the South's common problems—a shortage of necessities.[45]

Young Byars recalled that "if destitution had not revived the colonial handloom after it was supposed to be altogether out of date," he "would never have seen the skill of hand and eye, co-ordinated in the work of a 'born artist' on the handloom."[46] To be sure, county women became so proficient at spinning, weaving and tailoring that little town boys like Byars were never deprived of roundabouts and breeches to go with their copper-toed shoes, nor country lads the one-piece garments they wore in summer, which earned them the title "shirt-tailed boys."

As the war progressed, other primitive devices and practices had to be restored because of high prices and scarcity. For instance, when the supply of Northern oil was stopped, homemade candles were substituted for lamps. "When we went back to the tallow candles," wrote Byars, "helping to mold them became part of the education of which I am now proud."[47]

With the virtual disappearance of coffee from county tables, some families made a substitute from sweet potato fragments. "The worst destitution brought home to me," noted Byars, "came through operating a case-knife on sweet potatoes, to be cut first into small cubes then dried in the sun and finally parched as a substitute for coffee."[48] Other alternatives to coffee were made from blackberry leaves and sassafras roots.

By February 1863 county residents were paying exorbitant prices for nearly all goods. Calico was selling for $7.00 a yard; shoes, $80.00 a pair; cotton thread, $3.00 a spool; sugar, $7.50 a small keg; jeans, $6.50 a yard; and common shoe blacking, $4.00 a box.

Salt for preserving meat was also a scarce commodity by this time, but then so was meat. When a Federal detachment occupied Covington and stayed long enough to order bread to be baked by families found with flour, they were happy to settle for lardless loaves—"lardless because only the razorback, lean, fleet, and wary as a fox, could survive the 'requisitions' of both sides by taking to the deepest woods."[49]

Many of these wild hogs were, however, apparently not swift enough to escape hungry citizens, a fact corroborated by Byars.

> *The utmost opulence of these times can never give such memories as belong to a razor-back ham, well-smoked, after having had molasses, black pepper and spices rubbed into it. Day after day I have gathered chips and made the smoke under such hams, some of which escaped both armies and occasionally made the worst period of destitution so joyful to remember that Chicago* [with her stockyards] *cannot hope…for "love or money" to supply the like.*[50]

Many people, especially the country folk, were able to raise their own food so that starvation presented no real threat. Liza Culbreath, who was born a slave in 1852 on the Bob Taylor farm near Mason, later recalled that there was a Federal army camp near the farm and that the soldiers often asked the slaves to come to the camp and take leftovers from their meals. She said, however, that they had enough to eat during the course of the war, even if it was sometimes nothing more than fat meat and cornbread, with a small ration of flour twice a week per family. "We generally," remembered another resident, "had a sufficiency of the common necessaries of life to supply the wants of nature and keep starvation from our doors."[51]

Lieutenant Brown and His Incredible Red Monster

The Battle of Memphis on June 6, 1862, was a complete and one-sided victory for the North. Not only was the Confederate ram fleet destroyed and the city captured but the Mississippi River was opened as far south as Vicksburg. To be sure, Memphis had already been made untenable by the Federal occupation of Corinth, but the Confederate fleet's destruction ensured the North of river supremacy down to the next bluff.

Luckily, the Confederates had had the foresight, following the loss of Island No. 10 and Farragut's passage of the New Orleans forts, to destroy one ironclad under construction in Memphis, the *Tennessee*, and to move a second incomplete vessel, the *Arkansas*, to a place of greater safety. The latter was towed downriver to the mouth of the Yazoo then up that stream to Greenwood, Mississippi. Here the unfinished ironclad was safe enough for the time being, but the surrounding countryside was devoid of needed materials and work on the vessel proceeded as slowly as it had at Memphis.

It was clear that a strong resourceful leader was needed to finish the project. On May 28, Secretary of the Navy Stephen R. Mallory sent a wire to Lieutenant "Newt" Brown, a former Tipton Countian, ordering him to assume command of the *Arkansas* and to finish and equip her without regard to time or money.

Isaac Newton Brown, the Kentucky-born son of a Presbyterian minister, had shown an early interest in construction while living as a youngster in Covington. As a fatherless boy, he sauntered almost daily around the square watching workmen build Tipton County's first permanent courthouse. In 1834 he enlisted in the U.S. Navy as a midshipman and saw service in the Seminole and Mexican Wars as well as Commodore Perry's expedition to Japan. When the clouds of war began to gather, he resigned from the old navy that had been home for twenty-seven years and cast his lot with the Confederacy.

As it turned out, Mallory had made an excellent choice. A man of lesser determination would have been appalled at the sight that greeted Brown at Greenville: only five carpenters were working; the guns, without carriages, were strewn about the deck; the engines were in pieces; and the only portion of the railroad iron on hand for the vessel's armor was at the bottom of the Yazoo, the barge carrying it having foundered. As if that were not enough, the river was out of its banks, leaving the hulk of the *Arkansas* moored quite a distance from dry land.

Brown took one look at the chaotic situation and exploded into action. In just two days he had raised the armor barge, moved the *Arkansas* downstream to the higher ground of Yazoo City and acquired twenty blacksmiths from nearby plantations and two hundred carpenters from the army to work in shifts around the clock.

By July, Brown had turned the *Arkansas* into a formidable war machine. Measuring about 165 by 35 feet, she carried a casement covered with railroad iron on the sides and boiler iron on the quarter and stern. For armament she carried ten guns—three of mixed calibers in each broadside, two eight-inch columbiads firing forward and two rifled thirty-two-pounders firing aft. The vessel, however, had one great drawback, which it demonstrated on a short shakedown cruise across the Yazoo; her ancient homebuilt engines had a tendency to stop on dead center, and if one stopped, the other pushed the craft in a circle. In a narrow river, this almost certainly meant going aground.

As for looks, the *Arkansas* would have been ugly even if Brown had followed the original design. His modifications and compromises had done nothing to improve her appearance. She was a squat craft with a single excessively

Lieutenant Isaac Newton Brown. *Battles and Leaders*.

fat smokestack and vertical, instead of the usual sloped, broadsides. The ram was supposed to be chocolate brown, the same color as the river, but because of bad paint she was mostly red with rust.

While Brown had been busy finishing work on the *Arkansas* and gathering a crew to man her, Flag Officer David G. Farragut had run the biggest part of his fleet of big oceangoing sloops past the Confederate defenses at Vicksburg and he, along with the river squadron of Captain Charles H. Davis, which had destroyed the Confederate flotilla at Memphis, lay above Vicksburg, between that place and the mouth of the Yazoo. Both Federal naval officers knew about the *Arkansas*, but with the numerous men-of-war in their combined fleets, they refused to believe that any single opponent would dare challenge such odds; they could not have been more mistaken.

With the blessings of his superiors, Brown weighed anchor on July 14 and steamed down the Yazoo with the intention of surprising the enemy early the next morning while they were at breakfast. But it took the *Arkansas* all day to cover half the distance to the Mississippi. Besides the usual engine troubles, steam was discovered to have leaked into the forward magazine, wetting all the powder.

Fortunately, a clearing was found around an old abandoned sawmill near the mouth of the Big Sunflower River. Here Brown had the powder landed and spread upon tarpaulins to dry in the sun, a procedure that consumed most of the afternoon. With constant shaking and turning, the powder was dry to the point of ignition before sunset. That night the *Arkansas* lay at anchor near Haynes Bluff, and at 3:00 a.m. on July 15, was underway again.

At 4:00 a.m. the same morning, a Union squadron of three boats was dispatched for a reconnaissance up the Yazoo to find out about Confederate river defenses and to learn something of the *Arkansas*, which was reported to be on the move. The ram *Queen of the West* (Lieutenant James Hunter), the timber clad *Tyler* (Lieutenant William Gwin) and the ironclad *Corondolet* (Lieutenant Commander Henry Walke) entered the Yazoo, leaving behind the fleets of Davis and Farragut anchored along the left bank of the Mississippi. All lay with steam down because of the stifling summer heat and a shortage of coal.

Dawn found the *Arkansas* entering Old River, so named because at this point the Yazoo followed an old Mississippi channel, or cutoff, for a distance of about ten miles. As the sunshine filtered through the trees along the river's east bank, the three Federal vessels were spotted a few miles ahead steaming upriver in line abreast, the *Corondolet* in the middle.

Brown made a short speech and then ordered the men to their guns. Stripping to their waists in the morning heat, they tied handkerchiefs around their heads to keep the sweat from their eyes. The officers, too,

The *Arkansas* under construction at Yazoo City. *Battles and Leaders.*

except for Brown, had also removed their coats and were moving about the deck in their undershirts. The captain was conning in full uniform from the top of the shield just above the bow guns, which he ordered not to be fired until the fight was fully joined.

The sudden appearance of the Confederate ironclads bearing down on them caused the Federal commanders to act independently. The *Queen of the West* had orders to ram any enemy vessel encountered, but being unarmed and finding her speed advantage offset by the current, she rounded to and frankly ran. The *Tyler* and *Corondolet* remained on course, intending to make good use of their bow guns, then to swing their helms downstream and make a running fight of it with their stern pieces, expecting the noise to bring reinforcements from the rest of the fleet. Both fired their bow guns and missed. The *Arkansas*, however, found its mark, putting one of her shells through the wooden bulwark of the *Tyler*, killing six men on the gun deck.

As the Federal boats turned to run, the *Arkansas* closed upon the *Corondolet*, the slower of the two, sending shells into her unarmored stern. *Corondolet*'s projectiles glanced harmlessly from the slanting shield of the ram, doing little damage except to take off an Irish seaman's head when he stuck it out of a gunport to see how the battle was progressing.

Most of the missiles fired straight at the stern of the *Arkansas* were deflected upward and over by the inclined shield, but presently one caromed a little low, inflicting a severe contusion to Brown's head. He, nevertheless, remained at his post, relieved that he had found no brain particles in a handful of clotted blood drawn from the wound. At about that time, however, the *Tyler* slowed to help the badly damaged *Corondolet*. She put a shot into the pilot-house of the *Arkansas*, killing one pilot and disabling another.

The *Arkansas* was now within range of riflemen aboard the *Tyler*, who were concentrating their volley on the tall, bearded figure barking orders from his exposed position on the hurricane deck. Presently, a minie ball struck Brown over the temple, knocking him through an open hatch and down among the guns below. When he regained his senses, he was being placed below deck with the rest of the casualties. He promptly regained his feet, climbed back topside and assumed his former position on the shield.

The shells from the *Arkansas*, he noticed, were continuing to take their toll on the *Corondolet*. They smashed timbers, beams, lifeboats and the aft sections of her quarter and spar decks. They tore away her steam gauge, her steam escape pipes and some of her cold water pipes. She began to lose headway as the menacing prow of the Confederate ram drew closer. Seeing that the *Arkansas* intended to ram, Lieutenant Commander Walke, an old friend and shipmate of Brown in former days, took his vessel into the shallow water close to the west bank. At this point, a shot from the *Arkansas* tore away the *Corondolet*'s steering gear, and she became unmanageable and ran into the bank. Unable to follow because the water was too shallow, the *Arkansas* poured a broadside into the *Corondolet* as she passed the stranded vessel in pursuit of *Tyler* and *Queen of the West*. The Federal gunboat was left wallowing in the shallows one and a half miles from the mouth of the Yazoo with both steam and survivors escaping from her ports.

Gwin, who had held the speed of the *Tyler* down while supporting the much slower *Corondolet*, now put on full steam. The timber clad, battered and burning, rounded the last bend and entered the Mississippi, her captain swearing furiously because the *Queen of the West*, now tearing downstream toward the fleet, had not taken a hand against the *Arkansas*. Perhaps, too, he was angry with the fleet for obviously ignoring the sounds of the long running battle. The sailors of the fleet had indeed heard the shooting, but they believed it to be the gunboats shelling rebel positions in the woods. They were caught napping, and as a result none of the Federal ships had steam up or guns loaded when the strange red vessel came into view.

Although Brown had been informed earlier that more than thirty enemy vessels lay upstream from Vicksburg, he was nevertheless astounded by the sight of such an assemblage. Everywhere he looked, except astern, he saw a veritable forest of smokestacks and masts. Anchored in mixed order along the east side of the river were sloops, rams and ironclads; along the west side, steamers and mortar boats.

Noting that the Union rams were stationed behind the spaces between the larger ships, Brown ordered his pilot to drive the *Arkansas* close up against the enemy line of vessels to prevent the rams from working up enough speed to strike him. This maneuver, however, carried the *Arkansas* within point-blank range of the eleven-inch pivot guns of Farragut's steam sloops, and as she went down the line firing both broadsides, she took hit after hit in return.

Soon the Federal line of fire grew into what seemed to Brown a constantly closing circle. He found that in such a situation he could fire in any direction without fear of hitting friends or missing enemies. This did not hold true for the Federal vessels, some of which were accidentally hit by shots meant for the *Arkansas*.

The Confederate ram was now receiving about as much damage as she was inflicting, with shots from all directions ringing against her sides. As she passed the sloop *Richmond*, she was hit with a tremendous broadside, which filled her gundeck with flying railroad iron and splinters. An eleven-inch solid shot penetrated her casement armor, killing or wounding all of the members of a sixteen-man gun crew. A rifle bolt added eleven more to the casualty list. The smokestack was so full of holes that *Arkansas*'s furnace draft failed, causing her to drop from 120 pounds of team pressure to 20, just barely enough to keep her engine turning. The temperature had reached 130 degrees in the engine room, forcing men from the guns to relieve firemen and engineers at fifteen-minute intervals.

With one-eighth of her crew casualties, her lifeboats shot away and armor plating ripped from her stern, the *Arkansas* was still giving as much as she was taking. On the shield, Brown had never stopped giving orders through the speaking tube to his men below. Completely exposed to the deadly hail of iron, he, at one point, had his telescope shot from his hands.

Finally, one of the rams, the *Lancaster*, gained steerageway and headed straight for the *Arkansas* in a final, desperate attempt to block her way. Brown ordered the pilot to ram his way through, but the collision was averted when the *Arkansas* put a shot through *Lancaster*'s boiler at one hundred yards. The resulting explosion of steam scalded crewmen standing nearby and forced others overboard to escape a similar fate. The disabled craft drifted downstream with men clinging to her rudder.

The *Arkansas* was in the clear now. Limping badly, she rounded the point to Vicksburg, where a cheering crowd had gathered on the bluff to greet her. General Earl Van Dorn, the commander at Vicksburg and the man who had ordered the *Arkansas* to that town so that she might attack Federal transports below, witnessed her arrival and sent Brown his greetings. He felt that she should steam back up and sink some of the enemy ships, but Brown said no. He did not care to risk further either his ship or his crew just then. His immediate concern was the removal of his dead and wounded and the putting of the *Arkansas* into some sort of defensive posture for the attack that was sure to be launched against her.

Farragut, meanwhile, was infuriated, almost to the point of incoherence, at the Confederate ram's triumph. She now lay between his fleet and New Orleans, the place to which the falling stage of the river would soon force him to return. Besides that, a small number of Federal vessels including his own sloop, *Brooklyn*, were still below Vicksburg, where the seemingly unsinkable rebel ram might attack them at any time.

The more Farragut thought about the state of affairs, the angrier he became. He decided to charge down, without delay, and destroy the *Arkansas* where she lay, broad daylight and the Vicksburg forts notwithstanding. After a time, however, his staff was able to calm him down enough to delay the move until proper preparations could be made. Refusing to postpone the attack any longer than dusk, he ordered the guns loaded with solid shot and the *Hartford*'s heaviest anchor suspended from her main-yardarm, meaning to drop it completely through the rebel ram's deck and bottom. The river ironclads would provide covering fire, keeping the batteries on the bluff busy while the sloops did their work on the monster below. Supported by the ram, *Sumpter*, the saltwater fleet steamed downriver just before sunset.

Dusk was falling when Farragut's lead vessel reached Vicksburg. The wily Brown, anticipating the attack, had shifted the *Arkansas*'s position after sunset so that the move would not be noticed. As smoky twilight gave way to inky darkness, the red ironclad was well camouflaged against the clay of the bluff. The flash of her guns was all that could be seen of the ram as the Union ships passed in single file. By the time they located her, they had only enough time to reply with one swift broadside each before the current carried them out of range.

Perplexity among the men of the *Arkansas* at having to wage the day's third engagement, tied to the shore and with no more than half the ship's complement available for duty, changed to elation as the battle progressed. Rapidly firing their bow and port-broadside guns, they soon found that they had some marked advantages over their adversaries: they could shoot more accurately from their stationary position and they could see distinctly the Federal ships as they passed, their tall masts silhouetted against the last glow of daylight on the western horizon.

One by one the sloops glided so close to the *Arkansas* that her crew could hear not only the shot ripping through their sides but also the moans of their wounded. The rebel ram, however, did not go completely unscathed. The *Hartford*, groping blindly, put a chance shot through her engine room, disabling the engine and killing or wounding five men. She nevertheless kept firing until the last of the Federal vessels was out of range; then all was quiet once more.

This latest action cost Farragut five men killed and sixteen wounded. Although he had failed again to destroy the *Arkansas*, he had some consolation in the fact that he was now below Vicksburg. But he wasn't satisfied. He wanted the *Arkansas*, and he meant to have her, regardless of the cost. Early the next morning he sent a message to Davis, proposing that they converge with their fleets on the rebel at high noon and finish her. In his reply, Davis advised patience and self-control, and for the next few days continued to resist pressure from Farragut.

Finally, after observing movement on the part of *Arkansas* (she attempted a sortie, but her engine broke down again, and she was barely able to regain her former position beneath the bluff), Davis agreed on July 21 to a daring plan. Early the following morning, the gunboats *Essex* and *Queen of the West* from the upper fleet and *Sumpter* from the lower fleet would attempt to send the *Arkansas* to the bottom by ramming her. *Essex*, perhaps the most formidable vessel in the river navy, had just rejoined the fleet after having been completely rebuilt in St. Louis. Her commander, William D. "Dirty Bill" Porter, jumped at the opportunity for action, for he had been as inactive as his boat, and he was afraid his half-brother David, whom he despised, was getting more recognition than he.

The Federal commanders could not have picked a more opportune time for their attack. The morning of July 22 found some of the officers and all but twenty-eight of the *Arkansas*'s crew in the hospital suffering from battle wounds and sickness. The boat itself lay helplessly tied to the shore with a disabled engine.

As the *Essex* and *Queen of the West* steamed down at dawn, Brown slacked off the *Arkansas*'s bow-line, turning her sharp prow toward the enemy. The *Essex*, not being a ram, swerved at the last moment to avoid a collision that could easily have finished her, and both boats let go a broadside at close range as she slid past. One of *Essex*'s shells broke through the *Arkansas*'s gundeck, inflicting heavy casualties to what was already a skeleton crew. In return *Essex* took a shot, which damaged her engines and sent her drifting with the current to the fleet below. Just then the *Queen* rounded to and struck *Arkansas* a glancing blow that was too weak to do any damage. A broadside unleashed by the *Arkansas* raked the Union ram from stem to stern and forced her to crawl away, too badly shot up to try another blow. For some unexplained reason, *Sumpter* never got into action at all.

So, for the time being, the fighting ended at Vicksburg. Farragut, unable to stay so far north because of falling water, a low fuel supply and illness among his men, headed for New Orleans on July 26. Davis, who could do nothing without army support, steamed northward for Helena, Arkansas, the same day.

Vicksburg had been delivered, along with hundreds of miles of river both above and below. The naval siege had been lifted by a lone homemade ironclad, backed by the ingenuity and boldness of her commander and builder. She had repulsed everything that two victorious Union fleets could throw against her and as a result had prolonged the war by single-handedly disrupting a campaign.

When old-timers around Covington learned of Newt Brown's daring and heroic exploits, they were proud to boast that he had once been a citizen of Tipton County.

Two Confederate Generals

The rank of general in the Confederate Army eluded all of the brave and heroic soldiers that marched out of Tipton County to fight in the Civil War. However, at least two men who had lived in the county for a time prior to the war did attain that rank. One of these was William R. Scurry, the son of Thomas J. and Catherine (Bledsoe) Scurry, an early Covington lawyer. Born on February 10, 1821, in Gallatin, Tennessee, he moved to Tipton County at an early age. Here he attended school until the age of sixteen when he followed the lead of his brother and moved to Texas, settling in San Augustine.

Scurry became a licensed lawyer and then district attorney of the fifth judicial district before he reached the age of twenty-one. For a time following the Mexican War, in which he rose from the rank of private to major, he owned a newspaper, the *State Gazette*, in Austin.

After serving as a member of the secession convention of 1861, Scurry joined the Confederate Army as lieutenant colonel of the 4th Texas Cavalry. The following year found him under the command of General Sibley in the latter's attempted occupation of New Mexico Territory. Following battles of Valverde and Glorieta Cañon, Scurry was promoted brigadier general to rank from September 12, 1862.

General Scurry commanded the land forces in the successful recapture of Galveston on January 1, 1863, and took a leading part in the Red River Campaign of 1864, participating in the battles of Mansfield and Pleasant Hill in Louisiana against Banks. After Banks's retreat he went to Arkansas with Kirby Smith to oppose a Union advance under Steele and was there mortally wounded on April 30, 1864, in the battle of Jenkins' Ferry. Refusing to be taken from the field, where doctors might have been able to save his life, he died on the battlefield from loss of blood. Scurry County, Texas, is named in his honor.

Unlike Scurry, Cadmus M. Wilcox was not a native Tennessean, but like Scurry he spent many of his early years in Tipton County. A native of Wayne County, North Carolina, he was born on May 29, 1824, the son of Reuben and Sarah (Garland) Wilcox. His parents soon moved to Covington, where he grew up and lived until he entered college at the University of Nashville. Shortly thereafter, in 1842, he was appointed to the United States Military Academy, where he graduated four years later in the same class with T.J. Jackson, George E. Pickett and George B. McClellan.

Commissioned a brevet second lieutenant in the 4th U.S. Infantry, Wilcox joined the forces of General Taylor in Mexico and fought in the battle of Monterey. On February 16, 1847, he was promoted second lieutenant, 7th Infantry, and transferred to General Winfield Scott's army. He saw action at Veracruz, Cerro Gordo and so distinguished himself in the advance on Mexico City that he was made an aide to General John A. Quitman. He later distinguished himself again by leading the storming party at Chapultepec and received the brevet of first lieutenant for his gallantry.

In 1848, Wilcox served as groomsman in the wedding of his friend Lieutenant Ulysses S. Grant. Three years later he was promoted to first lieutenant and saw service in the Seminole War. Then from 1852 to 1857, he was assistant instructor of infantry tactics at West Point.

In 1858 failing health caused Wilcox to take a year's leave of absence in Europe. On his return the following year, he published *Rifles and Rifle Practice*, the first American manual on this topic, and in 1860 he translated from French to English a book on Austrian evolutions of the line.

Wilcox was commissioned captain on December 20, 1860, and was serving in New Mexico when his home state of Tennessee seceded. He resigned from the U.S. Army on June 8, 1861, and was commissioned colonel of the 9th Alabama Infantry. As such he fought at First Bull Run and until the final surrender at Appomattox, was with the Army of Northern Virginia in virtually all of its great battles. He established himself as one of the finest subordinate commanders in the Confederate Army.

On October 21, 1861, Wilcox was promoted to brigadier-general. In the Peninsula campaign his brigade lost more men than any other brigade—1,055 out of 1,800. At Second Bull Run, he capably commanded three brigades, and during the Chancellorsville campaign, his stubborn resistance while waiting for reinforcements resulted in the defeat of Sedgwick at

Major General Cadmus Marcellus Wilcox, one of Lee's most dependable lieutenants.

Salem Church. He made a charge at Gettysburg on July 2, 1863, which, had it been supported, might have broken the Federal center. The next day, however, he received a bloody repulse while supporting the famous charge of Pickett.

On August 13, Wilcox was promoted to the rank of major-general. He was given command of Dorsey Pender's old division, with which he augmented his reputation as a skilled tactician at the Wilderness and Spottsylvania. At Petersburg on April 2, 1865, a portion of his troops held Forts Alexander and Gregg until they were almost annihilated, enabling General Longstreet to cover the retreat of Lee westward. A few days later at Appomattox, Wilcox's division was scheduled to support Gordon's corps in an attempt to break through the Federal lines when operations were terminated by the Confederate surrender. While Lee and Grant negotiated, a group of Union generals, including Sheridan, Gibbon and Ingalls, rode forward to see their old friend Wilcox, taking him back to their lines to visit Grant.

After the war, General Wilcox, a bachelor, settled in Washington, D.C., where he resided with the widow and children of his elder brother, C.S. Congressman John A. Wilcox of Texas. He felt such a sense of responsibility for his sister-in-law (the former Emily Donelson, daughter of Andrew Jackson Donelson) and her children that he declined commissions in the Korean and Egyptian armies to remain with them.

In 1886, following two decades of varying fortune, Wilcox was appointed chief of the railroad division of the Land Office by President Cleveland, a position he retained until his death in 1890. "I know of no man of rank… on the Southern side who had more warm friends, *North* and *South*, than Cadmus M. Wilcox," wrote General Henry Heth.[52] That belief was borne out at his funeral, where four general officers of the Union Army and four general officers of the Confederate Army were pallbearers and General Joseph E. Johnston was chief mourner.

Days of Desperate Men

The Strange Demise of Handsome Jack

Quite a bit of excitement was created during the summer of 1941 when a fisherman named Henry Theis discovered the charred remains of a steamboat that had washed out beneath the bluff at Randolph. Most of the hull was embedded under 30 feet of earth, but from the shape of the timbers in the exposed portion, the boat was judged to have been about 230 feet long and some 40 to 50 feet wide. Several people from various parts of the county journeyed to Randolph to view the interesting relic of old riverboat days and enjoyed speculating about its history.

According to one theory prevalent at the time, the hull was that of a large steamer, which exploded her boilers near Randolph in 1841 and burned. An account of this disaster relates that the boat, en route from New Orleans to Randolph with a heavy cargo, drifted downstream a short distance from the town and sank.

Theis, on the other hand, was confident that he had found the skeleton of a Civil War transport or possibly even a gunboat. His assumption was based upon the fact that while working to uncover the wreck, he had found a bayonet, a canteen, a U.S. soldier's belt buckle and some cannonballs.

Judging, however, from its location, its proximity to the bluff and its apparent connection with the military, the wreck was more likely that of the *Mississippi*, a steamer that sank at Randolph in 1846 under very unusual circumstances. The boat, en route from Cincinnati to New Orleans, was carrying troops, supplies and equipment for the war that had just been declared with Mexico.

The story of the ill-fated journey of the *Mississippi*, as told by its pilot, David Homes, appeared many years ago in the Memphis *Commercial Appeal* in Joe Curtis's column, "In the Pilothouse." Here is Homes's narrative of what happened:

> *The* Mississippi *come to Cincinnati light—that means without passengers or freight. We took on a few soldiers there,—horses, cannon, ammunition and whatnot. Between Cincinnati and Louisville, which was our next stop, who should come into the pilothouse but John Simond, better known to us on the river as "Handsome Jack," a professional gambler from down about New Orleans.*
>
> *In answer to a question, he explained that he was going back to New Orleans to enlist for service in the Army. When I say handsome, I mean it too. I believe that he was the best lookin' man I'd ever set eyes on. Always wore fine clothes, and, being a college man, he had no trouble findin' associates mongst the best people.*
>
> *Down at Madison, Indiana, our boat was hailed, and we took aboard a family whose son was named Fentress Frazer. From all I gathered they were wealth people accompany'n their son who was to become a soldier after we arrived in New Orleans where an Indiana regiment was being formed for the war. Well, Handsome Jack discovered that Fentress Frazer was carrying considerable money, and his fingers got to itching for more of it. So, after we left Uniontown, Kentucky, they with three others started a poker game. At first it was a friendly affair; then they began bettin' small amounts like a quarter or a half dollar. Handsome Jack raised one time to bet $5. Young Frazer won. Ann was so interested that she stood by as a watcher. Later that afternoon the bettin' was brisk. Real money was changing hands. Frazer seemed in good luck, but when I went off watch that evenin' at six o'clock, I could see that Handsome Jack was just baiting him.*
>
> *The game broke up at Cairo with Frazer a good winner. In the meantime Handsome Jack was seen makin' love to Ann. Her father and mother objected, but she only laughed at what she said were a "lot of silly imaginations."*
>
> *But Handsome Jack didn't let any grass grow under his feet. He kept makin' love to Ann and won her over by the time we departed from Cairo. However, her brother, mother and father took her to a stateroom and must have pounded some advice into her head, for when she came out, she spurned further attentions from Handsome Jack.*
>
> *Later that day, Fentress Frazer and Handsome Jack met on the larboard cabin guards, talked and fought. Some of the crew, hearing the rumpus, ran to 'em just in time to prevent Handsome Jack from throwing Frazer overboard. After he had been pulled back into the guards, he shook his fist*

in Handsome Jack's face tellin' him he'd cut his throat from ear to ear if he ever spoke again to his sister Ann.

Handsome Jack jerked a knife out of his pocket and would have plunged its long blade into Frazer if Ann hadn't happened along and come between 'em.

That caused Handsome Jack to withdraw from the scene and when his actions were reported to the captain, he threatened to set him ashore unless he behaved himself. But Handsome Jack kept mooning around. Wouldn't speak to anyone. Appeared like he was waitin' opportunity to knife Frazer to death, but that young man stayed away from him.

We landed at Randolph late one afternoon when I was on watch and Handsome Jack come in the pilothouse very quietly, sat down on the high bench, leaned over with his face in his hands, and I heard him mumble to himself, "They can't do that to me. I love Ann, and I'm going to have her or pass out tryin'."

I said nothin' to him and he left a few minutes later. We took on some cotton at Randolph for the army at New Orleans. It was stored amidship 'mongst some other freight. Directly under the cotton and in the boat's hold was some kegs of powder.

We had just backed away from the landing at Randolph and I was swingin' er head down stream, when there was an alarm of fire. On account of the cargo and passengers aboard, there was a sort of panic. Our crew attempted to put out the fire, but in some unexplained way, sparks fell through an open hatch down in the hold where it caught other combustible freight stored next to the powder cans.

The captain ordered me to land. As I was now headed down-stream, I saw a place along shore a quarter of a mile below Randolph where there was good water. I headed her that way and landed safely. In the meantime, the crew had set about warning all passengers to get ashore quick as possible, and they did.

Fifteen minutes after the boat was deserted by crew and passengers, two or three powder kegs exploded, scattered fire in all directions, and in twenty minutes the Mississippi was a solid mass of flames.

The powder explosion tore a hole in the bottom and sides of her hull and she sank at shore her bow against the bank but tied to a tree. Her stern went down in deep water.

There was no loss of life except one man. And, maybe you'll guess who that was. He was none other than Handsome Jack, the famous river gambler, who concealed himself in the boat's hold. Water from two or three holes in the hull prevented him from bein' burned to death. He drowned. The crew who found his body in the sunken hull searched it and among *his effects was a note to young Frazer's parents that they had robbed him of Ann and they "shall not live, for I will destroy this boat and cause their lives to be snapped out with its flames."*

So after reading that scribbled note, the captain knew how the Mississippi *was set on fire and why.*

The Murder of Jo Bragg

The greatest menace to the citizens of Tipton County during the Civil War came not from the troops of either army but from roving bands of Confederate deserters who carried on a campaign of robbery, destruction and even murder. They were aided in their endeavors by the fact that the war had forced the suspension of civil government in the county. They could, therefore, carry out their depredations without fear of the law because it did not exist.

Ironically, a young Covington man was the leader of one of the first guerrilla bands to make its appearance upon the scene. He was Lou Davis, who joined Captain J.B. Turner's infantry company at the beginning of the war but who deserted at Corinth following the battle of Shiloh. Returning home, he soon realized that by remaining there, he ran the risk of being arrested as a deserter by Confederate authorities or of being captured by Federal troops. With such gloomy prospects looming very real before him, he decided to become a bandit and soon found henchmen in men named Shaver and Gardner, among others, to do his bidding.

Their avowed purpose was to prey only upon Union sympathizers, but their real objective was to take whatever suited their fancy even if they had to commit murder to get it. Their reign of terror lasted until the fall of 1863, when the brutal murder of a prominent citizen proved their undoing.

Jo Bragg was an old bachelor who supervised a number of newly freed Negroes on his uncle's farm near Covington. Since the old man was reputed to be quite wealthy and he lived alone, he became the target of Davis and his gang. They made plans to rob and kill him in the belief that he had a vast sum of money hidden in his house.

The story is included in an autobiographical manuscript by Samuel R. Shelton (1827–1920), a part of which was serialized in the *Covington Leader* in 1953 under the heading "Life Story of an Early Settler."

It was on a certain morning in the fall of 1863 that it was reported among the acquaintances and neighbors of Mr. Bragg that a herd of men had gone to his house the night before and he had gone off with them, but whether his

Days of Desperate Men

Samuel R. Shelton, taking a stroll along Elm Street in Covington, about 1900.

disappearance was voluntarily on his part or whether it was compulsory on the part of others, was not known.

Nevertheless he had disappeared very mysteriously and his absence was only conjectured. Great uneasiness prevailed in the minds of his friends and many of them were of the opinion that he had met foul play by those with whom he was last seen.

I was living two and a half miles northeast of Covington and Dr. Lafayette Hill rode out from town to my house and informed me of the disappearance of Jo Bragg from his house and of the suspicious circumstances of his disappearance.

I saddled my horse and went with him to the house of Mr. Bragg to make an investigation of his absence. In riding along a lane that led up to the house of Mr. Bragg's and being on the lookout for any sign or thing that would lead to the discovery of the missing man, or that would give any clue, as to the manner of his disappearance, I noticed the tops of some weeds that grew in the corner of the fence that had been broken or bent over as if for the purpose of concealing something.

I at once stopped and called Dr. Hill's attention to the broken weeds. On a close scrutiny I observed a garment concealed beneath the weeds. I got down off of my horse and running my arm through the crack of the rail fence I took hold of a garment and pulled it through.

This garment proved to be a pair of copperas pants, turned wrong side out and when I turned them right I discovered that the legs of the pants were covered with fresh blood.

On Dr. Hill and I smelling the blood to ascertain whether it was that of a human being or not—or that of an animal—we were convinced that it was human blood. We were so thoroughly convinced that the blood on the pants was that of Jo Bragg, and that he had been murdered, I took my saddle and blanket off my horse, folded up the pants and placed them on my horse.

I again replaced my blanket and saddled over the pants, remounted my horse and rode up to the house to make further investigation.

We found many people there ahead of us, searching for anything or indication that would tend to lead to solve the mystery of Mr. Bragg's disappearance. We took Esq. Ransom Winn and one or two others into our confidence and after moving out of sight of the negroes and others present, we took the pants from under the saddle and exhibited them to those men for their investigation and opinion.

From the character of the pants we were of the belief that they belonged to some of the negroes on the place and that this clue would lead to the discovery of the guilty party or parties who murdered Jo Bragg. We first approached Crockett Bragg, the leading negro on the place, and after taking him out of sight of the other negroes, we showed the pants to him and asked him if he could tell us whose pants they were. He immediately informed us that they were Peter's, a young negro man on the place.

We then proceeded to arrest Peter, and after facing him with the pants and accusing him of having murdered Jo Bragg, he at once acknowledged all about the murder, stating that he was killed the previous night, and where they had concealed the lifeless body. He informed us that by a preconcerted arrangement made between Lou Davis and himself, he was to let them in the house where Mr. Bragg slept, when they came to rob and kill him.

This was an easy matter to do as Peter being a house servant had free ingress and egress to the sleeping apartment of Mr. Bragg. He also stated that when Lou Davis and two other men appeared he quietly conducted them to the room where Mr. Bragg was sleeping; that after entrance to his room they then gagged him to prevent an outcry being made by him, that they compelled him to accompany them, telling him that as dead men tell no lies they intended to kill him and sink his body in Hatchie River; that after they had murdered him they returned and searched the house for money; that after taking him about a mile from his house and stopping in the woods where they had a long and threatening talk, Mr. Bragg suddenly attempted to make his escape by dashing for liberty through the woods; that they pursued him and shot at him several times as he ran but did not hit him until he jumped over a fence and got into a field; that at this place he was stricken with a bullet in the hip and he fell to the ground; that on account of being near the residence of Stephen Kent they decided not to fire their pistols any more for fear of arousing the gentleman and thus to be detected, but they would proceed to take his life in another way; that they then took a halter from one of their horses, tied it tightly around Mr. Bragg's neck and running a stick through the loop of the halter and by twisting it tightly endeavored to kill him by strangulation; that this crude mode did not seem to end his life as speedily as desired, they then dragged his body by the halter to a rail fence about 100 yards away and then took a rail from the fence and beat on his head with it until life was extinct; that they then dragged his body to an old well at an unoccupied house with the intention of throwing the body in the well and thus conceal their crime, but upon an examination of the well which was near a public road they found that it had not been used for so long a time that from caving earth and rubbish thrown into it that it had filled up nearly to the top; they then concluded not to put the body in the well but would take it to the Tipton graveyard, which was located in a somewhat isolated place in the woods not far way, and put the body in a grave where a Confederate soldier from Fayette County had a short time before been buried and then disinterred by his wife, leaving the grave open; that they then put the dead body across one of the horse's backs and made him [Peter] get up behind the body and hold it while they led the horse to the graveyard; that on arriving at the graveyard the body was thrown into the empty grave and then covered up with a short log and chunks of rotten wood; that they then left and he returned to his house.

After hearing Peter's statement, we made him guide us to the various places mentioned in his narrative. First we went to the place in the woods where they had the talk. There we discovered numerous horse tracks; we also found a small dogwood tree with a scrap [sic] freshly made with a bullet when they fired at Bragg while he was fleeing for his life.

We then went to the field where he was shot down, and there we found the spot where he fell. We saw where he was dragged by the halter to the fence, and there was a rail with one end covered by blood and a few strands of human hair plastered to it by dried blood; there was the old grave in which the lifeless body had been thrown, filled with rubbish, and on removing the same, we found the lifeless and nude body of the murdered man.

Peter was kept under guard until the afternoon of that day, when after consultation of the citizens of the neighborhood, he was then taken to the roadside east of Covington, and near the bridge over Town Creek, and there hung by a rope thrown over the limb of a hackberry tree in expiation of the foul crime in which he took a part.

The murder of a good man and respected citizen, for no other purpose than robbery, so incensed the people of Covington and vicinity that they resolved to mete out punishment to this gang of outlaws in the speediest manner possible. They quietly met together and discussed the best plan for their capture.

The courts of the country and all officers of the law having been suspended and made inoperative on account of the existence of the war at the time, the citizens of the county had to do something for their own protection. It was determined by them that a picket or watch should be stationed every night at certain places where it was surmised this gang of outlaws, or any one of their number, might pass.

This was kept up without intermission for about four weeks, and by the expiration of that time the whole gang had been captured, each one of them died dangling at the end of the rope that had so effectually suspended for all time the animation of Peter Bragg.

Thus the murder of Jo Bragg was avenged and the country rid of the most dangerous outlaws that ever infested it.

Smoke on the Hatchie

As the Civil War progressed toward a conclusion, the number of deserters from the Confederate army increased. So, naturally, the number of guerrilla bands, made up of deserters calling themselves cavalry, also increased. By late January 1865 conditions were so shockingly bad in West Tennessee and North Mississippi that General N.B. Forrest, the Confederate commander of the district, sent troops into the areas with orders to hunt these marauders down and to exterminate them if necessary. His efforts were only moderately successful.

By the time of Lee's surrender, there were "about sixty gentlemen of the bushwhacking persuasion in Tipton County."[53] Theses guerrillas, operating along the Hatchie River, preyed upon boats plying that stream. Between

Days of Desperate Men

April 10 and April 15, 1865, they captured three side-wheel cotton steamers, the *St. Paul*, the *Sylph* and the *Anna Everton*. The details of the capture are found in a statement later made by the captain of the *St. Paul*.

> *On Monday, the 19th instant, Lieutenant…Luxton, who claims to belong to Bill Forrest's command, and a half-brother of General Forrest, with 6 men, came on the steamer* St. Paul *at Brownsville Landing; said they had gone down on the* Elwood *and protected her out. Left Brownsville on Tuesday, the 11th, stopped at Lowry's Landing, waiting for cotton. They shot one of the deck hands at Lowry's and he either got overboard himself and swam ashore or they threw him overboard. On Wednesday, the 12th, 6 more men came on board with horses at Lowry's and got off at Bond's Landing; claimed to belong to…(W.C.) Quantrill's guerrillas. On 15th met steamer* Sylph *aground below Bragg's Landing in possession of party of about 20 of Quantrill's men. Three miles below, at Bryant's Ferry, another party, about 20 of Quantrill's men…took possession of the* Anna Everton…*They put the freight ashore and tore up the cabin, bar, etc; said they intended burning both the boats. The* St. Paul *came down to Morgan's Landing…and they burned the* St. Paul *Sunday morning at that point.*[54]

The captain of the *St. Paul* went on to say that he believed the leader of the band that burned his boat to be the "real Luxton." He was referring to Mat Luxton, who was being blamed for crimes all over North Mississippi and West Tennessee. Actually a number of guerrilla leaders had assumed the name of General N.B. Forrest's half brother in hopes, it seems, that the name would carry weight with the people of the region. At least four of these impostors bore such a striking resemblance to Luxton that some acquaintances could not distinguish the differences at the distance of only a few feet.

When news of this latest guerrilla activity reached Memphis, Major General C.C. Washburn issued Special Orders No. 102 "for the purpose of capturing Quantrill and his band…operating on the Hatchie River, and Mat Luxton, with his band…operating in the same region."[55] Washburn directed General E.D. Osband to scour the country along the Hatchie and to "pursue, destroy, and kill all guerrillas" that he might find.[56] All commanding officers were ordered to maintain strict discipline and to disallow marauding or the abuse of citizens.

Drawing three days rations on April 18, Osband proceeded up the Mississippi by the steamers *John Raine*, *Salle List*, *Dove* and *Pocahontas*. His command consisted of 250 men from the Fourth Illinois under Major

Search, 200 from the Eleventh Illinois under Major Davis and 250 from the Third U.S. Colored Cavalry under Lieutenant Colonel Cook. Plans called for the separate movement of the three detachments along and on both sides of the Hatchie with Brownsville as their rendezvous point.

The Third U.S. Colored Cavalry disembarked at Randolph on April 19 and rode through Covington toward Brownsville, which place they were unable to reach because of the flooded condition of the country in that area. They managed, however, to capture the guerrilla leader who had been passing himself off as Mat Luxton. It was discovered that his real name was Wilcox and that he was the son of a prominent Memphis physician.

The Eleventh Illinois Cavalry proceeded up the Hatchie, but because of unwieldy boats due to the pilot's being unacquainted with the river, they were forced to disembark at Van Buren's Landing. Marching from there to Brownsville, they arrived too late to cooperate with the Fourth Illinois, which had disembarked at Fulton on the 19th and had arrived at Brownsville on the 20th, capturing nine prisoners, none of whom were guerrillas.

On the afternoon of April 22, the Fourth and Eleventh Illinois returned to Fulton and embarked. At the same time the steamers *Salle List*, *Dove* and *Pocahontas*, accompanying the unburned *Anna Everton* and *Sylph*, reached the mouth of the Hatchie.

Arriving at Randolph, Wilcox, alias Luxton, was tried and convicted by a drumhead court-martial. At 6:30 p.m. he was hanged by order of General Osband from a cottonwood tree and "left hanging as a warning to his brethren in crime."[57]

Despite the loss of their leader the guerrillas remained active along the Hatchie. In early May they made a futile attempt to capture once again the *Anna Everton*. They cut a tree down along the riverbank, which fell into the water, but it failed to stop the cotton-laden vessel. Because of guards on board, the guerillas did not go near her.

This new policy adopted by the steamboat lines of posting guards on the boats of the Hatchie trade forced the guerrillas to look elsewhere for new sources of plunder. Their next major effort would be directed against the town of Covington.

The Covington Raid

Early on the morning of May 9, 1865, two men, uniformed, equipped and armed as Confederate soldiers, rode into Covington. Giving their names as Luxton and Wade, they told of discovering the plans of a band of guerrillas to raid the town later that night. According to the strangers, the bandits planned to rob the stores and to plunder the homes of citizens known to have money and other valuables. They inquired of the townspeople if they had sufficient arms with which to oppose such a force. Suspecting their motives, the citizens declined to give them any information regarding their means of resistance. The two men then rode away, saying that they would return in a short while.

Preparations were immediately made to repel the threatened attack if, indeed, one should be made. About thirty men, many of whom were ex-soldiers, were assembled with such weapons as they had and posted around the square and at points along all the avenues of approach to the town. They were instructed to let the raiders enter town but not to let them leave.

At about 9:00 p.m., the two strangers returned, as promised, with the intelligence that the raiders were nearby and would be in town in another hour. The citizens waited patiently in their concealed positions as one hour passed and then another; at 11:00 p.m., the guerrillas made their appearance. They entered the suburbs from the south, riding slowly and cautiously as if not to arouse anyone. On reaching the square, the gang, consisting of six men, halted and were about to dismount when the citizens fired a volley at them, knocking one of the bandits from his saddle. The rest put spurs to their horses in a desperate attempt to escape the trap. They were met by a withering fire from all sides as they ran a gauntlet of veterans, well trained and experienced in the use of firearms.

In a short time it was over. Three of the guerrillas lay dead, and another was critically wounded, his body riddled with buckshot. Three horses were also killed in the fray.

The events of the night made an indelible impression on W.V. Byars, the small son of Judge James Byars. Sixty-two years later he would recall:

> *I knew they were coming. I knew what would occur to them. I was not allowed to intervene or to participate—to my deep regret. But I heard the firing from our boys, ranged around the courthouse square as Company Q rode in…never to ride out again.*[58]

The dead men were identified as Scott Cleveland, Dick Shimble and James McIllvaine, alias Jim Gray. They had been part of the so-called Luxton gang that had burned the steamer *St. Paul* a month before at Morgan's Landing.

It appears that the two uniformed strangers had also been a part of the same gang. During their short absence from town, they were overheard by one of the citizen sentries having an earnest, confidential conference with the guerrillas. The sentry reported that the guerrillas seemed to have the utmost confidence in them.

The *Memphis Argus* of May 13 gave the indication that they had been part of the gang in this report of the fight.

> *It is but proper to say that the two men who acted strangely in giving the citizens the information joined with them in firing upon the guerrillas, one of whom was shot by his late comrade, for such they appear to have been.*

The following morning, as the ladies of Covington were pitying the handsome, smooth-faced boy wounded the night before, a large force of men rode out of town in pursuit of his comrades who had escaped the ambush. "The citizens and old soldiers [of Tipton County] are determined to get rid of such scoundrels," reported the *Memphis Bulletin*.[59]

This latest violent affair helped to point up the need for the restoration of civil government of the county. A mass meeting of Tipton County citizens was held for that purpose at the courthouse in Covington on May 15. The meeting was composed in most part of former Confederate soldiers, who, realizing that their cause had been lost, wished to turn their efforts toward what they thought would be best for the future.

On the motion of Nat Tipton, Colonel George T. Taylor was made chairman, and John T. Douglas was appointed secretary. The chairman made some pertinent remarks in regard to the purpose of the meeting and then appointed a committee to draft suitable resolutions for the assembly to act upon. The committee, whose members included T.R. Richardson, Major C.H. Hill, Colonel George U. Day and Dr. John S. Peete, retired and after a short absence made its report.

> *Whereas, the time has now fully arrived when it behooves all good citizens to lend their influence to suppress guerrilla warfare, robbery, theft, bush whacking, a murder and crime generally, and aid in reestablishing law and order in the state, under the Constitution and laws of the land, therefore.*
>
> *Resolved, that His Excellency William G. Brownlow, governor of the State of Tennessee, and the General Assembly of said state, he and they are hereby respectfully petitioned to authorize, empower and cause to be all such action as may be necessary and proper for the purpose of eradicating such evils, and the re-establishment of all the courts and offices in our midst. And we hereby pledge ourselves to use all the means at our command to sustain them in such action and measures as they may use.*
>
> *Resolved, that C.H. Hill and John T. Douglas be appointed delegates to bear and present to His Excellency William G. Brownlow, and the Honorable General Assembly, a copy of this petition, and to solicit their*

advice and instruction as to the best and most speedy means of effecting the ends and objects aforesaid.[60]

On the motion of Dr. Lafatette Hill, the report was unanimously adopted.

The petition was met with favor by Governor Brownlow and the General Assembly for they, too, wanted to crush the guerrilla menace in the state. This was evidenced by the fact that they made such crimes as horse stealing and house breaking capital offenses and prescribed hanging for all guerrillas.

In July 1865 Governor Brownlow appointed the following men to public office in Tipton County: George W. Reeves, Circuit Court Judge; Nat Tipton, Circuit Court Clerk; John W. Harris, Chancellor; W.F. Talley, Attorney General; William C. Harris, Sheriff and Tax Collector; Richard S. Barrett, County Court Clerk; John M. Clerkin, County Trustee; and Samuel Green, County Register.

Thus, civil government was returned to Tipton County, and the guerrilla reign of terror brought to an end.

The Quiet Visit

On a Monday in late September 1933 a small sedan pulled up in front of W.C. McDow & Co. in Covington. Its occupants, a stout youngish man and a slender stylish woman, got out casually and glanced up and down the street. Spying a number of eating establishment signs, they walked leisurely past several buildings and stopped at the Darby & Cravens Restaurant. After a short stay, in which the man drank two mugs of beer and the woman one, they departed as quietly as they had entered.

Mr. Darby might not have noticed them except for the fact that they were strangers who had appeared at the restaurant during a lull in business. He had no inkling as to their identity until a day or two later when their pictures appeared in all the Memphis newspapers. Although they had looked like anything but desperadoes to him, he discovered his recent customers had been George K. Barnes, alias "Machine Gun Kelly," and his wife.

Kelly, who was being sought for a series of crimes ranging from the massacre of four policemen at a railroad station in Kansas City to the successful collection of a $200,000 kidnap ransom in Oklahoma, was arrested in Memphis the day after his Covington visit. Police detectives, operating on a tip and armed with automatics and sawed-off shotguns, broke into the fugitive's hideout and nabbed him without a fight. One of the three arresting officers was Detective A. Oliver Clark, a former Covington resident.

Shortly after the arrest of the FBI's most wanted criminal, a Memphis salesman for a produce concern, in making his regular trip to Covington, called at the Darby & Cravens Restaurant and corroborated Mr. Darby's certainty that he had unknowingly entertained the desperado. Stating that he was a former schoolmate of Kelly, the salesman said he called at the county jail in Memphis and was permitted to talk for a short while with the criminal. In response to his questions Kelly mentioned in detail his visit in Covington, including the fact that he had parked in front of a store owned by a man by the name of McDow.

Reunion and Dedication

General Forrest's Last Speech

Following his surrender in May 1865 General Nathan Bedford Forrest returned to his two plantations in Coahoma County, Mississippi, to begin a struggle to try to remake his broken fortune. According to his own estimate, he had been worth a million and a half dollars in 1861, but four years of war left him little better off than he had been as a young bridegroom twenty years before.

For the two years immediately following the end of the war, Forrest gave his personal attention to the running of his plantations, but as soon as they were back in such condition that they could be operated without his personal attention, he moved to Memphis to head a fire insurance company. Here, he suffered the same lack of success in the same business and in the same town as another well-known ex-Confederate, Jefferson Davis. By February 1868 the general was bankrupt.

Despondent but not easily discouraged, Forrest found renewed hope for his future in late 1868 when he organized and became president of the Selma, Marion and Memphis Railroad, a proposed through line from Memphis to Selma, Alabama. But, with financing incomplete and the line sill under construction, disaster struck again. The panic of 1873 and the devastating yellow fever epidemic in Memphis that same year doomed the project to failure.

Forrest now returned for a living to the occupation he knew best—planting. His plantations in Mississippi having long since been sold to pay off his debts, he leased a plantation on President's Island just below Memphis. For labor he leased prisoners—a common practice in those days of inadequate prisons—from Memphis and the surrounding area, and he built a workhouse on the island in which to house them.

Tipton County's first involvement with Forrest's workhouse probably came in July 1875 with the escape of Jerry Hughs, who was sentenced from Bolivar to four years in the penitentiary. A trusted wagoner in Forrest's camp, Hughs stole a gun and made his way to Tipton where he was to linger until his mate joined him.

When Hughs walked up boldly to Sheriff Ben Locke in Covington one day and asked if he could see a fellow in the sheriff's "hotel," the keen-eyed sheriff immediately recognized him as the escaped prisoner for whom Forrest had offered a seventy-five-dollar reward. The sheriff was, therefore, more than happy to let Hughs enter his jail. The obliging convict was escorted back to President's Island by William Forrest, the general's son, who just happened to be in town that day.

In September 1875 General Forrest himself visited Covington and contracted with the chairman of the county court for the services of criminals sentenced to the workhouse. At that particular time there were only two men in the county jail. Both had been convicted of disturbing public worship, and neither had been able to pay his fine.

During the months that followed, rumors reached the county that living conditions at Forrest's workhouse were poor and that prisoners were receiving harsh and inhumane treatment. In order to find out if there was any basis for truth to these rumors, the Tipton County Quarterly Court appointed a committee to visit the workhouse and to examine the condition of the prisoners confined there.

In July 1876 committeemen S.E. Stevenson, H.M. Turnage and N.W. Baptist paid an unannounced visit to the facility on President's Island. At the October term of court the committee made its report of the visit.

> *In accordance with your instructions we visited President's Island some time during the month of July last, that we did not notify Gen. Forrest of the action taken by the court in the appointment of the committee or of our intended visit to said island. We were, on our arrival, shown through the prison, the sleeping apartments, dining room, kitchen, etc., and most cheerfully bear testimony as to the commodiousness and cleanliness of said apartments. In fact, the location and entire surroundings of said prison were as favorable to health and comfort as could possibly be had in that section of the country. We saw posted the rules and regulations governing the conduct of prisoners, and in our estimation saw nothing therein bordering upon barbarism, inhumanity or even extreme harshness. We conversed apart from the other prisoners with three convicts sent from this county and they were well fed and well clothed. We saw no indication nor marks of violence upon the person of any prisoners confined therein.*[61]

Reunion and Dedication

Forrest was no stranger to Tipton County, having served as a private in the camp of instruction at Randolph during the summer of 1861. Nor was he a stranger to the men of the county who had served in his command during the war. His devotion to these men brought him once again to Covington on September 22, 1876, to attend a reunion of the Seventh Tennessee Cavalry.

He was greeted by thunderous cheers that Friday morning as he rode along the line drawn up on court square. Present were more than one hundred veterans from the famous Seventh Tennessee as well as a number of veterans from various other commands.

From court square the ex-soldiers marched in columns of twos behind Arnold's Brass Band to the fairgrounds. Here, they were formed in the arena to hear speeches by some of their comrades. No uniforms were visible, for the time had not yet arrived when they could be worn again in public processions.

William Sanford made the welcome address, which was responded to in a fitting manner by Captain J.A. Anderson. Following an interlude of music by Arnold's band, General Forrest was called upon to speak.

> *Soldiers of the Seventh Tennessee Cavalry, ladies and gentlemen—I name the soldiers first because I love them best. I am extremely pleased to meet with you here today. I love the gallant men with whom I was so intimately connected during the late war. You can readily realize what must pass through a commander's mind, when called upon to meet in reunion the brave spirits who through four years of war and bloodshed fought fearlessly and boldly for a cause they then thought right, and who, even when they foresaw, as we all did, that the war must soon close in disaster, and that we must all surrender, yet did not quail, but marched to victory in many battles, and fought as boldly and persistently in their last battles as they did in their first. Nor do I forget these many gallant spirits who sleep coldly in death upon the many bloody battle-fields of the late war. I love them, too, and honor their memory. I have often been called to the side, on the battlefield, of those who had been struck down, and they would put their arms around my neck, draw me down to them and kiss me, and say: "General, I have fought my last battle and soon will be gone. I want you to remember my wife and children and take care of them." Comrades, I have remembered their wives and little ones and have taken care of them, and I want every one of you to remember them, too, and join with me in the labor of love.[62]*

This was not just rhetoric on the part of the general, for he had given a large portion of his income from the President's Island farm to the support

William Sanford of Covington, a veteran of Company I, 7th Tennessee Cavalry, made the welcome address at the 1876 reunion of his regiment. This engraving of Sanford was taken from a wartime photograph. *Seventh Tennessee Cavalry.*

of the disabled veterans of his command and to the widows and orphans of those who died fighting under his flag. Until the day of his death he would continue to help support these helpless people.

Leaving the subject of charity, Forrest next touched upon patriotism.

> *Comrades, through years of bloodshed and many marches you were tried and true soldiers. So through the years of peace you have been good citizens, and now that we are again united under the old flag, I love it as I did in my youth and I feel sure that you love it also. Yes, I love and honor that old flag now as do those who followed it on the other side; and I am sure that I but express your feelings when I say that, should occasion offer, and our common country demand our services, you would as eagerly follow my lead to battle under that proud banner as ever you followed me in our late great war. It has been thought by some that our social reunions were wrong and that they would be heralded to the North as an evidence that we were again ready to break out into civil war. But I think they are right and proper, and we will show our countrymen by our conduct and dignity that brave soldiers always make good citizens and law-abiding and loyal people. Soldiers,*

Reunion and Dedication

> *I was afraid that I could not bear the thought of not meeting with you (Forrest was suffering from chronic dysentery resulting from his war years), and I will always try to meet with you in the future. I hope that you will continue to meet from year to year, and bring your wives and children with you, and let them and the children who may come after them enjoy with you the pleasure of your reunions.*[63]

Forrest's desire to meet with his men again was not to be. He had addressed his comrades for the last time. On October 29, 1877, he succumbed to the wasting disease with which he had suffered for so long.

According to his wishes his wife Mary continued his charitable work until she had given away practically all of what the general had left her. A hint as to the means of her livelihood during these years can be found in the pages of the *Mason Call* for January 8, 1880: "The Tipton County authorities…have contracted the convict labor to Mrs. Mary A. Forrest for three years from the first instant."

THE BRIGHTON REUNION

> *The more our people mix and review the old memories of the war and its consequences the more we are united and devoted to the eternal principles of this great government, founded on the principles of justice and equal rights to all under the law.*[64]

In 1879, just three years after the great Seventh Tennessee Cavalry reunion in Covington, an annual Confederate Reunion was begun, which became an institution in Tipton County for more than sixty years. People came from miles around to attend the celebrations held each year on the second Thursday in August. Everyone, black and white, was invited and welcomed to share in the spirit of carnival and good fellowship. The event was described as "a typical Southern gathering" with "no drinking, no gambling, no amusements which would be objectional to anyone, no loud talk and no profanity."[65]

Originated by veterans of Company C, Ninth Tennessee Infantry, the annual reunion was held at different locations until sometime in the 1880s when Brighton became its permanent home. The reunion site, shaded by giant oaks, was located south of the old white frame Brighton School on land given by A.W. Smith.

Plans for the reunion were extensive and made well in advance. During the early years the veterans themselves made all of the arrangements,

L.P. Marshall, the county's last surviving Confederate veteran, at the last reunion of the Blue and Gray at Gettysburg in 1938.

Reunion and Dedication

which included inviting guests, selling concession privileges, electing young ladies as company sponsors and erecting tables on the grounds. They also procured hogs, which were taken to Brighton the afternoon before the reunion and barbecued all night over wire-covered pits.

The programs for the early reunions were generally the same every year. At mid-morning the veterans, in uniform, would gather at the Brighton schoolhouse for a reorganization meeting. Gray-haired men, who had not seen each other since young manhood, would grasp each other's hand and look inquisitively into each other's moistened eyes. The business at hand would frequently be interrupted with recognitions, introductions and inquiries to learn if members of this or that regiment were present.

Following the meeting, the old soldiers would fall into ranks behind a brass band and with battle-torn flags flapping in the summer breeze would march to the speakers' stand with the vigor of former days. Once at the stand, they would break ranks and take seats reserved for them.

Next on the agenda would come the speeches. The men chosen to make the addresses for the occasions would usually be public figures who would speak on important governmental problems of the day. They would include not only those who fought for but also sometimes those who fought against the Confederacy.

Invariably, before the close of the official exercises, someone would express a desire to hear the "Rebel Yell." When such a request was made at the reunion of 1889, the marshal called for the band to play "Dixie," and he waved the old blood-stained flag around the stand. It produced a wild, deafening cry from the nearly three hundred veterans present. This was an inadequate representation, though, of the true "Rebel Yell," for it was only heard amid the din of battle during a desperate charge when victory seemed within grasp.

The rest of the day would be spent enjoying dinner on the grounds and renewing old acquaintances. Young couples would stroll through the Brighton groves, which, according to legend, inclined young men to pop the question.

On the day of the reunion people arrived by every means of transportation available; they came on foot, on horseback, on trains, in wagons, buggies and ox carts. Those who lived any distance from Brighton usually came by train. Most Covington residents chose this mode of travel because there were not enough livery horses in town to begin taking care of the crowd.

Besides the regular trains a special was run out of Memphis, which brought a load up from the south. It then went to Ripley and back to Covington to finish loading. From Covington the train ran very slowly on to Brighton, allowing the conductor time to take up tickets and the boys time to drink ice water—a rarity in those days before the ice plant. For two or three days before the reunion, boys would drink very little water because they wanted to be able to drink plenty on the train.

Riding the train to the reunion had one major drawback—the journey home was hardest on those who had to wait at the Brighton depot for a train no one was sure would come. The indefinite wait in the broiling sun caused many to remark in haste that they would never return, but they usually did.

When the train finally arrived, a mad scramble ensued for any sort of position on any of the cars. Anyone fortunate enough to gain a good foothold waved smilingly back at those left behind.

Attendance at the early reunions varied from year to year, but the crowds were always large. The number present in 1889 was conservatively estimated at seven thousand; and in 1895 at ten thousand. The gathering at the reunion of 1897 was reported by the *Tipton Record* to have been the largest to that date.

Despite the tremendous throngs of people at these gatherings, there seemed never to have been a shortage of food. Everyone was urged to bring not only enough food for their own families but also enough to feed those visitors who might show up without food of their own. After one pre-1900 reunion, it was reported that more than twelve baskets of dinner fragments were taken up. Besides the ever-present barbecue, ice cream, cake and other delicacies were sold on the grounds.

Entertainment was provided for many years by the Brighton brass band, a traveling group that played at reunions, fairs and other social functions from Millington to Ripley. Some of the members of the band at the turn of the century were Ciecero Bolik, Dr. B.A.L. McLister, Will Huffman, Sunny Huffman and Lee Smith. Other members who joined the band in later years included DeLong McLister, Luke McLister, Waldo McLister, Russell Moore and Maben Moore. The Brighton band was succeeded at the reunions by a brass band from Woodlawn.

In 1903 a new mode of transportation was introduced to the reunions when Hawk Atkins arrived in his new Ford (Henry Ford had just established the Ford Motor Company that year). The frightening new contraption caused horses to rear, women to cry and men to curse, but before the end of the day, people were paying twenty-five cents each to ride in Atkins's "horseless carriage."

As the years passed, other innovations added even more to the general carnival atmosphere of the reunion. One of these was a mid-way, which arrived on the grounds several days in advance to set up rides. These rides were manually operated and somewhat rickety, but they were a source of genuine pleasure to a great many children.

Reunion and Dedication

L.P. Marshall and W.G. Cockrill pose at the depot in Covington prior to leaving for a Confederate reunion in Dallas, Texas.

Just when baseball entered the reunion picture is not clear, but the game, played each year on the field adjacent to the reunion grounds, became the highlight of the afternoon. Some years a local team was pitted against one from outside the county as was the case in 1932 when Tom Anderson's All-Stars played the Memphis Jolly Cabs and in 1933 when Covington played Ripley. Other years, like 1931, saw two local teams, Brighton and Holly Grove, play each other.

The weather was usually very cooperative for the annual affairs, but on occasion it did rain. In 1930, for instance, a shower during the morning of the reunion kept a number of people from the adjoining counties away and held the attendance figure down to between three and four thousand. Such a shower had at least one redeeming quality, however, since it made the grounds more comfortable by settling the dust, which by mid-afternoon was usually ankle deep.

The Joe Brown Bivouac of Confederate veterans was always a big hit at the Brighton reunions.

The worst reunion weather was probably that of 1921. With a large, enthusiastic crowd gathered early in the morning for an expected day of fun, a heavy rain began to fall, which caused creeks in the area to overflow. Many who had come by conveyances other than the train were stranded in Brighton for the night on account of bridges being washed out. People were forced to sleep in churches, in the school, in the gin and in practically every residence in town. Some two hundred passengers from Covington who had boarded the local southbound train that morning were able to return home by rail.

In 1936, after elaborate plans had been made, the reunion was canceled because of a polio epidemic in the country. Revival came in 1938 with a reunion that featured some new attractions—a movie and a softball game between teams of the Tipton County Softball League. But the interest of former years was lacking, and with a final effort in 1940 the Brighton Reunion became history.

No doubt the main reason for its demise was the passing from the scene of all the county's Confederate veterans. The ranks had grown so thin by 1929 that only eighteen old soldiers were able to attend. In 1930 the number was down to ten. That year saw the deaths of such venerable old veterans as Simon Peter Driver, John A. Shoaf, James Peyton Overall and

Reunion and Dedication

William Carleton Hanna. The last survivor was Leonidas Polk Marshall, a great-nephew of Chief Justice John Marshall and a relation of Confederate General Leonidas Polk. He died on November 4, 1938, at the age of ninety-five.

THE LIGHTER SIDE

Ciecero Bolick was the leader of the Brighton band when it made its first reunion appearance sometime during the 1880s. The band played well enough that day, but it was handicapped by a limited repertoire consisting of only two selections, "Dixie" and "A Flower from My Angel Mother's Grave." This situation resulted in an amusing incident, which was later recalled by Judge W.A. Owen in his "Do You Remember?" column in the *Covington Leader*, August 20, 1931.

> *My friend, Edwin Paine, told me that he lost half dozen cigars and soda waters at Brighton the first time the band played. In those days everybody in Covington attended the reunion, and everyone who had ever lived in Tipton County and had not moved over 100 miles away, came to Brighton on reunion day. Mr. Paine did not get to Brighton until the noon train, although we used to have a train about every two hours from Covington to Brighton to accommodate the reunion crowds.*
>
> *Paine joined a group of friends for dinner. After dinner the master of ceremonies called out "Music!" The bass drummer hit his drum a lick or two and the band began to assemble. One of Paine's friends said, "I bet the cigars I can name the piece the band will play." Mr. Paine took the bet, for he thought that it would surely be quite a guess for an outsider to name the air that the band would select. The friend named, "A Flower From My Angel Mother's Grave." Well, the band played the air named.*
>
> *When music was called for again, the friend offered sodas for the crowd that the band would play "Dixie." Again Paine covered and lost. So several times during the afternoon the friend named the air the band would play without failing. Finally Paine said, "Boys, I have been against a brace game. You fellows have been down here all day and knew that this band played only two selections." Then the crowd laughed at my friend's discovery. Paine took a chance, the others knew and it was a sure thing with them.*

True Tales of Tipton

A Fitting Memorial

We this morn, with swelling hearts,
This monument unveil,
To men unborn, in future years,
'Twill tell a noble tale.
This man in bronze, with head erect,
Stands ready for the fray—
Fit emblem of Tipton's sons
Who loved and wore the Gray.[66]

On the public square in Covington there stands a monument dedicated to the Confederate soldiers of Tipton County. Located on the south lawn of the courthouse and facing Main Street, it is made of Westerly granite and weighs nearly fifty thousand pounds. It is surmounted by a bronze representation of a Confederate cavalryman. "The figure is handsome, graceful, and soldierly looking, is attired in uniform, stands in the attitude of watchfulness and expectation with drawn sword in right hand and left hand resting on his belt."[67] On three sides of the monument are the names of battles in which county soldiers took a prominent part—Tishomingo, Harrisburg, Chickamauga, Perryville, Kennesaw and Franklin. The main inscription, located on the south side, reads as follows:

To the Confederate Soldiers of
Tipton County, whose courage
in war and virtues in peace
have illustrated the highest
type of American manhood.

"Nor braver bled for a brighter land,
Nor brighter had a cause so grand."

The idea of erecting a monument to the memory of the Confederate soldiers of Tipton County was first conceived by Richard H. Munford in the early 1870s. He began a fund for the purpose with a generous donation and worked zealously on the project until his death in 1884. Fortunately, he left the project in good hands. Prominent among those who never ceased in their efforts to raise the money for the memorial was Munford's daughter, Mrs. Sarah M. Holmes, who, along with Mrs. James Lemmon and Mrs. C.B. Simonton, organized the Memorial Association. This body worked closely with the older Tipton County Confederate Monument Association,

Reunion and Dedication

which was organized shortly after the donation of Munford. Composed of some of the most distinguished veterans in the county, the Monument Association was highly successful in collecting contributions at the annual reunions.

The design for the monument was selected by the executive committee of the Monument Association, which, at the time, included Captain C.B. Simonton, Chairman; Colonel J.U. Green, Secretary; Colonel William Sanford; Captain D.A. Merrill; N.W. Baptist; and Joseph Forsythe. The work was carried out by the Peter & Burghard Stone Co. of Louisville, Kentucky, at a cost of $2,000, a goodly sum in those days. J. West Green, the company's local representative, worked conscientiously to see that the contract was fulfilled to the letter.

Most of the week of May 19, 1895, was spent by employees of the stone company setting the monument into position. The brick foundation upon which it was placed was raised about two feet above ground level, and a mound of dirt was raised to the same elevation as the foundation. Future plans called for the mound to be paved with concrete, forming a walk around the monument. By Saturday, May 25, the monument was in place, and a veil was placed over the statue to await ceremonies scheduled for the following Wednesday.

May 29, 1895, was a proud day in the county's history as a crowd estimated at between thirty-five hundred and five thousand people gathered for the unveiling of the monument. Described as "the best looking and the best humored crowd ever seen,"[68] everyone seemed to be of one mind—that of paying tribute to the Confederate soldiers of Tipton County. Even with all six of the town's saloons open, not a single arrest was made for there was not the slightest disturbance.

The gray-haired and grizzled bearded veterans, each wearing a white ribbon with the inscription "Veteran, May 29, 1895," formed on Main Street just off the square under the command of Chief Marshal J.F. Dickson, assisted by S.H. Mitchell of Mason and Colonel W.F. Taylor of Memphis. The procession was led by the Brighton Band, companies falling in line behind. Upon reaching the square, the old soldiers filed off to the right, marched around the square and took their seats in a large stand built for the occasion on the east side. The *Covington Leader* of May 31, 1895, carried a full account of the proceedings that followed.

> *On the stand was seated the officers of the veteran company, the executive committee of the Monument Association, the speakers of the occasion, the forty-four young ladies representing the States, the choir, Mrs. Isabella Boyd, who represented "Mother of the Confederacy" and Mrs. W.A.*

Confederate veterans in line before the new monument, sometime before 1900.

Black, representing "Columbia." Mrs. Sarah Calhoun, who also had several sons in the war, was invited to take a seat with them. To the right of these noble ladies was seated Rev. W.H. Adams, who offered the opening prayer. A number of distinguished visitors and old Confederate soldiers were also given seats on the stand. Immediately on calling the assemblage to order, Col. Sanford, master of ceremonies, called on the choir, which sang, "America." He then invited Rev. Mr. Adams to invoke the divine blessing. Mrs. Isabella Boyd was then presented to the audience, after which she assisted the thirteen young ladies in singing, "My Maryland."

Mrs. Henry Sherrod recited "The Conquered Banner." Miss Sarah Hill then pulled the cord that unveiled the monument, with appropriate remarks. The band next struck up "Dixie" and the monument stood in full view and was greeted with shouts from thousands of voices. Mr. West Green then arose in behalf of the contractors and tendered the monument to the Association in brief, but appropriate remarks, which President Sanford accepted. The choir sang "Bonnie Blue Flag," the audience joining in the chorus. Miss Vivian Poindexter read an original poem written for the occasion…

Col. Sanford next called on the speakers present for addresses in the order of their names: G.W. Smitheal, Capt. Alex Merrill, Joseph Forsythe, Dr. T.W. Roane, Capt. Jas. I. Hall, Capt. D.J. Wood, Peyton J. Smith, N.W. Baptist and Dr. J.R. Sanford. Only three of the above responded to the call, viz: Messrs, Smitheal, Merrill and Baptist. Mr. Smith rose from his chair on the stand and made his apology for not speaking, in a few

Reunion and Dedication

The Confederate monument, flanked by cannon from Fort Pillow, as it appeared in 1915.

> *well chosen words. After this Mrs. Boyd, as "Confederacy," Mrs. Black as "Columbia" and forty-five young ladies representing the States of the Union, sang "Star Spangled Banner." Capt. C.B. Simonton was then called on and made a short address. The speakers confined themselves to historical facts and incidents of the war and were interesting and vivid in their portrayal, eliciting the loudest applause from the vast audience. The band, at the close of the speeches, played "Yankee Doodle," after which the choir sang "Columbia the Gem of the Ocean."*

This concluded the morning's exercises. The master of ceremonies then announced dinner and told the Confederate soldiers that their meal would be provided by the citizens of Covington and Tipton County. Dinner was spread on the yard around the courthouse and on most of the yards near the square.

Colonel Sanford called the gathering to order at 1:30 in the afternoon. General J.J. Dupuy, Colonels W.F. Taylor and W.L. Duckworth and Captains W.M. Carnes and J.P. Young responded to calls and made short speeches. Green Williams of Company A Confederate Veterans of Memphis then sang a couple of Stephen Foster songs, being joined in the chorus by the company. Nothing that transpired that day seemed to elicit more enthusiasm.

The day's exercises were then brought to a close by the veteran company, which formed and gave a short drill exhibition, firing three salutes. Altogether the program was one of the greatest affairs held in Covington and one that would be remembered by young and old alike for as long as they lived.

Amusements

"The Carlsbad of America"

In 1906, a plan was formulated by some of the leading business and professional men of the county to connect Covington and Memphis by an electric railway. Described by advocates as the "greatest enterprise in the history of Tipton County," the road promised to be worth thousands of dollars each year in the form of cheaper passenger and freight rates. With a car running every hour to Memphis, it would put people within easy reach of all the advantages and conveniences of the city while allowing them to enjoy the comforts and luxuries of the country.

A contract was subsequently made with the Palmer Engineering Company and Electric Road Builders of Kansas City, Missouri, to make preliminary estimates and surveys. Beginning on August 14, a force of engineers went to work surveying the proposed route, which was to run west of the Illinois Central Railroad from Covington through Munford to Memphis. On September 1, the engineers reported that the road could be built along that route at a minimal cost.

Munford was a strong supporter of the railway idea. The *Munford Times* was quick to extol the advantages of such a system to the town.

> *With these increased facilities the town of Munford will grow to be one of the best towns in West Tennessee, for she has the territory to back it up. Munford now handles more goods and does a better business than any town of its size in the entire state. It has a well drained and healthful location, is a splendid school town, and people will move in to partake of its many advantages. The town lies within easy reach of the famous Glenn Springs, whose waters are already known far and wide for their splendid*

This page and opposite above: Three views of the pavilion, which covered the main spring at Glenn Springs.

Amusements

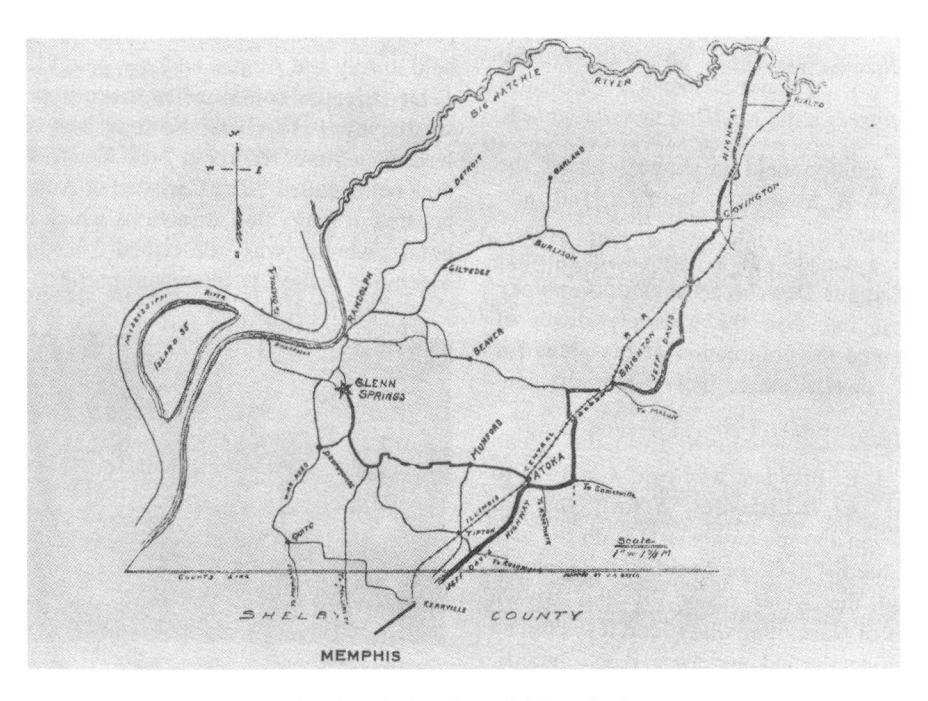

Map in Blaydes's brochure showing the location of Glenn Springs.

113

medicinal properties...This proposed railway will render these springs of easy access to the world, and people living in the crowded city, tired of its dust and smoke and heat, will come by the scores to spend their evenings at Glenndale.[69]

The project failed to receive the support that it needed to become a reality. The apparent reason for its failure was the inability of promoters to remove one of the biggest obstacles in the way of road construction—the purchase of the right of way. Appeals for people along the proposed route to make liberal concessions apparently fell upon deaf ears, thus dooming the project.

The hopes of drawing scores of people from the city to Glenn Springs, however, would be realized anyway. There would come a time when as many as 175 cars from Shelby County alone could be found parked there in one day.

The springs were discovered in the 1860s by a man named Ballard while boring for a well on his farm near Randolph. Following his death, the springs and adjoining farmland passed into the hands of Samuel P. Glenn of Fayette County.

Upon discovering that the water contained medicinal properties, Glenn at once began to develop the springs that came to bear his name. He erected a large summer hotel and provided his guests with places of amusement, one of which was a five-acre lake built principally with wheelbarrows. A levee some five hundred feet long and thirty feet high was built between two hills and held back the water of several large springs that fed the lake.

By 1880, Glenn Springs was a thriving resort. Principal among the activities that summer was a Confederate reunion held in August under the direction of C.B. Simonton, John G. Hall and Holmes Cummins.

For about a decade and a half Glenn Springs rivaled the famous Dawson Springs of Kentucky in popularity, but then the untimely death of Glenn prevented the completion of his plans for the springs' development, and the resort languished.

The property was purchased from the Glenn heirs by Dr. J.E. Blaydes, who sold it in 1914 to his son, Dr. A.B. Blaydes, a forty-year-old Atoka physician and spa enthusiast. With the idea of reviving interest in Glenn Springs, the younger Blaydes had the water tested by the Brown Laboratories of Nashville, which found it to contain numerous minerals and endorsed it as "good" and "very pure."

Dr. Blaydes spent more than $1,000 over the next few months improving the springs and grounds. He had the springs bored down and curbed with concrete to prevent contamination by surface water and erected a handsome pavilion around the main spring. A splendid pump, marble basin for wash water and a fine system of underground pipers were installed.

Amusements

Dr. A.B. Blaydes, *center*, with his father and his son at Kentucky's Dawson Springs.

Dr. A.B. Blaydes's young daughter, Thelma, *second from right*, waits her turn to drink from the spring. Note that the pavilion has not yet been built over the spring.

On August 5, 1914, Glenn Springs was formally opened again to the public with a very successful picnic. The only disappointment was the failure of the music to materialize. Dr. Blaydes's son, Victor, went to Memphis in his Hudson "Super Six" to pick up W.C. Handy's band, which had been hired for the occasion. On the return trip the car broke down at Woodstock. After spending several hours in a futile attempt to repair the car and reach the springs at anything like a reasonable hour, the band boarded the evening train at Woodstock and returned to Memphis.

Handy, who had just written "St. Louis Blues," failed to let this misfortune discourage him from playing at Glenn Springs. He went twice a year during the early years to the picnics held in July and August and was paid $125 a day.

Dr. Blaydes continued to make improvements so that by 1917 Glenn Springs was one of the leading summer resorts in West Tennessee. It was now being called "The Carlsbad of America" and boasted many fine attractions, which included a hotel that was described in advertising brochures mailed to interested parties.

> *The hotel is built in modern style, to harmonize with the surroundings, its broad verandas planned for quiet, comfort, repose and health.*
>
> *These verandas are a source of never-ending delight to the guests, and the spacious rustic chairs and rockers are in constant use from early morning until late at night.*[70]

Amusements

A large crowd gathered around the dance pavilion at one of the summer picnics.

Hotel rates were $2.50 to $3.00 per day or $12.50 a week.

Improvements were made on the lake built by Glenn, and it was stocked with fish furnished by the government. Other attractions that were added included a skating rink, which doubled as a movie theater, a dance pavilion, a bath house with dressing rooms, cabins, which rented for $4.00 per week, and a camping area where tenting privileges were fifty cents per week per tent.

Glenn Springs water sold for $0.25 for a gallon and $0.50 if the jug was not returned. A five-gallon jug sold at $2.50 with $1.25 being reimbursed if the jug was returned.

Automobiles met all trains at Atoka and Millington stations and conveyed guests to Glenn Springs at "reasonable rates."

Public interest in Glenn Springs continued until shortly after World War I. Then, as was the case with similar resorts in North America at the time, its popularity declined greatly, and it went out of business. Before long the spring and its picturesque surroundings became just another place by the side of the road.

THE LIGHTER SIDE

Throughout its history Glenn Springs was noted for fine music. From the beginning, bands were hired out of Memphis to play at picnics and various other functions at the spa. An amusing incident involving S.P. Glenn, proprietor, and one of these bands occurred in the summer of 1880 and was chronicled in the *Mason Call* of July 29.

Visit the Famous
Glenn Springs
and Stop at the Hotel

Thoroughly sanitary, everything new and clean; unsurpassed cuisine, excellent service.

Music for dancing and skating for those in attendance during the summer.

THE GLENN SPRINGS
A. B. Blaydes, Proprietor

Office: Baltimore Bldg.   Memphis, Tenn.

Front cover of advertising brochure mailed to interested parties by Dr. A.B. Blaydes.

Last Thursday evening Mr. S.P. Glenn, of Glenn Springs, accompanied his string band from the springs to Covington, where the members of the band were to take the train for Memphis next morning. After entering that town and taking in a breath of that atmosphere, and feeling quite blue in consequence, they caught revival in the nearest saloon, Mr. Glenn proposing to pay the expense thereby incurred. After being served by the barkeeper, Mr. Glenn handed him a $20 bill, but before he could get his change a friend called him to the door, and the barkeeper being in a hurry to wait on other impatient customers put the change on the counter. When the owner returned the money was gone, and no one could or would tell where it was. Suspicion rested upon a certain member of the band, he of the big fiddle, big noise and little music. Forthwith Marshal Cooper was notified of the

Guests on the front veranda of the hotel.

theft and the fiddler was shadowed. Nothing was done till next morning. As the band was in the act of taking the train the officer nabbed the man upon whom suspicion rested, and proceeded to "go through" him. No money was found, and the search was about to be abandoned when a happy thought struck the officer. Maybe the fiddle stole it! It was searched, and lo, out of the bowels of this instrument came the exact amount which Mr. Glenn had lost. The thief, whose name we could not learn, was placed in jail.

THE RUFFIN AMUSEMENT COMPANY

On the occasion of the Ruffin Amusement Company's twentieth anniversary in May 1947, William F. Ruffin, the president, was quoted as saying, "During the twenty years we have been in the theatre business, we have seen many changes and improvements in motion pictures."[71] He could just as easily have been saying these things about the Ruffin Amusement Company, for in two decades he had built it into one of the most successful enterprises in the county's history. Since 1927 he had put together a chain of theatres that stretched from Covington to Benton, Kentucky.

The groundwork for the beginnings of the company was actually laid by L.L. Lewis, an experienced theatre owner, who moved to Covington from Walnut Ridge, Arkansas, in 1924. On December 1 of that year, Lewis purchased the Palace Theatre from J.H. Paine, the son of William Henry Paine; the elder Paine had constructed the Paine Opera House Building in which the theatre was housed. In February of the next year, Lewis announced

Panoramic view of Glenn Springs in 1919. The hotel is seen in the upper left of the picture, the skating rink/movie theatre in the upper right and the pavilion-covered spring in the lower right.

plans for the remodeling of a building on the southwest corner of the square into a modern theatre with a seating capacity of five hundred.

The entire building was remodeled with a stone front and a beautiful lobby. The theatre office was located in the center of the front of the building; windows faced the two entrances. The floor was elevated so that the screen and stage could be seen perfectly from any angle.

A fifteen- by forty-eight-foot stage was constructed in the south end of the building topped by a twelve- by fourteen-foot modern screen. A balcony was built over the lobby and theatre office, with entrance from the street in front.

Covington had long felt the need for a modern theatre on the ground-floor level. The construction of the new Palace Theatre was welcome news to the theatre-goers of Covington and Tipton County.

Ruffin took his initial step into the amusement world in May 1927 when he succeeded Lewis as the owner of the theatre in the old Paine Opera House Building. The theatre, named "Pleas-U" by Agnes Paine Barret,

Amusements

Famed pianist, Blind Tom, performed at the Paine Opera House long before it was converted into a movie theatre.

opened with one of Paramount Studio's top hits of the day, *Knockout Reilly*. On June 20, a second theatre was added by Ruffin to his new company when he purchased the Palace from Lewis. It was also in 1927 that the Ruffin Amusement Company first stretched beyond the bounds of Tipton County with the purchase of the Dixie Theatre at Newbern. The new acquisition was renamed the Palace.

The first talking picture shown in Covington, *The Barker*, made its debut at a newly decorated Palace on the evening of April 1, 1929. Covington was the first town in Tennessee, outside the large cities, to have sound equipment—in fact, there were but few towns in the country the size of Covington with Vitaphone, a development of the Bell Telephone Laboratories and the Western Electric Company.

On September 14, 1931, the Ruffin chain began the operation of a theatre in the Ryan Building at Martin. The location was soon found to be unsatisfactory and the theatre, the Capitol, was moved to the Parker Building.

The Paine Opera House as it appeared upon completion in 1890.

In June 1934 work was begun to convert the Palace Theatre in Covington into one of West Tennessee's most modern playhouses. "No pains or expense," wrote the *Covington Leader*, "will deter W.F. Ruffin, owner, from competing for the patronage of theatre-goers in this section."[72] In addition to lengthening the theatre by nearly twenty-three feet, which increased seating capacity by two hundred, a new stage with the most modern equipment, orchestra pit, drops and other features was added. Improvements also included a new, larger screen, which offered better reproduction of pictures, a metal roof and a new floor.

Tragically, the refurbished theatre, with its entire contents, burned to the ground on January 29, 1936. Ruffin immediately announced plans to temporarily operate a theatre in the Ray Building on West Liberty Avenue at Munford Street, and two days later films were being shown at that location. Out of the ashes of the old Palace rose the modern, luxurious Ruffin Theatre, which opened on July 24, 1936.

The Palace at Greenfield was added to the Ruffin string of theatres April 8, 1937. In welcoming the theatre to the city, prominent citizens of Greenfield expressed themselves as follows:

Amusements

William F. Ruffin, the founder of the Ruffin Amusement Company.

> *The people of this section are thoroughly familiar with the Ruffin Theatres, having been regular patrons of the Capitol at Martin, and the friends of long years standing will extend to Mr. Ruffin a cordial welcome to Greenfield, and will lend to his organization their full co-operation in making his undertaking a complete success. Theatre goers in this territory already know that Ruffin Theatres offer only clean, highly respectable, standard shows and in securing a show for Greenfield it is gratifying to note that we are assured a theatre of this type.*[73]

The Hall Building, which had been used for show purposes in the past but which had recently housed a store, was converted into a beautiful, modern theatre.

The Ruffin Amusement Company enlarged its chain of four theatres in May 1937 with the purchase of the Chickasaw Amusement company, a concern operating theatres at Milan and Humboldt. Though president of both companies with a common board of directors and stockholders, Ruffin

W.F. Ruffin Jr. on the running board of a truck decorated for the Buck Jones Rangers Parade, an event sponsored by the Palace Theatre.

The Ruffin Theatre in Covington replaced the old Palace Theatre.

Amusements

The Ritz Theatre in Covington became the headquarters of the Ruffin and Chickasaw Amusement Companies when it opened in 1942.

operated them as two distinct firms. In December 1937 he added the two-year-old Roxy Theatre at Alamo to the Chickasaw Company.

Ruffin crossed the state line in 1938 with the purchase of the Benton Theatre at Benton, Kentucky. Another theatre was added in Kentucky when Ruffin began operation of the Ritz Theatre at Hickman on September 26, 1938. A second theatre at Hickman, the Rex, was also opened to the public in September 1938.

In 1939 a group composed of businessmen and citizens of Halls, Tennessee, asked the Ruffin Amusement Company to consider building a theatre in their town. Agreeing with the group that Halls was a promising location for a theatre, Ruffin began construction of the Halls Theatre in September 1939. The new theatre opened in December 1940.

The Ruffin Company's first and only competition in Covington came on May 7, 1942, with the opening of the Gem Theatre on the west side of the square. Owned by C.H. Whiteshorn, the Gem was modernistic in design with a seating capacity of five hundred.

Just three weeks after the opening of the Gem, Ruffin opened the Ritz Theatre in Covington. "'Palace' would have been a more appropriate name for it with all the developments in theatre accoutrement from the outer lobby under the broad marquee, through the tile-floored lobby into the heavily carpeted foyer and down the aisles or up the broad stairs to the

Pictured in their office on the twentieth anniversary of the Ruffin Amusement Company are William F. Ruffin and his wife Annie M. Ruffin, president and secretary-treasurer respectively.

balcony to the sink-down-a-mile cushions of the maple armed seats."[74] The headquarters of the Ruffin and Chickasaw Amusement Companies were moved to offices on the second floor above the lobby of the Ritz.

No new theatres were added during the next five years, but at the time of the company's twentieth anniversary celebration, plans had been drawn up for the building of another theatre at Martin, the deluxe Varsity with a seating capacity of one thousand. Extensive plans were also underway for improvements that would turn the Palace in Newbern into one of the most modern theatres in West Tennessee.

By this time the Ruffin Amusement Company had become a family corporation with W.F. Ruffin Sr., president; W.F. Ruffin Jr., vice-president; and Mrs. Annie M. Ruffin, secretary-treasurer. Though the heyday of motion pictures would soon come to a close with the advent of television, the company would persevere. The first twenty years would prove to be just the beginning.

The Courthouse and the Courts

A New Courthouse

The old courthouse built in 1832 was by 1889 in very poor condition. As far back as February 25, 1869, it had been described by the *Memphis Appeal* as a "tattered and worn structure." Extensive repairs in 1875 had only stemmed for a short period the ravages of time and neglect on the old building. It had lately been condemned and re-condemned countless times.

Conditions finally forced the circuit court to abandon the courthouse in "hot haste" in February 1889, and the county court appointed a committee to advertise for and to take bids on tearing it down and building a new one. Each project was to be bid upon separately.

The committee, composed of J.S. McIntosh, W.H. Dunlap, B.F. Lacke, W.C. Exum and John Y. Peete, reported at the July term of court that W.F. Boone & Son of Clinton, Kentucky, had submitted the lowest bids for both projects. The company had agreed to tear down the old courthouse for $500 and to build the new one for $24,500.

Following the closing of the contract by the committee on July 6, all the furniture was removed as were the window sashes and doors. Four days later a small workforce of two men arrived and proceeded to remove the bell from the courthouse dome. That afternoon one of the men emerged from the dome and climbed to the pinnacle where his hammering and banging attracted a great deal of attention and notified the town that the old structure, which "had stood in the center of the square like a lone sentinal [sic] of justice for more than fifty-seven years," was being torn down.[75]

Men gathered in small knots along the streets and in the shade of the awnings around the square to watch and to talk sentimentally about the venerable old landmark. They knew that the end of an era had been

Tipton County's first permanent courthouse, 1832–1889.

reached, for that old courthouse embraced a good part of the county's history. For some it seemed like vandalism, in spite of reason, to see it battered down.

Less interested croquet players on the courthouse lawn went on with their game, seemingly oblivious to the falling debris. However, when rubbish began to fall dangerously near, they picked up their wickets and found a more comfortable spot in the shade behind a nearby store.

Although a prevalent opinion that a small amount of pounding on the dome or roof would bring the whole building down was proved false, no other workmen rushed in to share the dangerous work that day. As the job became less hazardous, however, the number of workmen increased. By the next day four or five men reported for work, and by June 13, the roof having been removed, the number of workmen increased to eight.

The structure was torn down without the occurrence of a single accident, which is more than can be said of its construction. During construction, a young man named William Maley, while hauling brick, had been thrown from his wagon, run over and killed.

Work progressed rapidly on the new courthouse, and on September 23, the cornerstone was laid during impressive ceremonies at which Captain C.B. Simonton was principal speaker. A Gulf Coast visitor witnessed the event and made note of it in a letter home: "I was here in time to see the

The Courthouse and the Courts

The new courthouse in 1890.

cornerstone laid. The people are intensely Southern in sentiment and bedded in the stone were several mementoes of the 'Lost Cause'."[76] A short time later, unbeknownst to anyone, a second and more informal "time capsule" was placed in the courthouse. Will Boone and John Berryman, two of the carpenters, wrote a short note in pencil on a piece of yellow poplar molding and put it under the floor of the staircase landing. In the note Boone (probably the son in W.F. Boone & Son) identified himself as being a native of Clinton, Kentucky, born December 25, 1860. The hidden message would be discovered on March 23, 1956, while the flooring on the landing was being replaced. The writing would still be clear but not too legible.

The building was completed and formally received by the courthouse committee in May 1890. The *Covington Leader* of May 9 gave the following description of it:

> *The hall, which was the last part of the building finished, is spanned by two beautiful arches. The main entrance is on the north, which is adorned porch, stone steps, etc. The stairway to the courtroom is situated in the south end, which prevents the hall from showing to so good an advantage as it does from the north. The floor of the hall is made of Tennessee marble, the walls plastered and nicely finished. These walls are yet unadorned by the hands of the vandal scribbler. It may be due to the watchful eyes of the work men, or probably they want the taxpayer to get one view of it in its pristine beauty before the pencil decorations begin.*
>
> *The officers are located as follows: Entering the building from the north, the first of the left ground floor is the chairman's office; second, county*

clerk's; third, register's office; fourth, circuit clerk's office. On the right, entering from the same point, the first is the chancery clerk's office; second, chancery court room; third, trustee's, and fourth, the sheriff's office. There are two rooms at the landing of the stairs on the second floor, one on the right, the other on the left of the entrance to the courtroom. One of these will be used for a grand jury room and the other for a witness room. There are also two rooms on the same floor for the use of the petit jury and a consultation room just behind the judge's stand.[77]

W.F. Boone & Son was given credit for having done a good, honest job without any friction between them and those in charge of having the courthouse erected. It was judged to be a handsome building with an abundance of room.

THE MASTER FORGER

Covington had many fine lawyers in active practice at the time the new courthouse was completed in 1890. Members of the bar included: Colonel William Sanford, Major G.W. Smitheal, Harry S. Young, Captain Charles B. Simonton, John A. Tipton, Josiah H. Lauderdale, Peyton J. Smith, J.C. Boals and Colonel N.W. Baptist, who had the misfortune of being the defense attorney in one of the most unusual trials ever held in Tipton County.

It was at the June term of the circuit court in 1890. Colonel Baptist was defending Edwin Stoddard, a handsome young man who looked more like a successful banker than a criminal. Stoddard had been indicted under the name of Henry B. Davis, alias J.D. Allen, for forging and passing counterfeit checks.

Before coming to Tipton County, Davis had been a brilliant lawyer with an avid interest in politics. His interest in money soon overshadowed his political interests, and as treasurer of his political party, he absconded with its funds. He was caught and sentenced to prison. Serving his term, Davis later showed up in Tipton County. He was arrested for forging a check on McCain & Company, merchants of Idaville, and for passing a counterfeit check on an old man near Munford.

The term of court opened as scheduled on June 10, but was adjourned until the next day because Judge Thomas J. Flippin was unable to get to Covington from his previous spot on the circuit in time for the first day's business.

The usual court routine was carried on for two weeks with a jury being sworn in on June 24. Jurors were: W.J. Farris, E.H. Peete, B.G. Shelton,

The Courthouse and the Courts

W.S. Mays, E.B. Whitley, J.M. Forbess, R.T. Clanton, J.C. Mims, E.W. Smith, D.E. Haynie, Y.B. Turner and J.G. Pitt. General S.L. Cockcroft was prosecuting attorney, and at that time J.T. Talley was circuit court clerk. The officers who waited on the jury were Sheriff Dan H. Smith and Deputies D.H. Lauderdale and John H. Moose.

Davis was brought before the court under four separate indictments. The first case tried was on an indictment for passing a forged imitation bank check. The defendant entered a plea of not guilty, but the jury found him guilty.

Possession of a counterfeit check was the indictment in the next case, to which Davis again pleaded innocent. Again he was found guilty as charged.

The third charge was that of passing a counterfeit bank check. Davis again entered a not guilty plea with the jury again finding him guilty.

On the fourth indictment, carrying a pistol, Davis again declared his innocence, and this time the jury, after carefully studying the evidence, found him not guilty of this charge.

Judge Flippin sentenced Davis to a total of six years in the state penitentiary. On his way to jail following the trial, Davis told Deputy Moose that the penitentiary would not hold him long.

Shortly after entering prison, Davis managed to acquire some Covington newspapers. He then had his former defense attorney, Colonel Baptist, send him some of the colonel's own office stationery. By bribing a guard, he was able to have bottles of ink, pens with various size nibs and legal-size paper smuggled into his cell. He now was ready to put his fantastic scheme into operation.

Starting with a dozen replica signatures that he remembered from his dealings in the county, he proceeded to forge a petition for his own release. He managed in various handwritings to sign the names of 150 of Tipton's best-known citizens. All the names, with the exception of the first twelve, were acquired from the newspapers and included county officials, bankers, lawyers, farmers, merchants and all of the jurors who tried him.

Next, to accompany the petition, Davis forged a letter from Colonel Baptist on the office stationery the colonel had sent him. Ironically, Colonel Baptist was a member of the State Executive Committee and a member of Governor Buchanan's staff.

Within two weeks, Davis received his pardon, along with a note from the governor asking him to come to the state capitol to sign some papers for his release. This was to be done strictly as a routine formality. On the way to the governor's office, Davis eluded a guard who had been assigned to accompany him and boarded an eastbound train. Although he had no money, he managed to reach his destination by riding the mail car.

This wasn't the first time that Davis had boarded a train without a ticket. On a train trip a few years before, a minister mistook him for a well-known preacher, paid for his ticket and invited Davis to be guest speaker at his church. The invitation was accepted, and for three successive Sundays the impostor preached about the world's suffering poor. He took up a collection and left town with several hundred dollars in his pocket.

But this mastermind with the colossal nerve, who was able to pull off big coups, bungled the small ones. He was caught forging a fifty-cent telegram in New Jersey by a detective who wired Governor Buchanan asking if he wanted him and if there was a reward. The governor responded that he did not. He said that Davis had beaten him very cleverly and was too brilliant a person to be in prison. His only request was that the forger stay out of Tennessee.

Many Tipton Countians were surprised when they heard that Davis had been pardoned, but Colonel Baptist must have been the most surprised of all.

The Last Legal Hanging

In the days before the electric chair, public hangings in Tipton County were quite rare. Only two were recorded during the first two decades after the Civil War. A white man named Gardner was hanged shortly after the war for horse stealing, and a black man, Andrew Saunders, was hanged in 1881 for murder. The last legal hanging in the county came shortly after the turn of the century as the result of the murder of Mrs. Sarah C. Hill on July 16, 1903, a crime described as one of the cruelest in the annals of Tipton County.

Mrs. Hill had been apprehensive the day before her murder and had invited one of her neighbors, Mrs. Dyer Ferguson, to spend the night with her. The two ladies propped boards up on the inside of Mrs. Hill's bedroom window so that no one could see inside, and they left a light burning in the room. When Mrs. Hill retired for the night, she had six children in the room with her, the youngest being five-month-old twins and the oldest being twelve years of age.

At about 2:00 a.m. someone raised the window, pushed a gun between the planks and fired the fatal bullet. The victim, probably aroused by the raising of the window, was sitting up in bed at the time of the shooting. The light in the room made it easy for the killer to find his target.

News of the crime spread rapidly, and an investigation was immediately begun by authorities. Evidence pointed to the guilt of the husband, John Hill, who was arrested later that morning in Covington. He denied knowing of his wife's death until he reached town to attend, he said, the trial of their divorce case.

Hill was indicted and immediately taken to Union City to await trial. It was feared that the crime was of a nature that might provoke a lynching.

Hill's trial opened with the defense making a motion for a change of venue, which the judge denied. The defense counsel consisted of J.C. Boals, Sanford & McClelland and Stephenson & Tipton. The prosecuting attorney was assisted by Owen & Smith and Charles B. Simonton & Son.

A venire of three hundred men was summoned on the first day of proceedings from which to select a jury. The jury was completed by the next afternoon, and the taking of testimony was immediately begun. Of about fifty witnesses examined during the trial, the prosecution put thirty-four on the stand to testify.

The evidence in the case was all circumstantial, but the prosecution wove the circumstances into a network that strongly implicated Hill. It was proven that Mrs. Hill had indeed begun divorce proceedings against the defendant and that he had made a number of threats against her, beginning several months before the crime.

The evidence showed that the murderer used mustard on his tracks to keep bloodhounds from picking up his scent; it was proven that the defendant had bought a box of mustard a few days prior to the murder.

The men with whom Hill stayed on the night in question were unable to account for him for part of the night. Two witnesses testified that they saw a man on a horse, closely followed by a mule, riding on the road between the place where the defendant was alleged to have spent the night and the murder scene.

The killer was trailed from the bedroom window to where he mounted his horse. Evidence indicated that the mule remained unhitched and grazed around where the horse was tied. From this spot the murderer was trailed to the house where Hill allegedly spent the night. Here the animals were found, and their tracks examined and compared by authorities.

After two days of the testimony, final arguments were made, and the judge charged the jury before the afternoon adjournment. The jury reached unanimous agreement on the first ballot and brought in its verdict shortly after the opening of the next morning's session. "We find the defendant guilty of murder in the first degree with mitigating circumstances."[78]

Hill listened to the verdict with passive indifference. In fact, he wore a more unconcerned look than anyone in the large crowd attending the final proceedings. The only time during the entire trial that he showed the slightest emotion was when his son was called to the stand to testify about threats made by his father and about his father's behavior toward his mother.

That afternoon the defense filed a motion for a new trial on grounds that Hill did not receive a fair trial. They claimed that one of the jurors, J.M. Archer, had formed and expressed an opinion of the defendant's guilt prior to the trial. Archer stoutly denied the allegation and convinced the judge that such was not the case. The motion for a new trial was denied.

The wording of the jury's verdict had transferred to the judge the responsibility of levying the penalty. After reviewing the testimony, he declared that he saw no mitigating circumstances that would justify anything other than the penalty for murder—that those found guilty of this crime be hanged by the neck until dead. He accordingly passed sentence at 10:30 p.m. that night and set the date of execution for April 25, 1904.

An appeal was made to the State Supreme Court, which automatically gave the accused a stay of execution until such time as the court of last resort could hear the case. Hill's lawyers hoped that the Supreme Court would overturn the lower court's ruling, thereby ensuring their client of another trial.

Hill was returned to the Union City jail by Deputy Sheriffs Charles Webb and N.B. Portis. There he was held to await the Supreme Court's ruling. Authorities, still fearing the possibility of a lynching, considered the Union City facility a safe and proper place for him to be imprisoned.

In June 1905, more than a year after Hill was sentenced to hang, the Tennessee Supreme Court affirmed the lower court's decision and ordered that he be hanged at Covington on August 8, 1905. Information on the case becomes meager at this point, but it appears that Hill's lawyers appealed to the governor and were granted another stay of execution so that he could study the case and render a decision on whether the sentence would stand or the stay of execution would become permanent. Hill, in the meantime, was moved from Union City to the jail in Jackson, Tennessee.

In a letter to the condemned dated September 3, 1905, Mrs. J.C. Boals wrote:

> *Mr. Boals with some of the other lawyers went to Nashville and had an interview with Gov. Cox on last Friday. They plead your case very earnestly before him, and answered all the arguments that had been brought up by the other side against commutation; Mr. Boals came home more hopeful than when he went, though he has not much to encourage him.*
>
> *He thinks the Governor did not want to raise their hopes, and was careful not to give them any encouragement, yet he seems not to have fully made up his mind. The lawyers have left nothing undone that could be done for your commutation and they will hope to the last and Mr. Boals will stand by you as long as you need a friend.*[79]

The Courthouse and the Courts

Mrs. J.C. Boals, who wrote a letter to John Hill concerning her husband's commutation efforts on his behalf.

The county jail as it appeared shortly before being torn down in the mid-1970s. It was on a gallows in the yard of this jail that Hill's sentence was carried out.

J.C. Boals, a native of Fayette County, was a schoolteacher and later the editor of the *Tipton Record* before being admitted to the Covington bar in the late 1870s. According to one of his peers, "Mr. Boals always saw the beauties, the noble qualities and virtues of his clients' causes and his opponents' many wrongs. He believed in each client, regarding him as the object of persecution by the opposing side."[80]

Despite the tireless efforts of Boals and his associates, and the appeals for commutation by letter to the governor of between sixty and seventy people, Hill eventually lost his bid for clemency. He was hanged in the yard of the county jail on October 10, 1905, thus becoming the last person to be legally hanged in Tipton County. Thereafter, the condemned would be sent to the state prison in Nashville for execution.

The World Wars

WORLD WAR I: THE HOMEFRONT

When the nation entered World War I in April 1917 it was faced with the Herculean task of mobilizing its economic strength. In order to raise the finances needed to carry on the war effort, the administration developed a plan calling for increased taxes and the sale of war bonds.

In general, the citizens of Tipton County responded with enthusiasm to the program. They paid higher taxes without noticeable complaint and subscribed generously in the four Liberty Loan drives of 1917–1918.

These drives were headed by a county chairman and his staff, composed of a sales manager, a program director and a publicity director. They saw to it that volunteer salesmen were recruited, entertainments and rallies were held and campaign posters were widely distributed.

In an effort to encourage thrift, War Savings Clubs were instituted by such organizations as the Covington Business Men's Club and the Tipton County Farmers Union Bank; schoolchildren sold twenty-five-cent Thrift Stamps, which could be accumulated to secure interest-bearing savings certificates (Baby Bonds). War bonds were placed on sale everywhere. Small communities and even isolated farmhouses were canvassed. Reluctant buyers of these bonds and also people known to have money who refused to contribute to the Red Cross drives were subjected to social pressure, often being scorned as slackers or enemy sympathizers. An example can be found in the *Covington Leader* of March 14, 1918. In a proclamation calling for the continued purchase of War Savings Stamps, Mayor J.J. Green of Covington sounded the following warning:

Let there be no slackers in our midst. Remember that whoever is not for the government in support of the war is against it, and who is against the government now is an enemy of the American people.

The *Leader* in its issue of May 30, 1918, reported the case of a poor widow who gave her last $5.00 to a Red Cross solicitor. In contrast it pointed out that not a single dollar could be obtained from some men who were abundantly able to contribute much. "Needless to say," wrote the paper, "the names of these men have been furnished to the government authorities."

The success of the various fundraising drives was attributed to the fact that everyone pulled together. Each community assumed responsibility for its own people, organized and went to work. Special recognition was given to black citizens in all parts of the county for their fine efforts. They were credited with having aided not only in all the different drives but also in every possible way when called upon to assist in causes promoting the welfare of the nation.

The same spirit of cooperation was evoked when it came to programs for the conservation of resources. People signed a "Tipton County Citizens' Agreement," in which they pledged to follow conservation measures suggested by the government in its efforts to put the county on a war footing.

In accordance with the Food Administration's program for the conservation of food resources, citizens of the county planted victory gardens and observed meatless and wheatless days. Tuesdays were designated as meatless days, and Saturdays porkless days. Wheatless days were on Mondays and Wednesdays.

Similarly, the Fuel Administration, which meted out oil and coal, sponsored "heatless Mondays." They, however, were not voluntary but were ordered by the administration in the winter of 1917 to meet a fuel shortage caused in part by congestion on the nation's railroads. The order applied in Tipton County to offices, places of amusement and most stores, which were not allowed to furnish heat.

The fuel shortage was keenly felt during the winter of 1917–1918 because of the severity of the weather. An eight-inch snowfall on December 8 was followed by a number of others, which kept the ground covered for more than two months. Temperatures dropped below zero on a number of occasions, hitting a record low of fifteen below on the night of January 11.

On January 12, the Mississippi River at Randolph was frozen so solidly that people were able to walk across the ice to the Arkansas shore and as far down the river as Richardson's Landing, where an ice gorge had formed. Here cakes of ice were piled up as high as fifteen feet.

Since almost everybody depended on coal for heat, the frozen river posed a serious problem because it prevented the shipment of coal by barge. But this

The World Wars

Boat sunk in 1918 by the ice gorge at Richardson's Landing.

was only half of the double-barreled blow dealt by the weather that hindered coal delivery. On January 19 a heavy snow fell over a large area, including Alabama and Kentucky, which shut down mines, roads and railroads.

The coal famine caused many schools to close and people to cast about for wood as a substitute source of heat. Some businesses were able to remain open due to the generosity of others who shared with them their meager and dwindling supplies of coal. As an example, when the Munford Telephone Exchange was hit by a shortage and it was feared that the company would have to be closed, the Covington exchange came to the rescue by shipping them a small quantity of coal in sacks.

The crisis saw the elimination of electric advertisements, the diminution of street lighting, the discontinuance of church services at night and the introduction of daylight savings time—all measures designed to lessen nonessential demand for coal. Once the citizens of the county appreciated the necessity of such measures, they accepted them as cheerfully as they had those of food conservation.

Even after the fuel crisis was over and "heatless Mondays" were ended on March 25, the government continued to preach domestic economy with such slogans as "Save a shovelful of coal a day." The Covington War Fuel Company was formed to induce people to burn a large percentage of wood and to furnish wood to citizens at low cost.

Sol M. Rhodes literally dropped in on a friend, Paul Shoaf, on the Shoaf farm south of Covington. The Park Field flyer crashed his plane while trying to make an unscheduled landing to visit his friend.

Neither the fuel situation nor the special luxury tax on amusements had any noticeable effect on theater attendance during the war. When D.W. Griffith's film, *The Birth of a Nation*, was shown at the Cozy Theatre in October 1917, every seat was filled, and a number of people had to be turned away. Live shows continued to be popular at Paine's Opera House, and as before the war, people traveled to Memphis to attend concerts at the Lyric Theater.

At the theater and other places where people congregated, volunteer speakers made brief talks on government needs and appealed for cooperation. These were the "Four-Minute Men," a group composed of some of the county's leading citizens and best speakers, among whom were R.B. Baptist, L.E. Gwinn, W.A. Owen, W.M. Simonton, W.V. Bringle, Peter Fyfe and M.A. Walker.

Through the efforts of W.F. Bringle, the Business Men's Club and patriotic citizens of Covington, a twenty-five-acre field one mile north of Covington was secured in March 1918 as a permanent landing site for student pilots making their first cross-country flights from Park Field near Millington. Aviators from this, Tennessee's most important training base, had been using this field for a landing place since the previous year.

The World Wars

A Park Field flyer happily poses for this picture in a field north of Covington, then returns to his plane for the flight back to Millington.

The officer in charge of flying at Park Field gratefully accepted the site because he was impressed with its excellent location and splendid condition. He immediately had signs posted around it to keep trespassers out but reserved the eastern edge along the Jeff Davis Highway as standing room for visitors. Crowds often gathered there to get a close view of the airplanes.

Though slowed temporarily at times in their war efforts by such things as the devastating flu epidemic in the fall of 1918, the citizens of the county did all that was asked of them, and more. Everything expected of any citizenry involved in war—to keep morale high, to adhere to government policies and to feed the soldiers—was accomplished by the people of Tipton County through hard work and sacrifice.

Shouts of Farewell

A small portion of the county's contribution to the armed services was already under arms before America's involvement in World War I. They were members of the First Tennessee National Guard regiment, which was called upon June 19, 1916, to participate in General John J. Pershing's unsuccessful attempt to capture the Mexican rebel Poncho Villa. Their return from duty along the Mexican border preceded the United States' declaration of war by only a few weeks. Most of these men were called into service as members of the Thirtieth ("Old Hickory") Division.

On May 18, 1917, Congress enacted the Selective Service Act, calling for the registration of all men between the ages of twenty-one and thirty. The first of Tipton County's registrants to be called into active service left for Camp Gordon near Atlanta during the first week in September 1917. They were Ernest Allen, Mack Fred Jones and Thomas Parker. The remaining eleven members of the county's first quota left for the same destination shortly thereafter.

The departure of the county's second quota of forty-four men later that same month drew a large crowd to Covington. Not since the unveiling of the Confederate monument in 1895 had the county witnessed anything like it. Although it was not without its pathetic scenes, the occasion was overall a happy one.

The young soldiers had their picture taken on the steps of the Federal Building by local photographer J.W. McDaniel, and they were given sumptuous meals at the Hotel Lindo both at noon and at supper. For their journey, the ladies of the Red Cross gave them boxes filled with an ample supply of good things to eat.

The World Wars

This group of registrants was photographed on the steps of the courthouse by photographer J.W. McDaniel shortly before taking the train for camp.

The farewell program was set to begin at 4:00 p.m. Before that hour people began to stream into town from all parts of the county, filling the square with automobiles and other assorted vehicles. The throng was even larger than the great crowd that had gathered the previous April to witness a ceremony in which a ten- by twenty-foot American flag was raised atop the courthouse tower. It was estimated that three thousand people congregated in and around the courtyard to witness the proceedings.

During the exercises the honored guests were drawn up in line before a gaily decorated speakers' stand. Red, white and blue bunting decorated the stand's white backdrop. In the center in letters of red, white and blue were the words "Our Boys." On one side of this was a Confederate flag with the date 1861, and on other the American flag with the date 1917. Adding still more color to the scene was the presence of a number of Confederate and Spanish-American War veterans in uniform.

Patriotic songs were sung, and eloquent addresses were delivered by a number of distinguished speakers who all sounded a note of optimism and patriotism. Included among them were William Sanford, a Confederate veteran, and M.A. Walker, a veteran of the Spanish-American War.

Even more touching than the program was the scene at the depot later that day. Sad-hearted mothers poured out their grief over the departure of their sons, and sweethearts and young wives, though struggling to be brave, broke down as the train pulled out for Camp Gordon amid waving handkerchiefs and shouts of farewell. Scenes such as this would be enacted time and again throughout the war.

A Good Accounting

A total of fifty Tipton County men died while in service during World War I—twenty-nine white and twenty-one black. The leading cause of death was disease, which claimed thirty-seven lives. Of the remainder, seven were killed in action or died from wounds received in combat; two died of train wreck injuries; one died of injuries received in an airplane crash; one died of sunstroke; one died of injuries received in a fight; and one died of heart failure. The latter was Second Lieutenant Paul C. Calhoun, the first Tipton County soldier to lose his life during the war. He died suddenly on February 27, 1918, while drilling troops at Camp Wheeler, Macon, Georgia.

Ironically, Lieutenant Calhoun's cousin, Dan Calhoun, had been the first soldier from Tipton County to die in the Civil War, and another cousin, George Mayes, had been the first county soldier to sacrifice his life in the Spanish-American War.

As in previous wars the county was not without its heroes. One of these was W.H. McLaughlin, who entered the army shortly after the United States became involved in the conflict. Following his commission as a lieutenant in August 1917, he sailed for France and was assigned to Company F, 16th Infantry, 1st Division.

In late October McLaughlin's battalion was merged with a French counterpart and moved to the front line trenches. When German troops raided his platoon's sector in November 1917, Lieutenant McLaughlin was gassed and wounded by shrapnel. This action was said to have been the first of the war for any American unit, and Mr. McLaughlin was credited with being the first American officer serving with American troops to be wounded. For his heroic part in the engagement, he was awarded the French Croix de Guerre.

This nation's highest award for gallantry, the Congressional Medal of Honor, was given to only six Tennesseans during World War I. One of the recipients was Sergeant Alvin York, the country's most decorated hero. Another was Sergeant Joseph B. Adkison of Atoka, a member of Company C, 199th Infantry, 30th Division.

Adkison saw service along the Mexican border and at Camp Sevier in South Carolina before being shipped with his division via England to France

Lieutenant William Tipton.

in the spring of 1918. In early July he moved with the division across the Belgian frontier and into a sector in Ypres salient. Here, he took part in the defense of Ypres and beginning on August 19, 1918, fought in the Ypres-Lys offensive.

Early in the morning of September 29, near Bellicort, France, Sergeant Adkison found his platoon pinned down by murderous fire from a machine gun nest fifty yards away. Alone, he raced across the fifty yards of open ground straight into the face of the enemy machine gun, kicked the gun from the parapet and captured the three-man crew at the point of the bayonet. His quick decision and gallantry enabled his platoon to continue its advance and was a major contribution toward the allied breakthrough in the Hindenberg Line.

Adkison was wounded in the later stages of the battle in which he won fame. For the next several months, he was shuttled from one hospital to another, both in Europe and in the United States. He did not learn that he had been selected to receive the Congressional Medal of Honor until his discharge at Camp Pike, Arkansas, in March 1919. "They invited me

Lieutenant Bennett G. Buford.

to Washington to get the medal," he later recalled, "but I still wasn't very well, and couldn't make the trip."[81] So, instead, ex-Sergeant Adkison was presented the medal by an officer from Washington in ceremonies at the Presbyterian Church in Atoka. Besides the Congressional Medal of Honor, he was also awarded the Great War for Civilization Medal, the Italian War Cross and the Republic of Portugal Medal.

Another honor was bestowed upon Adkison in April 1929 when the new Jeff Davis Highway bridge over the Obion River was named in his honor. The dedication was in keeping with the policy of Governor Horton to so honor fifteen of Tennessee's outstanding heroes.

Lieutenant Roy Boyd.

The navy was well represented by Tipton Countians during World War I. These three sailors are, *left to right*, Troy McCall, Douglas Faught and Joe Payne.

The World Wars

Sergeant Joseph B. Adkison, Medal of Honor winner.

The Lighter Side

Ambia Roby was a young Red Cross nurse who volunteered for overseas duty along with two other Tipton Countians, Ruth Dennis and Ruth Beatty. She left for France in August 1918 and was assigned to duty at an American hospital near the United States Embassy in Paris. There she began a wartime career that included caring for the wounded of the Belleau Wood and Chateau-Thierry battles.

During the course of the war, General John J. Pershing visited the hospital on occasion to cheer the soldiers. Just prior to one of his visits, a basket of eggs was brought to the hospital, and Nurse Roby set about boiling them for the patients. While hurrying up a flight of stairs with the eggs in a steaming pot of water, she tripped on a step just as someone in boots was coming down. The eggs and water were on target. The wearer of the boots was General Pershing.

Ambia (who later became Mrs. Ferrell Pickens) was at a loss as to what to do. She had poured boiling water on the most important American in Europe. "All I could do was stammer an apology," she later recalled.[82] She was quickly reassured by the general that all was forgiven.

Ambia remained in Paris for nearly a year after the war's end and was a witness to the tumultuous welcome received by President Wilson when he arrived there to create a "lasting peace." While the president's party was in Paris, the illness of one of his aides prompted a call to the hospital for a nurse. Ambia and a friend were immediately dispatched to treat the patient.

When they arrived at the hotel where the party was staying, they passed a man in the corridor who bore a striking resemblance to the president. "Isn't that President Wilson ahead of us?" one of the nurses inquired a bit too loudly. The president, overhearing her, stopped and introduced himself to them. In the course of the ensuing conversation, he expressed his "personal appreciation" for the fine work they did during the war. "You played a vital part in our bringing about peace," he told them.[83]

Deeds of Valor—Quirks of Fate

More than half of the men in Tipton County were registered for the draft during the course of World War II. Only boys under seventeen and men over sixty-five were in the category of the unclassified. Of the 7,341 men who registered, more than 2,300 actually served in the armed forces. For some of them war proved to be the experience of a lifetime; for others a last, heroic moment of sacrifice.

From the beginning, Tipton Countians were very much in the thick of the action. Several were stationed in the Pacific area when the Japanese attacked Pearl Harbor on December 7, 1941. Onboard ships based at Pearl Harbor were Carl Whitaker of Covington, Dr. Langdon Newman of Covington and brothers Bill Jim and Rob Roy Davis of Charleston. Others stationed in Hawaii included Doc Wrotham, Sam Poag and Iral Johnson, all of Oak Grove; William C. Maharry of Brighton; W.O. Millican of Poplar Grove; and Reba A. Campbell of Atoka.

Fortunately, none of Tipton's sons were killed at Pearl Harbor, the county's first casualty being recorded much closer to home on April 30, 1942, when the destroyer *Jacob Jones* was torpedoed off Cape May, New

Captain Hays E. Owen, *left*, Major Joe Foss, *center*, and Colonel Charles A. Lindbergh, *right*, strike a pose on Guam, May 30, 1944. Captain Owen of Covington was ground crew chief for Foss's crack air combat unit.

Jersey. Sanford Farris Ray of Mason was among the one hundred officers and men who went down with the ship.

Ray was one of only three Tipton County men in the navy killed during the war. The marines listed three killed in action, and the army headed the list with forty-two who were either killed in action, died of wounds received in the combat zone or were declared dead after a period during which they were listed as missing in action. Another seven died of non-battle causes while serving in the army.

Ironically, the mortality rate for Tipton Countians was as high outside the service as it was in. Records show that forty-one registrants died before they had a chance to enter the armed forces.

Corporal Farris O. Massengill of Covington was awarded the French Croix de Guerre on January 25, 1945, for exceptional service of war rendered in the course of operations in the liberation of France.

    While the casualty percentage for Tipton County was on a par with the state as a whole, the percentage of county men decorated for heroism probably exceeded the state norm. Deeds of valor were so numerous that only a few of the most outstanding can be presented as examples.

    At least two Tipton County men were cited for outstanding courage in action at Bouganville in the Solomon Islands. One of these was William A. Dyson, a black private who had been reared by his grandparents, Hance and Francis Bond, on the F.B. Williamson farm near Mason. On July 5, 1944, the platoon of which Private Dyson was a member came under heavy fire as it approached an enemy ridge. Though suffering a head wound in the first volley, Private Dyson continued to fire his Browning automatic. Repeatedly exposing himself to heavy Japanese fire, he silenced a machine gun on one of the flanks, permitting the men up front to withdraw to safety. But for his courageous action, these men would most likely have been trapped.

The World Wars

Major A.S. Witherington Jr., a native of Munford, was also cited for bravery at Bouganville. When an ambushed combat patrol left three wounded men lying on an open section of beach, Major Witherington voluntarily crawled out under devastating enemy fire and dragged them all to safety.

In a similar incident, Sergeant Marvin E. Cox of Rialto was leading a combat patrol through a wooded ravine on Luzon in the Philippines when the Japanese opened fire with small arms and automatic weapons. Cox led his men out of the ambush, and then with complete disregard for his own safety returned under heavy fire and dragged two wounded men to safety.

Between January 2 and January 27, 1945, the 15th tank Battalion, 6th Armored Division, was under constant enemy fire in the vicinity of Bastogne, Belgium. The fire was so intense that the men could not leave their tanks. Staff Sergeant Robert E. Faught of Covington risked his life to carry hot food to each tank.

During that same period, on January 4, Sergeant Alfred M. David, also of the 6th Armored Division, exhibited conspicuous gallantry. When two of his comrades in a nearby foxhole were buried alive by a near hit, Sergeant David fearlessly exposed himself to heavy enemy fire from rocket and artillery barrages to dig the men out and evacuate them to medical aid.

Courage at sea was exemplified by Seaman William F. Cates, who was killed at his gun on the cruiser *San Francisco* in battle off the Solomon Islands in November 1942. The twenty-three-year-old Drummonds native was cited posthumously by President Roosevelt for his "extraordinary courage" in bringing down a Japanese torpedo bomber; he stayed at his post, firing at the plane until it crashed into his ship, taking his life. The USS *Cates*, a navy destroyer escort, was christened in his honor at Tampa, Florida, on October 10, 1943.

The navy paid a like tribute to Lieutenant Alfred Naifeh, a native of Covington who attended Covington City Schools before moving to Oklahoma in 1930. Young Naifeh died in the line of duty on October 16, 1942, and was later posthumously awarded the Navy and Marine Corps Medal by the president of the United States "for heroic conduct and outstanding devotion to duty in caring for survivors clinging to life rafts after the sinking of the *USS Meredith*." The award of the medal was accompanied by the following citation:

> *With complete disregard for his own personal safety, Lieut. Naifeh persisted in constantly swimming around the rafts, rendering invaluable aid to the men who were wounded or exhausted. As a consequence of his continued valiant efforts to hold these men to the rafts, he himself was completely overcome by exhaustion which ultimately resulted in his death. He gallantly gave up his life in the service of his country.*

Sergeant Alfred M. David of Covington braved enemy artillery fire to extract two of his comrades from a foxhole where they had been buried alive by a near hit.

The brilliant University of Oklahoma graduate died on a life raft following his heroic efforts and was buried at sea. In February 1944 the navy assigned the name USS *Naifeh* to a new destroyer escort vessel launched at Orange, Texas.

Tipton County itself had a navy ship namesake during the war. The USS *Tipton* was one of 310 cargo and transport ships of the navy carrying the names of counties of the United States. It was constructed by the U.S. Maritime Commission and became a naval vessel, on a loan basis, upon completion and acceptance by the navy.

Almost as numerous as the deeds of valor were the instances where Tipton Countians, both at home and abroad, found themselves involved in rather unusual and even bizarre situations. For example, there was the case of a Solo woman who was almost killed when her house was bombed. Lethe Harper was in the kitchen of her home on the afternoon of August 4, 1943, when a bomb tore through the roof, missing her by only four feet.

The missile, which went through a table and through the floor to the ground beneath, was dropped by a bomber crew from the Dyersburg Air Base

The USS *Cates*. *National Archives*.

on maneuvers over the nearby Solo Auxiliary Field. Fortunately for Lethe, who was not injured, the bombs used in the target practice by the Dyersburg flyers contained mostly sand with only a small charge of powder.

Planes from the Millington Naval Air Station were also seen in the skies over Tipton County, but it was an army plane from an unknown base that provided two Covington men with a strange and unforgettable experience. On May 1, 1944, the craft was seen circling a field on the W.C. Harris farm, about a mile north of Covington, by Charlie Porter Forbess, who operated the farm, and Charles Keltner. The two men watched as the pilot set his plane down in a freshly planted cotton field. Any thoughts that engine trouble had forced the craft down were quickly dispelled when the pilot confessed to Forbess and Keltner that he was lost and wanted to know the way to Memphis.

After receiving the information that he desired, the pilot's attempted takeoff from the cotton field proved unsuccessful. But with the assistance of the two Covington men, the plane was pulled manually to a nearby oat patch where the takeoff was made.

While all this was transpiring, two other army planes of the three-plane squadron circled the area where their comrade had landed to seek directions. When he took to the air for Memphis, they followed after him. Although the plane that landed apparently escaped damage, a considerable strip of Mr. Forbess's cotton had to be replanted.

The lost pilot certainly received a much better welcome then did an uninvited visitor who dropped in, literally, on Private First Class Milton E. Murphy of Burlison. The incident occurred during the American drive for Munda Airfield on New Georgia Island.

It was late one night and the GIs were dug in. The Japanese night fighters were on the prowl, chattering and screeching and calling the Americans by their first names, information they had obtained during the daytime.

Murphy and a buddy were in their foxhole, keeping low as they had been ordered to do, when suddenly in jumped a Japanese man with his knife swinging. Murphy and his pal, with machetes already in their hands, went to work on the intruder. After a few seconds the enemy soldier disappeared out of the foxhole as quickly as he had entered.

The assailant was pulled out of the hole by his comrades who had a rope tied around him. When the going got too tough, they yanked him out and dragged him to safety. Murphy never knew how much damage he and his pal had inflicted on their uncous guest. Murphy himself came out of the melee with only a slight cut on one finger.

Private George Robert Blalack of Brighton believed so firmly that a small pocket testament with a metal cover saved his life that he refused to send it home until his mother had bought another and he had received it. Blalack, a member at the time of General Mark Clark's Fifth Army in Italy, was carrying the testament in his pocket when it was struck and dented by a bullet.

A "close shave" of a different type was had by another private in the Fifth Army in Italy. According to a story filed by a war correspondent, William J. Martin of Mason astounded members of his unit by calmly shaving while the Germans lobbed shells in his immediate vicinity, pinning down his whole platoon. When finished, he nonchalantly washed up at a small spring he had found. "I just had to shave," explained Martin, "and I thought there was no time like the present."[84]

The threads of an almost unbelievable story came together on January 8, 1944, when John M. Walker, owner of Walker Chevrolet Co., received a card from Lieutenants Jimmy Turner and Bert Johnston stating that they were roommates in a German prison camp. Both had worked together before the war as employees of Walker.

The two men were born in different Mississippi towns, attended high school in different states and were not acquainted until both moved to Covington where they worked for the automobile company. After Pearl Harbor, both entered the U.S. Army Air Corps, received commissions as navigator and pilot, respectively, went overseas to different theatres of war, were shot down over different countries and finally were reunited as roommates in the same prisoner of war camp in Germany.

The World Wars

The USS *Naifeh*. *National Archives.*

As the *Covington Leader* so aptly put it on January 13, 1944, "strange things are happening every day in this war."

The Incredible Flight of the *Night Raider*

In early 1943, B-24 Liberators of the Army 8th Air Force took off from a field in England for an attack on important industrial targets in Wilhelmshaven, Germany. Among the heavy bombers was one called the *Night Raider*, a veteran of numerous missions over enemy territory. Lieutenant George Pinner of Covington was the bombardier of the plane, which despite its name had never participated in a night raid. It was his responsibility from his position in the nose to line the bombsight on the target.

Trouble began for the plane before it ever reached its objective. One of the crewmen lost consciousness when his oxygen mask failed. Another crewman, in his effort to administer aid, loosened his own mask and also passed out.

Flak from enemy anti-aircraft guns puffed all around as the plane neared its target. Shrapnel sprayed the fuselage everywhere. Enemy fighters, which had already made about thirty passes, continued to attack the B-24s even in the heaviest flak. Then the *Night Raider* began its run with its bomb-bay doors wide open. Wilhelmshaven was rocked by the bursts. Lieutenant Pinner had pinpointed his target.

As the crippled B-24 limped back toward England, enemy fighters and anti-aircraft guns on the ground opened up with all they had. The *Night Raider* was soon left behind by her sister ships. She was in serious trouble now with one engine dead and the radio out of commission. The two crewmen without oxygen were still unconscious.

Losing altitude rapidly, the bomber was set upon by twenty German fighters. Lieutenant Pinner and the navigator, both in the nose, fired their guns at every enemy plane that came into sight. Three attacking fighters were shot down, and three more probably.

Finally, the guns of the enemy began to find their mark. The radio operator's right arm was shot off as he manned a gun, and the waist gunner was wounded by the same shell.

By this time gas and ammunition were getting low. The *Night Raider*, flying on only two engines now, lost precious altitude when the pilot flew her into a cloud bank to escape the enemy fighters. Since a ducking in the cold waters of the North Sea seemed eminent, Pinner moved back in the plane to help the wounded adjust life preservers.

The plane struggled onward, and just as it passed over the coast of England, the gas ran out. The tires had been punctured, the undercarriage shot out and the hydraulic system rendered useless. A crash landing was the pilot's only choice. Lieutenant Pinner went back again to help place the wounded in such positions as to lessen the shock.

There was no shock, however, as the pilot set her down with a perfect belly landing. The wounded were hurried to a hospital. Both unconscious men had regained consciousness during the fracas.

After checking the plane, the ground crew chiefs reported the following damage: power and hydraulic lines in the tail section shot out, as were the carburetors, primers, oil coolers, oxygen regulators and intakes; tires punctured; undercarriage out of order; five 20-millimeter holes and forty-seven 30-caliber holes in the rear fuselage; a large hole in one of the tail flaps; four cannon and sixteen 30s in the left fin; one cannon and seven 30s in the right fin; one cannon and five 30s in the right aileron; thirty-six 30s in the left wing; twelve 30s in the fuselage; twenty-seven 30s in the bomb-bay doors; all gun barrels burned out.

One member of the ground crew was heard to mutter, "This one shouldn't have come back."[85]

A sad postscript was added to this story on April 26, 1943, when Mr. and Mrs. Virgil Pinner were informed by the War Department that their son, Lieutenant Pinner, had been missing in action since April 16. The news came just a few weeks after the raid on Wilhelmshaven.

Disaster Years

A Fire Department

A new era in firefighting was begun in Covington when its first engine arrived by railroad car in February 1921. The $12,000 triple combination car built by the American La France Fire Engine Company of Elmira, New York, was the last word in firefighting machinery. In little more than twenty-five years, Covington had come from the bucket brigade to a motor machine capable of pumping 750 gallons of water a minute.

The old-time bucket brigade had provided Covington citizens with their only defense against fire until the 1890s. This system failed to materially protect property, and as a result Covington was the scene of several big fires during the late 1800s, which literally burned themselves out. The first broke out shortly after midnight on May 27, 1875, and burned the entire east side of the square. But for the fact that things were still wet from a rain the previous night, the north side would have also been consumed.

This fire was noted for its many ludicrous scenes, which caused smiles even under such terrible circumstances. One gentleman grabbed the outer end of a bolt of material and rushed out into the street trailing it behind him, leaving the other end in his store. Another was seen emerging from a burning building carrying his clothes under one arm and a washboard under the other. Sill another, "forgetful that it is contrary to Scripture to pray on the house-tops, began to offer up supplications on the top of Crofford & Clark's Store, and rolled off, fortunately sustaining no injury by his fall."[86]

On the night of December 7, 1882, with a stiff wind blowing out of the north, a fire began in a small frame, two-story house on the west side of the square. Volunteers with buckets used water from the courthouse well and fought the blaze for a time but to no avail. Both the west and the south sides of the square burned as did a number of structures on South Main Street from the square to Church Street. One of the buildings swept by the blaze was the Shelton House, a three-story wooden hotel located on the corner of South Main and the square.

The west side of the square was quickly rebuilt after the fire of '82 but burned again in October 1890. This blaze originated in the hayloft of Boone and Wimbish's Livery Stable. Again the volunteer firefighters used buckets and ladders, getting their water from the well in the courthouse yard and from wells behind the livery stable. Though a large crowd assembled, very little assistance was rendered other than the removing of goods from buildings adjacent to the stable. One of these being a saloon, many of the firefighters took the opportunity to refresh themselves. According to one observer, instead of fighting "the fire to the last ditch" some "fell in the ditch."[87]

With the advent of city water mains just prior to the turn of the century, a volunteer fire department was created with M.P. Garrett as its first chief. Two hundred feet of hose, a hand-powered reel and a hand pump were acquired and housed in a small frame building located in a corner of the courthouse yard.

Ed Wall, the blacksmith who made the hose reel, joined the department in 1897 as plug master. Since the mains in those days were not strong enough to carry the full force of the water pressure, it was his job to regulate the force of the water coming into the mains in accordance with the capacity of the mains to withstand the pressure. In 1900 Wall became chief of the department and served in that capacity for more than a quarter of a century.

The crude wheel cart proved adequate for small fires, but fortunately the city faced no general conflagration during the period that it was in use. In February 1906 the hand-drawn cart was replaced by a one-horse fire wagon, which was in turn replaced the next year by a two-horse outfit. The department at that time, in addition to Chief Wall, consisted of driver John T. Eckford, Jim Keathley, Ed Klingman, Virge Ogilvie, John Maley and Charles Stancliff.

The department was located on the lower floor of the city hall just off the square on the west side of South Main Street. The firemen lived and slept on the same floor with the horses; the firemen slept in the section next to the street while the horses were kept on the main floor next to the alley.

The horses, named Ed and John (for Ed Wall and John T. Eckford), were put in charge of a fireman hired especially to feed, curry and train them and to keep them in readiness for a fire. They were put through their paces every day getting into position between the shafts of the wagon. When the alarm sounded, the horses tugged at their tethers, ready to jump between the shafts. The harness, which was hung over the shafts, could be dropped on the horses

Disaster Years

Members of the fire department pose on March 1, 1906, with their new one-horse fire wagon.

below and buckled up in a matter of seconds. It was said that the horses appeared proud of their task as they raced through the streets whirling the red wagon around corners on the two wheels, raising clouds of dust.

With the arrival of Covington's first engine, the old firefighting wagon and apparatus was kept at the station in case of a breakdown in the new equipment. The horses were eliminated from the service and utilized by the city for dray purposes. Ironically, the team that had galloped to the rescue of so many burning buildings in Covington was itself burned to death in a fire that destroyed the city barn on August 16, 1922.

Chief Wall and his firemen were justly proud of their new engine. Some of the specifications of the machine were: 105-horsepower motor; single front and double rear tires; artillery-type wheels; ten-inch electric search light; rotary gear pump with 750-gallon capacity; 1,200-foot hose capacity; 40-gallon chemical tank; 200 feet of chemical hose; two 3-gallon extinguishers; two extension ladders; and all necessary operating tools. One of the chief advantages of the new machine was the chemical tank, which would put out an average fire without the usual damage caused by water.

The first real test of the new equipment came when the fire alarm sounded at 4:50 on the morning of May 2, 1921. The Covington Supply

Chief Ed Wall, under whose leadership the Covington Fire Department went from bucket brigade to modern pumper.

Company Building at the corner of West Liberty and the square was on fire. Although the department responded immediately to the call, by the time they reached the scene, flames were leaping from doors and windows and the entire building was ablaze.

The firemen, under the leadership of Assistant Fire Chief John T. Eckford, turned their efforts to saving the structures in the immediate vicinity. The Hotel Lindo across the street caught fire but was quickly extinguished and sustained only slight damage. The front porch of the courthouse also ignited, but it, too, was quickly put out. Although the four-story brick Supply

Disaster Years

The Supply Company Building shortly after its construction in 1897. The burning of this structure on May 2, 1921, provided the first real test for the fire department's first fire engine.

Company Building was completely destroyed, the Tennessee Hardware Company next door suffered only heavy water damage.

The *Covington Leader*, in reporting the fire on May 5, wrote the following:

> *All those who suffered loss expressed appreciation for the efficient manner in which the fire department handled the situation, which looked at one time as if the whole west side of the square would be swept away, and everyone who witnessed the fire expressed themselves as highly pleased with the results given by the American-La France fire engine which the city recently purchased.*

On May 11, 1926, the city purchased another firetruck from the American-La France Company. The machine was similar to the one already in use except that it was a 360-gallon capacity pumper and had a four-cylinder engine instead of a six. It carried the same hose, ladders and chemical equipment as the other truck.

The machine was not new, however, having been first purchased by the city of Greensboro, North Carolina, and then returned to the company because it was too small for their needs. The truck had been used for two years and then only as a hose truck. The pumper had seen only about fourteen hours of use. Covington was able to buy the apparatus, which cost $12,000 new, for only $6,800.

To Chief Wall went the credit for getting the additional equipment. He had been advocating its need for several years because of the large truck's inability to function properly on the small water mains in the outlying sections of the town. It was felt that the new machine with its smaller pumping capacity would not suck these mains dry as had the old one.

Before long, the advantage of having two fire engines was made apparent. One of the most potentially dangerous fires in Covington's history occurred on the night of March 23, 1928, when seven tank cars and two box cars of a northbound freight derailed one hundred yards north of the Illinois Central Station. All seven cars burned in the resulting fire, but luckily the contents of only two of the tank cars ignited. The tank cars were loaded with gasoline, kerosene and crude oil.

When the oil in the tank cars caught fire, flames shot hundreds of feet into the air, holding in awe the hundreds of citizens who had gathered to witness the spectacle. The streets leading to the depot were filled with people throughout the night. Fear of an explosion caused many to leave the scene for a time, but their curiosity got the best of them, and they returned to see what progress was being made in the efforts to extinguish the flames.

Adding more potential danger to the situation was the fact that the fire occurred directly between the Federal Compress (in which thousands of bales of cotton were stored) on one side of the railroad right of way and two wholesale gasoline and oil stations on the other. Although all three places were constantly threatened, the good work of the firemen kept the flames away.

The big pumper was stationed at the north end of the compress yard. To reach the plug, it was necessary to go through the compress yard, but the gate was locked. An attempt to break the lock with an ax proved too slow, so Dick Bryant charged the gate with the big truck and sent it flying in every direction.

The light pumper, in the charge of Herbert Fuller, was stationed south of the compress yard on Liberty Avenue. For eight hours his pumper supplied constant streams of water from the city mains.

Water, of course, was useless in fighting the oil fire, but as the oil seeped from the tanks and went burning toward the adjoining property, the firemen used their hoses to sweep it back to the railroad. In this manner they were able to confine the fire to the burning cars. Besides the derailed cars, four boarding cars on a nearby siding were also consumed.

Disaster Years

Although no serious injuries were recorded during the eight hours that it took to extinguish the flames, there were a number of close calls. I.R. Calhoun, one of the firemen, was temporarily blinded by the fire's bright glare and fell into a ditch filled with several feet of water. He was rescued by Asbury Malone, a black employee of the local ice company.

Another fireman, C.W. White, became entangled in fallen telegraph lines and went down in water and mud. As fire crept toward him, his comrades sprayed water on him until he was able to free himself and regain this feet.

In a similar incident, veteran fireman E.G. McIntosh and two or three other firemen were handling the big hose when one slipped, throwing all of them to the ground. Before they could get up, the burning oil was within a couple of feet of them.

The containment of this fire was proof that the infant Covington Fire Department had come of age. An expert fire official from Atlanta credited Covington with having the best firefighting equipment of any town of its size that he had ever visited. The equipment put Covington into a class with much larger towns in regard to fire protection.

Funnels of Death

One of the earliest recorded tornadoes to strike Tipton County was one that swept over the lower part of the county on the night of March 21, 1835. Eight people were killed and a number badly injured in what was termed "one of the most noted tornadoes ever in the state."[88] Due to the low survival rate of early county newspapers, information on any other such storms prior to 1900 is relatively nonexistent.

During the first three-quarters of the twentieth century, the two most devastating tornadoes to visit the county struck within five years of each other. The first made its appearance on the morning of April 21, 1928. Entering the county in the neighborhood, it split into two separate whirlwinds, one going through Mt. Carmel and vicinity and the other through the Melrose and Liberty communities. The storm was christened the "Atoka Tornado" for it was there that most of its fury was spent, the entire business district of the little town being leveled by the blow.

Before the storm, six store buildings and the Planters Bank Building constituted the main business section of Atoka; one building was occupied by the general merchandise store of I.D. Templeton with the lodge rooms of the Knights of Pythias located upstairs; another building housed the local barbershop; other structures were occupied by McDill and Quisenberry, Dr. J. Fleming, C.T. Walker and H.G. Sullivan. On the second floor of the

Atoka a few years before it was leveled.

Planters Bank Building were the office of Dr. A.B. Blaydes and the watch repair shop of A.J. Fite. Located in the rear of the same building was the blacksmith shop of Mike Gaines.

In the wake of the storm, all that remained of the business district was a portion of the walls of the bank, the floor of the building occupied by I.D. Templeton and one corner of the building occupied by McDill and Quisenberry. This corner housed the local post office, the equipment of which was later salvaged from the ruins and temporarily set up in the freight office of the Illinois Central depot, which had sustained only minor damage.

Not even the garage of Wallace Thompson, located several hundred yards north of the main business section of town, escaped the raging winds. The structure was practically destroyed as were all of the automobiles inside at the time.

The only building to escape damage in the central portion of town was the Methodist church. Strangely enough, it stood untouched by the twister while only a few feet away the store building of H.G. Sullivan was completely demolished.

Although a number of people were injured in the storm, miraculously, only one fatality was recorded. Paul Forbess, the fifteen-year-old son of

Bunyon Forbess, was killed instantly when the residence of his father collapsed. The remaining six members of the family were injured severely enough to require hospitalization.

The only other serious injury in Atoka was sustained when the H.H. Hunter house collapsed by the wind. Hunter's son, Malcolm, was pinned beneath heavy timbers, and it required rescue workers two hours to free him from the wreckage.

In view of the fact that fifteen of the residences in the town were totally destroyed and most of the rest suffered varying degrees of damage, it is remarkable that the total of dead and seriously injured was not greater. By nightfall, practically all of those left homeless by the storm had been cared for either by neighbors and friends or by the Memphis Chapter of the Red Cross, which was on the scene early with emergency supplies and tents.

The second and more disastrous of the two tornadoes occurred late on the afternoon of May 7, 1933. Following a period of almost midnight darkness, accompanied by heavy rain and hail, a light yellow cloud bank formed over the central part of the county, and out of it swooped one of the deadliest twisters the county has ever witnessed. Striking with rapier-like quickness, the rapidly revolving funnel first touched down just south of Brighton. From there it cut a hideous fifteen-mile-long swath through the heart of the county to the vicinity of Charleston, where the greatest damage and loss of life was recorded.

Rain and hail continued to follow in the wake of the twister over all the eastern and southeastern portions of the county. Between seventy-five and one hundred families were left without shelter and at the mercy of the elements.

With power lines down, it took some time for help to be secured even at points lying near accessible roads. Night set in quickly, adding to the already terror-stricken condition of the victims. Many were dazed and wandered aimlessly about after the severe shock of the precipitate blow, which had left them homeless and, in many cases, bloody from injuries.

Shortly after word of the storm reached Covington, the Red Cross office was opened by Secretary John C. Wilson, who with the assistance of dozens of volunteers started a search of the storm area for isolated cases of injury.

Within a short period of time automobiles began arriving in Covington from the south and east, each bearing its quota of injured. Available doctors in town lent their services and administered first aid to the crushed and bleeding victims, who were lifted from the automobiles and rushed into the various medical offices for examination.

The more seriously injured were sped to Memphis hospitals in privately owned automobiles and in a Ripley ambulance that had been made

John Cullum Wilson, vice-president of the American National Red Cross from 1962 to 1970.

available. The Covington ambulance was being held in readiness for the Aubrey Deverell family of near Charleston following word that the entire group was casualties.

Efforts to reach the Deverell family with medical aid proved fruitless for hours. Secretary Wilson, accompanied by Drs. L.J. Lindsey and J.J. Roby, Vernon Pickens and Henry Baxter, was finally able to make his way on horseback through the flooded and tree-strewn bottom between Charleston and the Deverell home. Volunteers then rushed into the inky darkness with timber saws and literally cut a road out so that a wagon could be used to bring the family to the nearest gravel road. At about midnight they were brought out of the bottom, sped to Covington and sent on from there to Memphis by the waiting ambulance.

Disaster Years

The Deverell family was hardest hit by the storm. The youngest child, three-year-old Stanley, had been killed in his father's arms during the storm; Mrs. Deverell died in Baptist Hospital, Memphis, on Monday, the day after the storm; Mildred, age eight, and brother Aubrey Allen died there the following day. The surviving members of the family, the father and six-year-old Louis Leon, were both hospitalized in serious condition.

The only other fatalities occurred on the Benton G. Calhoun farm six miles south of Covington, where Matti Cook, forty-five, and Fan Ethel Reed, sixteen, were killed. Four other blacks living on the same farm received injuries, which necessitated their being admitted to the General Hospital in Memphis.

That the number of dead and injured was not greater was attributed to the slow advance of the tornado. Although the twister revolved at a tremendous rate of speed, it moved slowly, permitting many to seek the relative safety of pits and ditches. Some, however, miraculously escaped with no harm or with only slight injury, even though they were not able to reach such shelter.

With the approach of the storm that leveled his house, W.H. Brammer and three members of his household raced for the protection of a nearby ditch. Brammer and one family member reached the ditch safely. The other two, just as the twister struck the residence, threw themselves to the ground with their arms around each other. Despite the hail of bricks, timbers and other deadly missiles, all escaped without a scratch.

After the full fury of the wind had struck the Jess Turner residence, only one room of the substantial structure remained. This room was constructed of boarded logs, a fact to which the family attributed their miraculous escape, they having hovered there as the storm approached.

An amazingly similar incident occurred on the Sigman farm. Timbers of the big two-story house on that place were scattered over several hundred yards. The only room left intact was the one in which the family had luckily taken refuge.

At least one person took advantage of the rare opportunity to watch a tornado's approach. C.L. Shoaf, a farmer in the Tabernacle community, sent his wife and children into a nearby ditch and then stood on the high ground in front of his house and watched the slow-moving funnel suck up trees and buildings as it advanced. When it reached a relatively short distance from his residence, he joined his family in the ditch just before flying timbers, trees and other debris passed overhead. Though his house was only twisted by the tornado, Shoaf lost several tenant houses and a splendid barn.

A bright, beautiful day dawned on Monday, disclosing clearly for the first time the results of the appalling disaster of the day before, which had left as many as four hundred people homeless.

A trip by daylight over the area…revealed the full extent of the worst catastrophe of the kind which has visited Tipton County in years. Death, injury, and destruction left a black mark 15 miles long and from a quarter to a mile and one-half wide through the center of the county. More substantial citizens were surveying their losses with a certain degree of composure, although many were still…shaken from their proximity to death. It was upon the poorer people that the greatest blow befell. They were found to be dazedly walking about the sites of their little homes, many young mothers with babies in their arms, while tears ran unheeded down their checks. Eyes gave forth little light as they dumbly surveyed the scenes of waste and desolation, their every earthly possession lying broken, twisted and rainsoaked beneath the huge piles of tangled wreckage.[89]

Red Cross headquarters were established in the Charleston School on Monday morning, and before noon, shipments of food, clothing and tents were being sped to the stricken area. For Secretary Wilson, the Charleston tornado was to be the first of many disaster experiences in which he would participate during a long and illustrious career with the Red Cross.

John Cullum Wilson was born on April 16, 1905, in Martin, Tennessee, but spent his early childhood on his grandfather's farm near Tabernacle. Upon the death of his grandfather in 1914, he moved with his mother, grandmother and two sisters to Covington where he attended the Covington Grammar School and graduated from Byars-Hall High School in 1924.

After attending the West Tennessee State Teachers College in Memphis and Emory University in Atlanta, Wilson received his degree in 1928 from Peabody College in Nashville where he also did graduate work in psychology and sociology. He then served for two years as teacher and principal at Holmes School in the Tipton County school system.

Wilson entered Red Cross service in 1932 as executive secretary of the Tipton County Chapter. A year later, after his fine relief work following the Charleston storm, he joined the national staff as a field representative in Tennessee to assist in the administration of emergency relief. In 1934 he transferred to the Midwestern area where he served for two years as a general field representative in Missouri.

Following a series of promotions, Wilson was named manager in 1944 of the Southeastern area of the National Red Cross with headquarters in Atlanta. Three years later he returned to St. Louis as manager of the Midwestern area.

In 1951 Wilson was transferred to the national headquarters of the American Red Cross in Washington, D.C., as vice-president responsible for supervising fundraising and disaster relief for the four area offices located in

Disaster Years

The Charleston Baptist Church, erected about 1903, was totally destroyed by the tornado of 1933.

Atlanta, St. Louis, San Francisco and Alexandria, Virginia. In 1962 he was elected executive vice-president by the Board of Directors with responsibility for the operation of the total organization. In this capacity he supervised a staff of more than four thousand scattered throughout the United States and in thirty-one foreign countries. He held this post until 1970 when he retired after thirty-eight years of service in the Red Cross.

During his career Wilson traveled extensively, assisting in many foreign disasters. For his services he was decorated by the Japanese Red Cross, the Greek Red Cross, the Austrian government and the Turkish Crescent. He was best known for his knowledge and experience in the area of disaster relief and for his skill in handling people.

The Lighter Side

The usual number of oddities that accompany tornadoes was noted in both the Atoka and the Charleston storms. During the Atoka twister, store invoices were blown from Atoka to Mt. Carmel, a distance of about ten miles. In that same storm, a sixteen-foot-long, two- by six-foot timber was blown through a door like a bullet. It broke one of the door's four- by eight-foot panes of glass but left the others completely intact.

An Atoka child's life was saved when falling timbers lodged against his bed, shielding him from falling debris. After the wind had passed, the mother found her four-year-old son safe and sound under the rubble, he having slept through the entire storm.

During the turmoil of the Charleston tornado, as her house was being destroyed, a woman pulled a chair over her head so tightly that she became wedged between the rungs of the chair. The rungs had to be broken before her head could be extracted.

The most bizarre incident of the Charleston storm involved Buster Williams, occupant of a house that was leveled near Tabernacle. With the approach of the twister, Williams sought shelter in a ditch near his house. When the wind with its dust, trash and flying missiles had passed overhead, he opened his eyes to find an eleven-hundred-pound bull standing directly over him. The animal had been picked up by the wind from a nearby field and gently deposited astride the ditch directly above his prostrate body.

Tipton County's Own

Augustus Hill Garland

In 1833, Rufus Garland, one of the county's earliest settlers, moved from his home four miles northeast of Covington to Miller County, Arkansas. A fellow citizen recalled meeting him and his wife, Barbara (Hill) Garland, near the Shelby County line when they were moving. The father was driving a wagon, and the mother was walking behind with one of her sons in her arms. This was probably Augustus Hill Garland, who was born on June 11 of the previous year.

Shortly after the family arrived in Arkansas, Rufus died. Mrs. Garland subsequently moved to Washington, Arkansas, where, in 1837, she married Thomas Hubbard.

Augustus received his early education in a private school in Washington. He then attended college in Kentucky at St. Mary's in Lebanon and St. Joseph's College in Bardstown. Following his graduation from the latter institution in 1849, he returned to Arkansas and taught school for a short time in Sevier County, studied law in his grandfather's office and was admitted to the bar in 1853. In that same year he married Virginia Sanders.

Garland practiced law in Washington, Arkansas, until 1856 when he moved to Little Rock and went into partnership with Ebenezer Cummins. In 1860 he was admitted to practice before the United States Supreme Court and was a presidential elector on the ticket of Bell and Everett.

In 1861, as a member of the state secession convention, Garland voted against an ordinance to secede; however, following the fall of Fort Sumter, he voted with the majority in favor of secession and was elected a representative in the first Confederate Congress. He was joined in the Congress on May 22, 1864, by his brother, Rufus K. Garland, who had also been born in Tipton County.

Augustus continued to serve as a representative until November 8, 1864, when he was sent to the Confederate Senate to fill the vacancy created by the death of Charles B. Mitchell. The committees on which he ably served as representative and senator included Judiciary, Enrolled Bills, Medical Department, Territories and Public Lands, Military Affairs and Post Office and Post Roads.

Upon his return to Arkansas after the war, Garland was asked by Governor Harris Flanagan to negotiate with Federal authorities for recognition of the state government. He obtained a pardon from President Johnson and immediately applied for the reinstatement of his license to practice before the United States Supreme Court.

An act of Congress had disbarred those who could not take the oath that they had never taken up arms against the United States or held an office in a government hostile to it. Garland argued that the act was unconstitutional since it was ex post facto, and that even if constitutional, the president's pardon had removed his disability. Both views were upheld by the Supreme Court, which ordered that he be reinstated.

In 1867, after the Democrats had gained control of the state legislature, Garland was elected to the United States Senate but was not permitted to take his seat. When the carpetbag regime was defeated in 1874 and a new constitution adopted, he was elected governor. Among the problems he inherited from the carpetbag regime was an enormous state debt. In order to finance the state he issued bonds, provided a sinking fund and halted the guaranteeing of railroad bonds.

In 1877, the year his wife died, Garland was again elected to the United States Senate, and this time was allowed to take his seat. Soon after taking office, he introduced a bill calling for an investigation of the effects of the tariff. He was a strong supporter of both tariff and civil service reform. Following the flood of 1882, he initiated legislation giving the Mississippi River Commission authority to build and repair levees along the Mississippi. He held that the matter was of national concern and so should be the responsibility of the federal government and not that of the individual states.

On March 9, 1885, Garland resigned his Senate post to become attorney general in the cabinet of President Grover Cleveland. Being an ex-Confederate, it was not surprising that he was subjected to a thorough congressional investigation. When he retired from the cabinet, Garland, who had spent a large portion of his life defending the Constitution and overcoming political obstacles, resumed the practice of law in Washington, D.C. He also gave some attention to writing and authored a little book, *Experience in the Supreme Court of the United States*, published in 1898, and he collaborated with Robert Ralston on *A Treatise on the Constitution and Jurisdiction of the United States Courts*, published the same year.

Tipton County's Own

Augustus Hill Garland. *Library of Congress*.

On January 26, 1899, Garland was stricken while arguing a case before the Supreme Court. Within minutes he was dead. His body was taken back to Arkansas and interred in Little Rock's Mount Holly Cemetery.

Confederate congressman and senator, Arkansas governor, United States senator and attorney general of the United States, Augustus Hill Garland deserved and won the esteem and confidence of his fellow countrymen. Tipton County is proud to claim him as her most outstanding native son.

"B. Baptist—rattling bones"

James I. Hall, George D. Holmes and Phillip A. Fisher were among the more noted educators in the county between the end of the Civil War and the turn of the century. Hall conducted the Mountain Academy, which he reopened in 1865, the old school having burned in 1860. Holmes succeeded his father, James, in 1868 as master of the Tipton Female Seminary in Covington. Fisher headed a school in Covington that was a common school when private schools were in session and a private school when the others were out for vacation.

At least one county youngster studied, at various times, under each of the above mentioned gentlemen. He was Richard Banister Baptist, who grew up to become judge of the Court of Appeals of the State of Tennessee. Known for his keen sense of humor and his gift for storytelling, he wrote an autobiography in 1936 in which he included some personal experiences and impressions of his primary training under the tutelage of Hall, Holmes and Fisher. That portion of his manuscript follows:

Richard Banister Baptist shown in later life. He served as circuit judge of the Judicial Circuit of Tennessee from 1918 to 1942, and as judge of the Court of Appeals of the State of Tennessee from 1942 to 1953.

Tipton County's Own

The first school I attended was conducted by Mrs. Harry Boyd in her residence. Who my schoolmates were or what progress I made in this institution of learning I am unable to recall. Perhaps I learned my "ABC's"; at any rate I was shortly transferred to the Tipton Female Seminary. This was an institution founded by Dr. James Holmes [Professor E.T. Alling was actually elected the first principal of the school when it opened in 1855. Dr. Holmes took charge in 1857 upon Alling's resignation.] *and conducted by his son Prof. George D. Holmes who was in charge during my attendance. It was strictly a girls' school, but boys up to ten or twelve years of age were permitted to attend, after which they were removed from these refined and refining influences. Prof. Holmes was splendidly qualified to be at the head of such an institution, a Godly man who exercised great influence over his pupils.*

This school flourished until the Public School was organized and this latter—the Grammar School building—now occupies the site of the Tipton Female Seminary. Again I am unable to recall the progress I made in this institution devoted to the education of the female of species. All I know is that I have no medals to remind me of any victories there won.

Dr. James Holmes. He founded the Mountain Academy in 1832 and served as principal of the Tipton Female Seminary from 1857 until his retirement in 1868.

True Tales of Tipton

George D. Holmes replaced his father, Dr. James Holmes, as head of the Tipton Female Seminary in 1868 and served in that capacity until the school closed in 1894.

Again I was transferred and this time to the Tipton Male Academy. Just why it bore this high sounding name I was never able to ascertain. There was only one teacher, Mr. Philip Fisher, affectionately called "Old Man Phil." I hardly think he could have been more than forty years old, but as he wore spectacles and a red beard swept his breast I thought then that he bore the weight of many years. It was [an] unruly and boisterous set over which he reigned, but he was equal to every occasion if discipline was needed, and these occasions were many. He was sparing with the rod, but woe betide the transgressor if he felt called on to use it. His punishments were varied and usually unexpected. There was a large black board at the end of the school room and when a misdemeanor was committed the culprit was required to go to this board, write his name, with the offense committed, and to remain after school was dismissed and get whatever was coming to him.

At one time I was the owner of a pair of "bones," that is to say two flat sticks of hard wood about ten inches long and when placed between the fingers and expertly used made a noise calculated to wake the dead. Mr. Fisher was engaged in teaching a class with his back to the school room. My "bones" were in my desk and a foolish inspiration caused me

Tipton County's Own

The Tipton Female Seminary.

to reach in there and bring them out, and then the rattle of those "bones" smote the stillness of the schoolroom. I softly replaced them in my desk as the teacher with great deliberation turned around and surveyed the room, and then quietly turned again and resumed his teaching. A second foolish inspiration came over me and I repeated the offense. Mr. Fisher arose and came to my desk as deliberately as if he had seen me commit the act [and] *said, "What did you do that with"; I hung my head for a moment and replied, "With my bones." "All right." He said, "go and write your name on the black board." I went to the front and wrote "B. Baptist—rattling bones." That afternoon I staid* [sic] *and waited wearily as each offender was dismissed and as he went he rubbed out his name. Finally, he turned his head and there upon that board stood my name alone. He read it aloud and said, "Get out your bones." He examined them with great care and had me to demonstrate the use of them, commenting the while on their remarkable quality. And then he suddenly said: "Now young man, you mount that rostrum and rattle those bones until I tell you to quit, and if you do quit before I tell you I'll give you the worst thrashing you ever had in your life." I proceeded to obey that command; at first with alacrity, then with moderation and finally awed pain and suffering. I had no means of knowing how long he kept me at it. It seemed for weeks, at least I know it was until my knees smote one against the other; until the arm hung limply*

Professor George D. Holmes with alumni and members of the class of 1894. The latter, *sitting on the ground*, were the last to graduate from the seminary.

>*by my side and my eyes were fixed in a glassy stare. He permitted me to quit just a moment before I expired, and from that day to this I have taken little interest in the art of "rattlin bones."*
>
>The water supply for the school was a spring located about a quarter mile from the building and to reach it a creek and two fences had to be crossed. The water was brought in turn by the boys, but this was considered no hardship; in fact each one was happy when his turn came to bring it and escape from the school room. There was never any hurry on that journey. This spring was a favorite place of deposit for bottles of milk which some of the more thrifty students brought to be consumed with their dinner. I thought at that time the school house and the spring were located in exactly the right spots but I have often wondered since why the house was not built by the spring as there was plenty of room in each direction for such a building. However, I have heard my Grandmother Boyd tell that the house she lived in before the Civil War was located a half mile from the spring, the only source of a water supply, and the reason was that carrying of water was a job for the little negroes and that it kept them continually busy and consequently out of mischief. At this school I advanced to some degree in the art of hand writing (not evidenced at this time.) by the diligent use of

copy books; to [sic] use of the multiplication tables in arithmetic; spelling learned from the "Blue Back Speller," and United States History. Mr. Fisher has long since been gathered to his Father and his memory has been honored for years by his students. After a few years at his school my Father decided to enroll me in the school kept by Captain James I. Hall at Mount Carmel. Captain Hall had conducted this school for many years and it was noted throughout this section of the State not only for what was supposed to be the thoroughness of training in the classics, but because of the character of its principal. Captain Hall, I think, was born in Iredell County, North Carolina and had come to Mount Carmel when a lad with his Father, and when that community was settled by the Halls in 1834. He was a captain in the Confederate Army, a gallant soldier and had been severely wounded in battle. He lived about two miles from the school house and his invariable custom was to walk that distance by a path through the fields and woods, always alone, and in cool or cold weather wearing a long military coat. There were several students from other localities who boarded with some family or families in the community. Some of the students who lived within a few miles walked the distance, while those at a greater distance came on horseback or in some sort of conveyance. I lived five miles from the school and went horseback. Although the weather was frequently bad and the road sometimes "belly deep to a horse" I remember no hardships in connection with those daily journeys on the contrary as one of the most enjoyable periods of my life. I rode whatever animal happened to be convenient at the time; sometimes the family buggy horse old "Bonny"; occasionally [sic] a mule and for a short time a small mustang mare, which my Father had secured from a drove shipped from Texas, and which was as vicious as a wild cat; so much so that she was disposed of after a short time, and I returned to a quieter and safer mount. I had a sack split in the middle, in one end of which were carried a few ears of corn for feeding, and in the other end my dinner and school books.

    The community of Mount Carmel, as well as the school, was noted. It had been settled in 1834 largely by the emigration of a part of a Presbyterian Community known as Old Bethany in Iredell County, North Carolina. My wife's Grandfather, Mr. John Nesbit Hall, came with that emigration and had a part in the settlement and up-building of the community and in the organization and growth of the Mount Carmel Presbyterian Church. This community, church and school grew and prospered for many years. I think I can add that our county has produced no finer type of citizenship than was here produced. Unfortunately, like many others, the community has been broken up with few of the old families remaining. Captain Hall was, for many, [sic] years a ruling elder in the

James I. Hall, who reopened the Mountain Academy in 1865.

church and was a man of great piety as well as learning. The public school building is now where his school house was. There was very little discipline in this school, or if there was, it has left no impression on me. I think Captain Hall was a great and conscientious teacher, but I also think it was largely left to the pupil as to whether he would take advantage of the opportunities. I attended this school for one school year and then, perhaps because I was not taking proper advantages of the opportunities offered my Father and Mother decided to send me to Webbs School at Bell Buckle, Tennessee, a famous preparatory school for boys, and presided over by the famous "Swaney" Webb.

Tipton County's Own

Men of Congress

During the summer of 1878, the Democrats of the 9th congressional district of Tennessee held their convention at Alamo, county seat of Crockett. Yellow fever was raging at the time, so it was deemed necessary to hold the convention away from the railroad. Alamo was considered a good location because of its distance from the nearest tracks.

Nearly every county in the district, except Crockett, had a candidate for Congress at the convention. Since a two-thirds majority of delegate votes was required to win the nomination, the convention was deadlocked for several days. C.B. Simonton of Covington finally emerged victorious and went on to win the election, becoming Tipton County's first representative in the United States Congress.

Charles Bryson Simonton was born near old Portersville in Tipton County on September 8, 1838. He received his primary education in the common schools of the county and graduated from Erskine College in Due West, South Carolina, in 1859. He taught school in Portersville until 1861 when he enlisted as a private in Company C, 9th Tennessee Infantry. Rising to the rank of captain, he was severely wounded in the Battle of Perryville and was rendered unfit for active duty for the remainder of the war.

In 1870, following a number of years as head of the school in his old neighborhood, Simonton was elected circuit court clerk of Tipton County. In this capacity he took advantage of the opportunity to study law and in 1873 was admitted to the Tipton County Bar. Four years later he resigned as circuit court clerk to fill a seat in the Tennessee legislature.

In 1886, following two terms in the United States Congress, Simonton served as chairman of the Democratic Convention of Tennessee and six years later was a presidential elector on the Democratic ticket of President Cleveland. He was appointed United States district attorney for the western district of Tennessee by Cleveland in 1897 and ably served as such for four years.

Simonton was eminent as citizen, soldier and statesman, but it was as Simonton the lawyer that the people of Tipton County knew him best.

> *He threw into the practice of his profession the intensity of his nature, his great love for justice and fair play, his thorough knowledge of the law. His magnificent powers as a debater and his intense and magnetic manner of expression made him a great and successful lawyer. His professional adversaries and the court found him prepared and ready to give his authorities and the strong and attractive manner in which he put his case and made his application of the law to the facts was the admiration of all*

Charles Bryson Simonton, one of only two men from Tipton County elected to the United States Congress.

who were fortunate enough to hear him. He was necessarily and naturally the leading counsel in every cause in which he was employed, and in the battle which followed was plodding pedestrian, skilled gladiator and soaring eagle. His pathos deep, strong and tender brought tears to his listeners' eyes and his sparkling humor provoked rounds of laughter and applause.[90]

One of the most touching traits of Simonton's character was his deep devotion to the people of the Salem community. Though he lived the last forty years of his life in Covington, his heart was always in the place of his birth with the people of his early years. They knew him to be a man who was willing, if necessary, to sacrifice all of his worldly goods and hopes for them.

Simonton died at his home in Covington on June 10, 1911. In resolutions adopted on June 28 by his peers, the members of the county bar, it was said that "there never lived in Tipton County a man who more thoroughly impressed himself by his character upon the minds and hearts of the people."[91]

Tipton County's only other United States congressman to date was Zachary Taylor, a man of genial disposition and Chesterfieldian manners who drew friends readily to him. A handsome man, his erect military carriage and physical appearance gave him a striking resemblance in his late years to General Robert E. Lee. Though not a native of Tipton County, he spent his boyhood and young manhood there.

Taylor, a son of Thomas Taylor, was born on May 9, 1849, in Haywood County, Tennessee. After receiving his preparatory education at James I. Hall's School at Mt. Carmel, he entered the Virginia Military Institute at Lexington, Virginia, where he graduated as senior captain of the cadet corps on July 4, 1872. He then studied law at Cumberland University, Lebanon, Tennessee, and was admitted to the state bar in January 1874.

In 1878 Taylor opened a law practice in Covington and at the time had an avid interest in the publication of law books. He was elected to the Tennessee Senate in 1880 and served as Covington postmaster from July 1, 1885. In the election of November 1884 he won a seat in the 49th Congress as a Republican for the 10th Congressional District of Tennessee.

During his term, from March 4, 1885, to March 3, 1887, Taylor investigated land deals in Illinois and was sent on a congressional Indian mission to Oklahoma. Following his defeat in a bid for reelection, he moved to Memphis and engaged in the insurance business. He later moved to San Antonio, Texas, but soon returned to Tennessee.

In 1896 Taylor was a delegate to the Republican National Convention, which nominated William McKinley. He spent his retirement years at Ellendale in Shelby County and died there on February 19, 1921.

THE LIGHTER SIDE

When C.B. Simonton made his bid for a second term in Congress in 1880, he ran into some opposition at the convention being held that year at Humboldt. Early balloting found him a few votes short of the required two-thirds necessary for nomination.

In their search for additional votes, Simonton's campaign workers observed that Gibson County was solidly behind Tipton's favorite son with the exception of one civil district. The old squire who controlled the district was soon besieged by friends of Simonton who wanted to know why he was against their candidate. His response was, "I don't like Simonton."[92]

After much persuasion the squire was finally induced to give the cause of his aversion to Tipton's candidate. He exclaimed angrily, "Simonton has scattered garden seed all over Gibson County and has never sent me ary paper."[93]

One of Simonton's supporters put his arm around the old squire and told him that he would see that the candidate sent him a whole bag of seed. On that promise Gibson County voted solidly at the next roll call for Simonton, and he received the nomination. Thus, the day was saved by a promise of garden seed while the distribution of free seed almost cost a congressman his nomination.

"Miss Fanny"

The Boyd family of Mecklenburg County, Virginia, received a lovely gift on Christmas Day 1867. It was a baby girl who, from the first moment of her life, seemed destined to make people happy. Frances, as she was christened, was her parent's first child and gladdened their hearts from the moment of her first weak cry. Years later she would spread joy all over the nation and coax laughter from young and old alike with her book, *Miss Minerva and William Green Hill*.

Frances Boyd lived in Mecklenburg County for about eleven years. (Boydton, the county seat, was named for one of her ancestors, and another of these ancestors, her great-grandfather Townes, had lived at "Occoneechee," one of the most famous of the antebellum homes of southern Virginia.) In 1878, Townes Boyd, her father, moved his family south to Warrenton, North Carolina. Two years later, he bought a Tipton County newspaper business, the *Tipton Record*, and moved to Covington.

Frances attended the Tipton Female Seminary in Covington, a handsome two-story building, which, with its four white columns and its steeple, looked very much like the old courthouse of that day. Graduating in 1885, she furthered her education at a school in Bowling Green, Kentucky.

In 1896, Frances took a position as a fifth-grade primary teacher in the Covington City School. "Miss Fanny," as she was known to her pupils, proved to be a good teacher for two reasons—she loved children, and she had the rare gift of turning the monotony of daily lessons into a real adventure.

Poetry was one of Frances's loves, and she had her classes memorize and recite with gestures such poems as "Maud Muller on a Summer's Day Racked the Meadows Sweet with Hay," "The Charge of the Light Brigade" and "Horatio at the Bridge." Being somewhat of a poet herself, she had a few verses published in one of the Memphis daily papers and others printed in her father's newspaper, the *Record*.

Frances was especially fond of dancing and playing cards. She played euchre, a popular card game of the day, at every opportunity. A keen sense of humor not only made her good company but also caused her to be in demand at the parties of the young people of Covington. She planned games and charades that the teenagers loved, and they knew that her presence always meant a successful party.

Frances Boyd Calhoun, who disliked having her picture taken, posed for this photograph at the request of her publisher.

Frances returned from these parties to several different homes during her years in Covington. One of the earliest, and possibly the first, was located near the square on South Main Street. Another was at the corner of Maple and Washington, next door to Dr. Lafayette Hill. It was here that she came to know William Green Hill, Dr. Hill's son, and the other children of the neighborhood whom she was later to use as characters in her book.

In 1903, Frances gave up her teaching career to marry George Barret Calhoun, a longtime sweetheart. With his death a year later, she kept busy by devoting most of her time to writing and being active in the Daughters of the Confederacy. "While eligible," she once wrote, "to join the Daughters of the American Revolution, I never have done so, preferring to give my time and attention to the Daughters of the Confederacy—of which organization I am a most enthusiastic member, being president of the local chapter."[94]

In the spring of 1908, Frances sent a manuscript to the Reilly & Britton Co. of Chicago. When the modest little package reached its destination, it was laid aside because the publishers were busy making preparations for that year's publications. No attention was given the manuscript until the publishers received the following little poem on August 22:

> *On the seventh of March, nineteen hundred and eight,*
> *Mr. Reilly, I sent you my book,*
> *And sure since that date for a letter from you*
> *Each day I've continued to look.*
>
> *Is it pigeon-holed now where the bookworm alone*
> *May laugh and grow fat on each joke,*
> *Where canker and rust will eat out the hearts*
> *Of my dear little, quaint little folk?*
>
> *Or, alas, has it vanished from all human ken,*
> *The hard work of two long, long years?*
> *Will the public ne'er know of its merit and worth,*
> *Its laughter, its sighs and its tears?*
>
> *Or has it already been published in full,*
> *And the 'steenth printing given it fame?*
> *And instead of the title I gave it myself*
> *Is it christened with some other name?*
>
> *If naught has befallen it, may I still hope*
> *You'll send my lost child back to me?*
> *And I'll start it anew on its difficult path.*
> *Please ship it at once C.O.D.*
>
> *Frances Calhoun*
> *Covington, Tenn.*[95]

This unusual appeal brought immediate action from Mr. Reilly. He found the "treasure" and took it home. That night he read with delight and surprise

Tipton County's Own

Frances Boyd Calhoun's *Miss Minerva and William Green Hill*. Others who read it were equally impressed, and so the novel was published on February 6, 1909.

The book, with William Green Hill as the central figure, was an immediate success and became a bestseller of its day. It has been enjoyed by thousands of men, women and children "because of its infectious humor which brings a laugh with the reading of every page" and "because Miss Minerva is a living expression of her type of womanhood, Billy a real, human, lovable little boy, and the other characters easily recognizable as those we meet every day."[96]

The book was based on real people who lived in the neighborhood with the author: William Green Hill, Lina Hamilton, Jimmy Garner, Frances Black and Ed Sanders. Many believe that Frances Boyd Calhoun put herself in the role of Miss Minerva and her husband in that of the major, the old maid's persistent suitor.

Some of the incidents included in the book were based on actual happenings. One such humorous episode was deleted from the book by the publishers. It dealt with a country church in a community west of Covington called Centre.

The Children of the Book *Miss Minerva and William Green Hill*

Jimmy Garner and William Green Hill.

True Tales of Tipton

Jimmy Garner.

William Green Hill and Wilkes Booth Lincoln, whose real name was Ed Sanders.

William Green Hill.

Lina Hamilton.

One Sunday a Mr. and Mrs. Simpson, who attended to the Communion, took a bottle out of the closet and used it to serve Communion. By mistake they got the wrong bottle, which contained, instead of wine, an old-time laxative called "Simmon's Liver Regulator." The results can be imagined.

Through the years *Miss Minerva and William Green Hill* has delighted people of all ages in all parts of the country. It was said at one time that the novel had been read by more Americans than any other with the exceptions of *Tom Sawyer* and *Gone with the Wind*. Its popularity over the years can best be attested to by the fact that it has gone through more than fifty-five printings.

Frances Boyd Calhoun never knew of the success of her little book, nor of the thousands who would laugh at "the doings of the wonderful creatures of her imagination."[97] She died on June 8, 1909, just a few months after her book was published. "This was her first and her only book, and it is a pity to think that her untimely death came just when she gave promise of adding so much to the story of human happiness."[98]

The "Rice Pipes"

In early 1917, William A. Owen became a candidate for the Court of Civil Appeals and made an extensive campaign covering eighty-eight counties. Having never run for office before, he soon realized that people enjoyed getting some small souvenir from a candidate. He, consequently, had two thousand pipes made, from two to two and a half cents each, which proved popular, especially among the people of the mountains. Not only did the men there like to smoke, but many also requested pipes for their mothers. The maker of Owen's pipes was James Newton Rice, one of Tipton County's most unique businessmen.

Rice, who was born on August 16, 1838, was taught the art of pipe making by his father. He had molds for both ladies' and gentlemen's pipes, which imprinted a face on the front of the bowl and inscribed "J.N. Rice, Maker, Covington, Tenn." on the lower part of the bowl and shank.

The bowls, made of clay found in Tipton County, were baked outdoors in a pit. During the hot summer months the baking was done at night because it was cooler then. The pipe stems were made by forcing a piece of red hot wire through sticks carved from box elder branches.

Rice made frequent trips to sell his popular pipes, his travels by train often carrying him as far north as St. Louis. He was assisted in this phase of his business by such people as Benjamin G. Shelton, sergeant-at-arms of the Tennessee House of Representatives, who sold the "Rice" pipes when the House was not in session.

One of the most prominent owners of the "Rice" pipe was U.S. Senator E.W. Carmack of Tennessee. In a letter to Rice, dated October 11, 1902, the senator thanked him for a "splendid pipe," which he had just received and he acknowledged that he had been a constant user of the "Rice" pipes for a long time.

Rice's wife, Betty (Goforth), assisted in making the pipes until her death in 1905. After Rice's death on April 16, 1918, his nephew Jimmy Rice took over as maker of the "Rice" pipes.

A Credit to the Game

Harvey Hendrick acquired the nickname "Gink" sometime during his prep school days, but even he did not know its origin. He certainly did not have the appearance of a gink but rather that of a sedate doctor or lawyer when not dressed in the attire of his chosen profession—baseball. His Major League career spanned eleven years, during which time he played with and against some of the great names in the game.

Hendrick was born near Mason on November 9, 1897, the son of Richard T. and Nannie Harvey Hendrick. He attended elementary school at Brownsville and went from there to Fitzgerald and Clark High School in middle Tennessee. Following graduation he attended Vanderbilt University for three years, where he was a member of the baseball, football and track teams. His college career was interrupted when he entered the army during World War I as a lieutenant. After the war he served as assistant football coach to Jess Neely at Southwestern in Memphis.

In 1920 Hendrick first entered the world of professional baseball by signing a contract with the Memphis Chicks of the Southern Association, then under a fiery manager named Spencer Abbott. But his career hopes almost immediately received a setback. An argument between the rookie and the manager resulted in "Gink" being dropped from the team.

Undeterred, Hendrick went to Chattanooga the next year and played in 141 games, then on to Galveston of the Texas League in 1922, where he recorded a hitting percentage of .311. Near the close of the season he was called up to the Majors by the Boston Red Sox but did not break into the records. That same year he married Lyda Shelton and made his permanent home in Covington.

In 1923 Hendrick joined Lou Gehrig as a rookie with the New York Yankees. Although he had a rather inactive season, he did play in more games than Gehrig and participated in the World Series against the New York Giants (Gehrig did not appear in a World Series game until 1926).

Tipton County's Own

Harvey Hendrick in one of the many different uniforms he wore as a professional baseball player.

Miller Huggins, the great Yankee manager, saw potential in his young left-handed hitting outfielder. Prior to the 1924 season, he talked about Hendrick's prospects as a Yankee:

> *Somebody said if our regular outfield broke down that we would be strained to the breaking point. We will, will we? Hendrick today is one of the best outfielders in the American League. He was coming on last season. The world series made him. He did not play any conspicuous part in it, but he got in, and the mere fact of being a participant has…him…ready to go. And when I say ready to go, I mean that if Witt is hurt, or Ruth is hurt, or Meusel is hurt, a ball player will step to that outfield who will hit hard enough to keep the Yanks in the race—and I don't care how hot the race may be.*[99]

True Tales of Tipton

The Yankees were in the pennant race in 1924 but finished second behind the Washington Senators. Hendrick, after a second season of relative inactivity, was farmed out for the 1925 season to Providence of the International League. He next appeared in the Majors later that year with the Cleveland Indians but was back South again in 1926 with New Orleans of the Southern Association.

At New Orleans, the tall man from Covington came into his own as a baseball player. He was the premier first baseman and leading hitter of the Southern League, batting at a .371 clip.

Hendrick's prowess as an athlete was not better exhibited than at the 1926 Fourth of July celebration at Spiller Field, the home of the Atlanta Crackers. He literally ran away with the lion's share of honors in a field meet held between games of a double-header. The event was recorded in the sports section of an Atlanta newspaper.

> *Gink Hendrick, former 10 second man for Vanderbilt University, had something on the rest of the boys in the Cracker-Pelican Fourth of July field meet, and found little trouble copping three first places for the high score of the day.*
>
> *Gink was first in the distance throw, with 337 feet; first in the dash to first base, which he made in three seconds flat, and first in the 100-yard dash, which he made in 10⅖ seconds. Very good time indeed, considering that he was handicapped by a baseball uniform and the fact that he had already played one ball game that day.*[100]

Hendrick's great showing at New Orleans earned him another shot at the Majors. This time he made good. From 1927 to 1930 he played outstanding baseball with the Brooklyn Dodgers, averaging over .300 in hitting over the four-year period.

In 1929 Hendrick, at age thirty-one, had his best year in the big leagues. Before the start of the season, while the Dodgers were training at Clearwater, Florida, manager Wilbert Robinson had several opportunities to make advantageous trades involving the big fellow but refused to consider any deal that even mentioned his name.

"Gink" won his starting berth on the 1929 club during a two-game exhibition series with the Yankees just prior to the opening of the campaign. He "knocked down" the fences at Ebbets Field with his terrific hitting and as a result found himself at third base when the season opened at Boston.

Hendrick was later shifted to center field when the regular at that position went into a hitting slump; then when the shortstop was injured, he stepped in to fill the gap. By the end of June, he was playing first base and leading the league in hitting with a .410 mark.

Most players would have balked at being moved from position to position as Hendrick was, but he would just smile and say that any position was all right with him so long as he could bat every ninth time. In fact, it was his ambition to catch one game before the season ended. Although he failed to win the batting title in 1929, he finished among the leaders with a hefty .354 average.

Hendrick remained with the Dodgers until the beginning of the 1931 season when, after playing in only one game, he was traded to Cincinnati. The Reds played him in 137 games that year, all at first base—the position he preferred.

Near the close of the 1932 season, Cincinnati traded Hendrick to the St. Louis Cardinals. Before the start of the next season, he was acquired by the Chicago Cubs, who needed a backup at first base for the aging Charlie Grimm. He closed out his big league career with the Philadelphia Phillies in 1934.

During his eleven Major League seasons, Hendrick compiled some impressive statistics, including a .308 lifetime batting average. At six feet two inches and 190 pounds, he was extremely versatile for a man of his size, playing, at one time or other, every position except pitcher and catcher. He fielded the ball equally well in the infield or the outfield, and in the vernacular of baseball he had a "rifle" for an arm. If he had a weakness, it was his tendency to throw the ball away while making a hurried toss.

Hendrick had the perfect temperament for a baseball player. To him baseball was a serious proposition. He seldom took part in storytelling bouts but would discuss the finer points of the game he loved as long as anyone cared to listen.

When asked, toward the end of his career, about notable achievements at bat or in the field, Hendrick could remember none involving himself. That was the way his professional life had been ordered—just doing the best job from day to day that his talents would permit. The 1932 edition of *Who's Who in Major League Baseball* called Hendrick "quite a credit to the game."

Two Trails to Hollywood

In 1946, Ina Claire Klutts of Covington was crowned "Miss Tipton County" and Martha Lee Estes, also of Covington, was alternate. A few years later, both were promising Hollywood starlets, appearing in movies and on network television. Their rise as newcomers in the world of show business was meteoric.

It all began in 1953 when Martha Lee won a modeling contest in Memphis and got a chance to model for the House of Charm Modeling Agency in San Francisco. She made her way to Hollywood during the summer of 1954 as the beauty queen of a sportsman's show. One fateful day as she was gaping, open mouthed, at a new insurance building, an agent happened by and promptly discovered her.

Leigh Snowden.

On a visit home, Leigh Snowden and Ina Poindexter pose with Lanier Ferguson Jr.

Tipton County's Own

Ina Poindexter.

Martha Lee, now known as Leigh Snowden, was given her first network television chance by comedian Jack Benny. She then appeared in rapid succession on one of the *Mr. District Attorney* shows and on the Mickey Rooney and Eddie Cantor shows. But it was her second appearance with Benny on his 1954 Christmas show from a naval base that launched her on the road to stardom. Besides being given a plug by the veteran comic, she drew loud applause and wild cheers from several thousand sailors and gained nationwide publicity through the news media. After viewing the show, famed columnist Earl Wilson likened her to Marilyn Monroe, and indeed she was often mistaken for the blonde movie queen.

A scout for Universal International Studios, who also saw Leigh on the Benny Christmas show, signed her to a long-term movie contract in January 1955. She went to work immediately on the movie *All That Heaven Allows* with Rock Hudson and Jane Wyman, having previously been cast in the Mickey Spillane movie *Kiss Me Deadly*. The announcement of her pact with Universal was followed the next day by the report that she was to be one of the featured players in the *Bob Cummings Show*, a new television comedy series. She had already worked in two of the Cummings shows filmed for future release as well as another with Mickey Rooney. It had been just five months since her arrival in Hollywood as an unknown.

Ina Claire was by this time well known in Memphis as a fashion model. She was happily married to C.T. Poindexter Jr. of Mason and was the mother of two small children. Any thoughts of a show business career took a back seat to her family. Then in January 1955 her husband was killed in a tragic highway accident. Three months later she visited Leigh Snowden in California and decided to give Hollywood a try.

During the summer of 1955, Ina worked with the Pasadena Playhouse, appearing in a production of *Sabrina Fair*. She also landed a part in a Warner Brothers film, *Giant*, and was featured on network television in an episode of the *My Favorite Husband* comedy series. In October she was selected by screen producers and directors as one of the thirteen most promising starlets for 1956.

Ina and the other "Wampas Baby Stars" (a name derived from Western Association of Motion Pictures Advertisers) were presented to the nation on television's *Variety Hour* on the evening of October 30, 1955. Her selection gave her an inside track in the race for movie stardom.

Covington now had two beauties in the Hollywood limelight. It had all happened in less than a year's time.

An Admirable Admiral

During the summer of 1944, Lieutenant Commander W.F. Bringle was credited with playing an important role in paving the way for Allied ground forces in Southern France. His squadron of rocket-firing "Hellcats" from the baby aircraft carriers *Tulagi* and *Kasan Bay* wreaked havoc on Nazi trains, tanks and motor vehicles. "Comdr. W.F. Bringle pours it on Germans," wrote the *Covington Leader* at the time.[101] He was decorated for heroism for his part in the action.

This was but one phase of a brilliant naval career, which helped establish Bringle as Tipton County's most prominent military figure to this point in its history. Through subsequent promotions he attained the rank of rear admiral, to date from January 1, 1964; vice admiral, to date from November 6, 1967; and admiral, to date from July 1, 1971.

William Floyd Bringle was born in Covington on April 23, 1913. After graduating from Byars-Hall High School, he received an appointment to the U.S. Naval Academy, which he entered on July 6, 1933. As a midshipman, he was a letterman on the Naval Academy football team.

After his graduation from the academy on June 3, 1937, Bringle was commissioned ensign and assigned to the USS *Saratoga* operating in the Pacific. In April 1940 he began flight training at the Naval Air Station, Pensacola, Florida, and in December of that year was designated naval aviator. In January 1941 he left Pensacola and joined the USS *Milwaukee*, serving as that cruiser's senior aviator until December 1942. During the next eight months, he served as commanding officer of Cruiser Scouting Squadron Two.

From September to November 1943 Bringle received training at the Naval Air Station, Melbourne, Florida, and in December formed and commanded the navy's first Observation Fighting Squadron in World War II. For outstanding service while commanding that squadron during the invasion of Southern France and operations in the Pacific, he was awarded the Navy Cross, six Distinguished Flying Crosses, seventeen Air Medals, the Navy Unit Commendation Ribbon with two stars and the French Croix de Guerre.

After the war, from October 1945 to October 1946, Bringle served as air group commander of Group Seventeen. He then returned to the Naval Academy and served as battalion officer until June 1948, then for two years was air group commander of Carrier Air Group One, based on the USS *Philippine Sea* and the USS *Tarawa*. Back at the Naval Academy, from June 1950 until July 1952, he served as a member of the superintendent's staff. The following year he attended the Naval War College in Newport, Rhode Island, and from July 1953 to December 1954 was executive officer, or second in command, of the newly recommissioned and famed aircraft carrier *Hornet*.

In January 1955 Bringle reported to Washington, D.C., to head the Operational Intelligence Branch in the Office of the Chief of Naval Aid to the Secretary of the Navy. From August 1957 until June 1958 he commanded Heavy Attack Wing Two and then was transferred to duty as commandant of midshipmen at the Naval Academy until August 1960.

Ordered to the USS *Kitty Hawk* (the world's first guided missile aircraft carrier), which was under construction in Camden, New Jersey, Bringle served as prospective commanding officer until she was commissioned in April 1961, then as commanding officer. In June 1962 he was again assigned to the Navy Department's Office of the Chief of Naval Operations, where he served as assistant director of the Aviation Plans Division until January 1963 when he took over as director.

On April 6, 1964, Bringle took command of Carrier Division Seven. "For exceptionally meritorious service as Commander Attack Carrier Striking Force SEVENTH Fleet and as Commander Task Groups SEVENTY-SEVEN POINT SIX from March 29 to June 29, 1965, and as Commander Task Force SEVENTY-SEVEN from May 28 through June 27, 1965." He was awarded the Legion of Merit with Combat "V."[102]

On July 12, 1965, Bringle became deputy chief of staff for Plans and Operations to the Commander in Chief U.S. Pacific Fleet and was awarded a second Legion of Merit for his outstanding direction and supervision over the operations conducted by the Pacific fleet. In November 1967 he was given command of the 7th Fleet and for meritorious service was awarded two Distinguished Service Medals for combat operations during the Vietnam conflict.

Bringle became commander, Naval Air Force, U.S. Pacific Fleet in March 1970, with headquarters in San Diego, California. For distinguished and

Admiral William Floyd Bringle.
Official U.S. Navy Photograph.

dedicated service in that capacity, he received a third Legion of Merit. In July 1971 he took over as commander in chief, U.S. Naval Forces, Europe, with additional duty as United States commander Eastern Atlantic. For meritorious service from July 1971 to August 1973 he was awarded a third Distinguished Service Medal. The citation read in part:

> *Admiral Bringle displayed inspirational leadership, outstanding executive ability and exceptional foresight in directing the complex and manifold operations of his command in the execution of United States national policy.*

Upon his return to the United States, Admiral Bringle had temporary duty in Washington, D.C., and on January 1, 1974, officially retired from the U.S. Navy. In addition to the awards already mentioned, he received the American Campaign Medal, American Defense Service Medal, European-African-Middle Eastern Campaign Medal with one operation star, Asiatic-Pacific Campaign Medal with four operation stars, Navy Occupations Service Medal, World War II Victory Medal, China Service Medal, Europe Clasp, National Defense Service Medal with Bronze Star, Philippine Liberation Ribbon, Armed Forces Expedition Medal with two stars and the Republic of Vietnam Campaign Medal.

Appendix A

Terrific Storm

No true-life oddity can match the "remarkable and ludicrous scenes and incidents" of a fictitious tornado reported many years ago in a Covington newspaper. With headlines telling of "Immense Destruction" in Covington, the article gave no indication in the beginning that the story was pure fantasy, leading the reader to believe at first glance that it was true. Regardless of whether the article was written as a comic satire or as a filler due to lack of news, it remains even today a very humorous tale.

Published in the *Tipton Weekly Record* July 23, 1875.

> *Tuesday last, about half past four o'clock in the afternoon, as we sat at our table, oppressed by the sultry weather and annoyed by the cry of "copy" from our printers, we were suddenly made aware of the near presence of a fearful storm or cyclone. We immediately thought of Prof. Tice of St. Louis, the great meteorologist. He is said not to have missed in a single one of his predictions, which are made upon scientific principles. A plague upon his last prediction, which was that the Mississippi Valley would be visited with terrible storms within two weeks. It is less than two weeks since the prediction was made, and here is the storm, sudden and terrific. It is true some clouds have been lying around for an hour or two, and there was the appearance of a summer shower. The sun was scarcely obscured, however, when there came a roaring, rushing, and crackling noise as of a thousand immense sails flapping in a fearful gale. Oh, the wild consternation and terrific grandeur of the scene! It was as if some awful demon, enraged with the agonies of the pit, were gathering a whole area of country, embracing*

Appendix A

forests, houses, men, women and children, animals, loose timbers, fence rails and dust, and, having mingled them with his giant hands in one indescribable mass, was hurling them through the air. Where is safety now? Oh, God, protect the helpless! We all are helpless now. We rushed to the front window, and even then the storm in all its terrible fury had struck our village, coming from the east, and was playing sad havoc. The roof of the courthouse was plainly distinguished as it came sailing over like an inverted cone. The walls of this structure were completely scattered almost in the twinkling of an eye, and some of the brick doubtless reached Randolph within ten minutes. The wind seemed to move in a circle, and the extent of the circle was but little greater than the width of the square. The row of buildings on the north of the square was lifted off their foundation and thrown off their pillars, but were not much moved out of place. It is thought to be owing to the fact that the buildings were all frame and situated so near as to act as braces to each other, that they were thereby enabled in so great a measure to resist the violence of the storm. The row presents, however, a very singular and dilapidated appearance. Every porch and awning is gone.

Mr. Lippman was just receiving a load of freight from the depot by a dray, and was superintending the moving of it into his house, when the storm suddenly burst upon the village. Kegs, barrels and boxes went flying through the air, followed by Mr. Lippman himself at fearful speed, but it has not yet been clearly ascertained whether he was carried away by the violence of the storm of his own sudden emotion to get back his goods. On the south side of the square, the volume of wind entering under the roof of the hotel that projects over the porches found a chance to display the fiendish fury. The roof and front columns were borne away with a terrible crash, and have not been heard of since. No further damage was done to this immense structure except the old part on the west was detached and swung back off the pillars, nearly capsizing. The wind entering the room occupied by Dr. J.J. Moore scarcely left an article remaining. One immense trunk was gathered up by the violence of the wind and hurried along with fearful velocity. The hinges of the lid were soon broken by the rough manner of its getting along, and its contents were scattered, whitening the whole atmosphere like a fall of snow. It proved to be full of photographs and perfumed letters, which unfortunately were scattered for miles around. The Covington depot was picked up bodily and carried away; the younger White was in there at the time with some person from the country, whose name we could not learn. It required the full power of the terrible storm to move the immense structure of the depot, but it succeeded, as it is though the storm god desired it for a place for himself and the storm queen. The falling

Terrific Storm

of the courthouse walls unfortunately caught Mr. J.R. Sloan and Thos. Barret. They were completely covered up in debris for twenty-four hours and were supposed to be dead, but when dug out were just a little frightened and hungry. All the records were blown away except the "Main Assessment Roll Book;" it defied the storm. After the storm subsided we received three agonizing missives from as many young ladies in town, inquiring after the fate of Mr. Thos. Barret. The fair but disconsolate writers hinted that their relations to the gentleman in question emboldened them to write, from which we concluded that the cold-hearted gentlemen had been coqueting. As for Mr. Sloan, we cannot recall the number of such missives received from the village and county—in fact we don't know, as we were compelled to employ a friend to answer them, but remember that several of them were from widows. W.J. Harris, Esq., the only other person who was in the courthouse, had well nigh beat the storm, sudden as it was. Being on the alert, he heard the first crash of its coming, and rushing out the north door reached Lippman's and, seizing that gentleman's coat tail to draw himself upon the porch just at the unfortunate moment when that gentleman began his ride on the chariot of the storm, he unfortunately was taken off with him, holding tight to his coat tails. When last seen he had a splendid hold and it is supposed that he is safe. Our enterprising friend that sells cigars, candy, etc., was seen to go off like a balloon on a fitful gust, but it is supposed that he was merely after some fellow that owed him a quarter. The scene in town beggars description, but it is supposed the village will soon rise; Phoenix-like, from its ruins. The late committee that formerly examined the courthouse to ascertain if it might not be repaired, have gotten together and are exceedingly sanguine that, with Architect Cook's assistance they will be able to show how it may be restored to its former grandeur, with a trifling cost, and yet be made to stand much longer than any other of them would dare to live. We cannot enumerate one of a hundred of the singular incidents that occurred during the passing of the tornado. A well known jeweler was heard to speak above the storm, "Mine Got! If I is permitted to live beyond dis ting, I vill quit all my ways," A clerk on the east side of the square was picked up by the wind and ran a very narrow escape of being blown away, but fortunately his cravat reached around the awning of Hall's brick store and held him suspended like a steamer during the fury of the wind—he was saved.

One of the most thrilling incidents of the day occurred at the very height and fury of the tornado. Two men were observed nearly in the center of the cyclone, where the moving tides of the storm were somewhat regular, at the fearful height of about ninety feet, both of them astride of a barrel—the more simple and unsuspicious all pronounced it a coal oil barrel. It was

Appendix A

doubted for some time whether they were citizens of our town, or the inhabitants of some other unfortunate section, but from the official looks and the homelike and comfortable appearance of the gentlemen on the barrel, and the very dexterious manner in which they managed it, they were ascertained to be, the one a staving constable and the other a late tax collector. Great solicitude was expressed for one unfortunate fellow that went whirling through the air, but all apprehension was relieved as he was seen to alight in safety on the belfry of the Catholic church and having raised to his Aeolian lips a certain historic flute, strike up in solemn notes, that welled up above the roar of the retreating storm, "Farewell, vain world."

The attaches of this office behaved with remarkable coolness. The most disconsolate thing we saw was a countryman who came in hastily not knowing of the storm, to get his marriage license. He was awfully broken up. There has been a great deal of speculation as to the cause of the tornado. A wit suggests, as the county court adjourned that day, it had some connection with that highly respected body—perhaps the explosion of the accumulative gas of two weeks. But the scientific theory is—"Copy, more copy" shouted the printer, and awoke us from reverie, and we looked out to find the courthouse still there, looking only a trifle older, and everything as it was an hour ago. "Ah, yes, sir, here is your copy."

Appendix B

Tipton County Men Who Died While in Service

World War I

Adams, Clark, Covington, died of pneumonia
Adkison, Barney A., Brighton, died overseas of tuberculosis
Albritton, Elmo, Mason, died of pneumonia
Ashe, John B., Tipton, killed in action overseas
Calhoun, Paul C., Covington, 2nd Lieutenant, died of heart failure
Doggett, Ahmid, Mason, died of tuberculosis
Dyson, Richard, Covington, died overseas of pneumonia
Essinger, Trice H., Covington, died of wounds received in action
Foster, Roland M., Covington, died overseas, injured in fight
Friedman, James H., Covington, died overseas of pneumonia
Givens, Samuel O., Atoka, died of pneumonia
Goode, Ernest M., Covington, killed in action
Greer, Hugh W., Richardson, died of pneumonia
Harris, Nelson, Mason, died overseas of meningitis
Harris, Wilson B., Covington, died at Nashville; train wreck injuries
Hindman, James Robert, Atoka, died overseas of pneumonia
Hines, Joe, Covington, died of pneumonia
Hunt, Jess C., Covington, killed in action overseas
Hunter, Cleveland, Tipton, died overseas of pneumonia
Hutchison, Shannon, Atoka, died of pneumonia
Johnson, John, Reverie, died of pneumonia
Kinney, Charles L., Covnigton, died of airplane accident wounds
Kosminski, Robert R., Covington, died overseas of pneumonia
Lewis, Lee, Munford, died of erysipelas

Appendix B

Malone, Will, Covington, died of pneumonia
McGowan, Joe, Covington, died of pyemia
McKee, George H., Atoka, died of abscess
Moore, William E., Covington, died of pneumonia
Murphy, Paul, Covington, died of pneumonia
Nelson, Thomas L., Brighton, died of pneumonia
Paine, Frank Troy, Covington, killed in train wreck
Payne, James, Brighton, died of pneumonia
Ralph, Thomas E., Brighton, died overseas of meningitis
Rice, Paul L., Covington, died of wounds received in action
Ruffin, James F., Covington, died of pneumonia
Sherrill, Ernest, Covington, died of pneumonia
Simmonds, John, Atoka, died of pneumonia
Smith, George, Mason, died of pneumonia
Somervill, William, Mason, killed in action
Starnes, Olian F., Munford, died of pneumonia
Strain, Willie, Brighton, died of myelitis
Tates, Charle, Covington, died of pneumonia
Ulin, James V., Munford, died of pneumonia
Van Meter, David M., Covington, died of sunstroke overseas
Waldran, Raleigh, Drummonds, killed in action
Whitmore, James D., Mason, died of meningitis
Whitson, Uncus, Quito, died of typhoid fever
Williamson, Samuel, Mason, died overseas of pneumonia
Womble, William H., Brighton, died of pneumonia
Wood, James F., Burlison, died overseas of pneumonia

World War II

Army (includes dead from all causes)

Atkins, William R., Jr.
Baker, Benjamin W., Jr.
Baskin, Lydle A.
Beaver, Solon M., Jr.
Blalack, George R.
Blankenship, C.C.
Bomar, George R.
Burgess, James O.
Cain, Richard S.
Camp, Ernest M.
Carr, Dalton W.
Davidson, Robert H.
Forbess, Harris, Jr.
Fritzsche, Orville V.
Glass, J.W.
Gross, William E.
Hadley, Winford T.
Harris, Robert H.
Hathcock, John P.
Hazlerig, Solon T.
Hocutt, Robert O.

Tipton County Men Who Died While in Service

Holmes, John W.
Jackett, William F.
Kelley, John C.
Kidd, Andrew E.
Kuykendall, Leonard O.
Lumpkin, Harold W.
Manley, John A.
Marbery, Woodrow W.
Mathis, Bill
McDaniel, Floyd L.
Mills, Adran V.
Parham, William O.
Pilkington, Bryson H.
Pinner, George A.
Pool, Woodrow W.
Posey, William A.
Sanders, Clarence R.
Sanders, James B.
Smith, Gordon C.
Somerville, Willie L.

Starnes, Nath H.
Thompson, Homer R.
Throgmorton, Reuben W.
Tracey, James W.
Trobaugh, Ott C., Jr.
Ward, Richard E.
Wilson, Jake
Wright, Robert T.

Navy (killed in action)

Forbes, Billy Gene
Goldsmith, Charles, Jr.
Jones, Thomas Booker
Ray, Sanford Farris

Marines (killed in action)

McKee, Rufus S.
Smith, William E.

Korean War (dead and missing)

Bringle, Newton W.
McDivitt, George
Moreno, Beningo
Rose, Darrow A.

Tate, Thomas E.
Vinceson, Otha R.
Wright, James L.

Vietnam War (dead)

Alston, Billy Clyde
Blalack, Jimmy Dale
Buford, Leroy
Craig, Odell
Glass, Billie
Hill, Lonnie O'Neal

Hughlett, John Albert
Jackson, Charles Sid
McCullough, Jerry Wendell
Smith, Ronald Gordon
Watkins, Glenn A.
Webb, Alfonso Augustus

Chronology

Some notable dates gleaned from 150 years of Tipton County history.

*All asterisks within the chronology denote dated items that can be found in the text.

1823

October 29: Tipton County is established from territory within the limits of Shelby County by an act of the legislature sitting at Murfreesboro. About one-third of the new county lies north of the Hatchie River.

December 1: The justices named in the act of October 29 and commissioned by Governor Carroll meet at the home of Nathan Hartsfield to organize the county court. Besides Hartsfield the justices include John T. Brown, George Robinson and John C. McKean. Jacob Tipton, a commissioned justice for Shelby County but a resident of the territory embraced in Tipton County, also takes his seat as a member of the court.

After taking the necessary oaths prescribed by the constitution and laws of the state, the justices proceed to elect the officers of the court; Andrew Greer, clerk; John T. Brown, sheriff; Nathan Hartsfield, register; John Robinson, trustee; William Henson, ranger; and George Robinson, coroner.

December 2: The county's first tax levy is ordered. This levy, for general purposes, is twelve and a half cents on each white person and twenty-five cents on each black person (to be paid by the slave's master), and the levy on land is set to be the same as the levy made by the state. There is also a special tax levied for the poor and for people who kill wolves, consisting of six cents on each white poll, twelve cents on each black poll and six cents on each one hundred acres of land.

Alexander B. Bradford and Robert Hughes become Tipton County's first lawyers when they appear in open court and take the oaths prescribed by the law for practitioners.

1824

March: The first jury is impaneled, consisting of the following citizens: Thomas Ralph, Anderson Ralph, Henry Allen, Hopson Ferrell, John Eckford, Alexander McCullough, Thomas Hodge, James Hodge, John Person, William K. Kulbreath (now spelled Culbreath), Jesse Benton (a brother of Senator Thomas Hart Benton), Michael Holshouser, William Henson, John Robinson, William Robinson, George Keller, Samuel Robinson, Adam Logan, Joseph G. Stone, Samuel Young and Hubert Ferrell.

June 1: The first deed is recorded in the register's office. It conveys 640 acres of land in Tipton County "on the waters of Big Creek of Loosahatchie River" from Thomas Hickman of Davidson County to Samuel Perkins of Williamson County.

October 11: Joshua Haskell appears at the home of Nathan Hartsfield and organizes the circuit court. Thomas Taylor is appointed clerk, and William Stoddart is sworn in as an attorney-at-law.

December 11: The commissioners appointed by the state legislature to locate sites for the county seats of the counties of West Tennessee, viz: James Fentress, Benjamin Reynolds, Robert Jetton and William Martin, appear before the county court and officially announce that they have "located the county site of Tipton County on the lands of John C. McLemore and Tyree Rhodes in range 4 and section 8 of said county and to be called Covington" (in honor of General Leonard Wales Covington, a native of Maryland who was mortally wounded in the battle of Chrystler's Field, November 11, 1813). The commissioners are paid $36 each by the county court for their services in locating the town of Covington.

John Eckford, Alexander Robinson, Robert G. Green, Elias F. Pope and Marquis Calmes are elected commissioners of Covington and superintendents of public buildings to succeed the commissioners appointed by the legislature.

1825

January 5: The commissioners of Covington petition the county court for enough money to build a temporary courthouse. The court appropriates $100 to be paid immediately and $150 to be paid when the building is completed. The money is to be refunded in eighteen months.
April 12: The commissioners of Covington begin the sale of lots in that town. The sale is scheduled to continue on a daily basis until all lots are sold.
July 4: The county court, sitting at Nathan Hartsfield's, adjourns to the newly completed frame courthouse located on the northeast corner of the square in Covington, The center of the square has been left vacant so that a permanent brick courthouse can be erected there at a later date.

The county trustee is ordered to pay Nathan Hartsfield $50 as payment for the court's use and occupation of his house.

John Robinson, Thomas Ralph and John Ecksord are appointed judges to superintend the election on the first Thursday and succeeding day in August for the purpose of electing a governor, representative to Congress and member of the state legislature.

Aquilla Davis is appointed road overseer and has workers assigned to him for the purpose of opening a road to the county line in the direction of Brownsville. A jury of view is also appointed by the county court to lay off a road to the county line in the direction of Somerville.
October 3: The first lots are sold in the new town of Covington. Jeptha Hardin of Gallatin, Tennessee, purchases lots 70 and 71 on Pleasant Street for $110.

A jury is appointed to lay off the McKean's Ferry Road to the Hatchie River.

1826

Covington is incorporated. It contains a courthouse, a jail, two taverns, seven stores, the Eleventh District surveyor's office, three or four lawyers, about the same number of physicians and between thirty and forty families.
January 2: The commissioners for the town of Covington are ordered by the court to pay John Payne $100 as additional compensation for his services in building the courthouse.
September 5: The court, seeking connection with Dyersburg, appoints a jury to lay off a road in that direction.
December 4: William L. Parrish is appointed overseer by the court to open a road from Covington as far as Indian Creek in the direction of Kelsey Douglas's warehouse on the Mississippi River.

CHRONOLOGY

1827

October 11: The town of Randolph, located about a mile below the mouth of the Hatchie River, is founded by Kelsey H. Douglas and John T. Brown on land acquired from John Terrell.
*November: Felix D. Robertson discovers a well-burnt brick and some European articles in a deep gully about a mile and a half east of Covington. It is his belief that the location is the site of a camp of the Spanish explorer Hernando De Soto.

1828

Kelsey H. Douglas and John T. Brown sell an interest in the town tract of Randolph to Hiram Bradford, Joseph W. McKean, Robert Cotton, David W. Wood and Robert Bedford. The seven above-named gentlemen, being the joint owners, proceed to lay the town off and to sell lots.

A post office is established at Randolph, and James M. Gibson becomes the first postmaster

1829

July 4: Davy Crockett, candidate for reelection to Congress from the Big Hatchie District, speaks at a barbeque being held on the hill southwest of Covington where extended revival meetings are usually held. Several other candidates for the post, including James H. Clarke of Covington, also deliver speeches on the occasion.
December: The first recorded division of a vote in the county court comes over the construction of a bridge over Hurricane Creek on the road from Randolph to Somerville by way of Simpson's tan-yard. Rivalry is the reason for the contest. Several justices hold the belief that no important road should be opened or bridged unless it leads to or by the courthouse. Interests that enter at Randolph, led by Kelsey Douglas, triumph, and that town has communication opened to other towns besides Covington.
December 7: The Covington and Raleigh Road is established. Robert Hughlett is appointed overseer and ordered to open the road from Hartsfield's to the south corner of his own farm; Nicholas L. Wood from there to where it crosses the Somerville and Randolph Road at Simpson's tan-yard; and William Simpson from that point to the county line.

Chronology

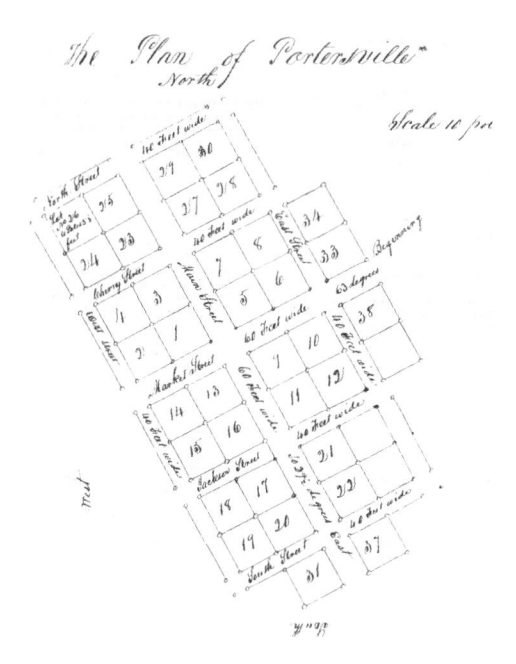

Plan of the town of Portersville as laid off by James Hodges.

1830

The General Assembly authorizes the county court to appropriate funds for the construction of a permanent courthouse and empowers the commissioners of Covington to draw from the trustees such funds as are necessary for that purpose.

January: A party of immigrants from South Carolina, consisting of John Miller, Gardner Miller, Robert Clark, William Simonton, William Wilkins and others, passes over the Covington and Raleigh Road to their future homes the day after the road is completed. They are the first persons to travel it.

March 4: The plan of the town of Covington is produced in open court and, being acknowledged by the town commissioners, is ordered for registration.

March 6: Andrew Greer is removed as county court clerk by order of the court, and Robert W. Sanford is elected to replace him. Greer's failure to turn over revenue that he has collected is the reason for his removal.

1831

A charter of incorporation is given the town of Randolph by the General Assembly. An unusual feature in the charter is a clause which provides that the town's ordinances are not applicable to nonresidents who might violate them unintentionally.

1832

*The Big Hatchie Turnpike and Bridge Company is organized for the purpose of constructing a turnpike from Haywood County to the Hatchie River. All of the members of the board of directors are from Covington and Randolph.

Portersville, a post town located about twelve miles southwest of Covington, is established on land owned by James Hodges.

June 25: The first session of court is held in the new permanent courthouse. Phillip Tackett pleads guilty and is sentenced to spend six months in jail, to be branded on the brawn of his left hand with the letter M and to pay court costs.

1833

March: James Crawford is the first of a handful of Revolutionary War veterans living in the county to go into open court and file his declaration so as to obtain the pension benefits provided by an act of Congress passed on June 7, 1832.

June 24: The first four-horse mail stage arrives in Covington. The new mail line runs from Jackson to Randolph through Brownsville and Covington. James Brown is proprietor.

1834

***June 21:** The first edition of the *Randolph Recorder*, Tipton County's first newspaper, is issued by F.S. Latham. The twenty-six-year-old printer believes that Randolph will become the principal city of West Tennessee.

1835

November 24: Lauderdale County is created by the legislature from parts of Tipton, Haywood and Dyer Counties. The formation of the new county leaves the Hatchie River as the northern boundary of Tipton County.

November 28: In answer to Sam Houston's call for volunteers, several young men from Randolph depart for Texas. They follow by only a few days a volunteer company from Covington.

Chronology

1836

H.R. Hill, who owns the 5,700-acre Marseilles Farm a few miles northwest of Covington, makes the first attempt in the county at raising stock as a business.

March 6: Sam Houston, having been named on March 4 to head the Texas army, leaves Washington-on-the-Brazos for Gonzales to take command of the troops there. He is accompanied on the journey by Colonel George W. Hockley and Lieutenant Richardson Scurry, both of whom are Covington volunteers.

March 27: Tipton Countians Samuel Wilson and Charles Haskell are among the 320 volunteers killed by the Mexicans in the "Fannin Massacre" at Goliad. Unlike the defenders of the Alamo who died fighting, Fannin's men are shot down after having surrendered.

June 16: The citizens of Covington give a public dinner in honor of Colonel George W. Hockley, inspector general of the Texas army, who arrived home for a visit on June 12. Many toasts are made to Hockley and to other Tipton County heroes of the Texas Revolt.

June 26: The steamer *Tuskins*, with three hundred Kentucky volunteers aboard, lands at Randolph for supplies. The citizens are furnished with music from a fife and drum corps, and the elite of the town go on board to distribute flowers among the soldiers. The troops are on their way to Texas.

*September 23: F.S. Latham announces that he has sold the *Randolph Recorder* to Allen M. Scott.

October 22: David Lauderdale kills a bear weighing four hundred pounds.

November 25: As part of a three-man escort appointed by Houston to take the captured Mexican leader Santa Anna to Washington, George W. Hockley sails with the party to New Orleans where they will depart for the capitol.

1837

November 14: F.S. Latham, who moved to Memphis following his sale of the *Randolph Recorder*, marries Jane Catherine Smith in Covington.

1838

*January 6: The first number of the *Randolph Whig* is issued by David M. McPherson, who has his office in a room over the Randolph Post Office.

This modest little headstone marks the grave of Jacob Tipton in Covington's Munford Cemetery.

1839

September 17: Jacob Tipton, one of the founders of the county and son of the man for whom it is named, dies at the age of forty-nine and is buried on the Tipton place east of Covington. His remains will later be moved to the cemetery in town.

1840

A county agricultural society is formed that plans to hold annual exhibits.

1841

Edward Burleson, an early settler in the county who moved to Texas and played a conspicuous part in Houston's victory at San Jacinto as colonel of a regiment, is elected vice-president of the Texas Republic.

A new political club is organized in the county. Joseph T. Collier is president, and Samuel A. Homes, Jordan Brown, William B. Vincent and Joseph G. Boon are vice-presidents.

CHRONOLOGY

1843

*March 25: Robert Holmes Dunham, formerly of Tipton County, dies a hero at Hacienda Salado, Mexico, following the "Black Bean Incident" or "Lottery of Death" ordered by Santa Anna. T.A. Thompson and William A. Clopton escape Dunham's fate by drawing white beans instead of the fatal black ones.

1847

*Company G of the 4th Tennessee Infantry Regiment is organized at Covington under the War Department's second call for volunteers to fight in the Mexican War. The company is made up of an equal number of men from Tipton and Lauderdale Counties.

*July: The Tipton contingent of Company A, 1st Tennessee Cavalry Regiment, which answered the War Department's first call for volunteers, arrives by steamboat at Randolph, having just served out its term of enlistment.

1851

August 4: Richardson A. Scurry, who practiced law in Covington from 1830 until he went to Texas in early 1836 to fight with Sam Houston, is elected to the House of Representatives of the Thirty-second United States Congress as a Democrat from Texas.

1855

*September 1: The Tipton Female Seminary opens under Prof. E.T. Alling as principal at a salary of $100 a year for five years. Two sessions of twenty-one weeks each will constitute the school year.

1857

The General Assembly authorizes a third and final referendum to be held by county voters to establish whether the county seat should be moved. As in the earlier referenda of 1851 and 1854, Covington is kept as the seat of government.

CHRONOLOGY

1858

April 10: The jury in the sensational change-of-venue murder trial of Memphian Isaac Bolton delivers a verdict of not guilty. The trial has brought little credit to the integrity of Tipton County. It will result in four of the jurors being indicted and tried for perjury and in the Tennessee Supreme Court handing down an opinion that witnesses and jurors had been bribed. Elsewhere, the case will result in one of the bitterest lawsuits ever fought in the courts and in a tragic feud that will claim the lives of seven people.
September 6: Nathan Bedford Forrest pleads not guilty and Wade H. Bolton, guilty, in circuit court to charges of gaming. A jury finds both guilty, and Judge J.C. Humphreys fines them five dollars each plus court costs.

1860

*Covington's first newspaper, the Covington *Weekly Spy*, is founded by R.C. Russ. The printing office is located on the second floor of the Masonic hall, west of the square.

1861

***May 14:** The "Tipton Rifles," the first Confederate company raised in the county, leaves its camp in Covington for Germantown, where it will be mustered into service.
May 18: The little cannon arrives that Covington blacksmith J.W. Wilson molded and bored out recently in Memphis. The three-foot, five-hundred-pound weapon, referred to as a "baby-waker" by the local newspaper, attracts a number of people to Wilson's shop to see it.
***May 20:** Mollie Thompson, a teacher at the Tipton Female Seminary, presents a Confederate flag, made by the ladies of the county, to the "Southern Confederates" at ceremonies held on the eve of the company's departure from Clopton Campground.
***May 31:** The county's first cavalry unit is organized by Charles H. Hill at Mason's Depot. Known as "Hill's Cavalry," it consists of men from Tipton, Fayette and Haywood Counties.
***June 10:** Tennessee's ordinance of secession passes by a vote of 108,511 to 47,338. Tipton County casts 943 votes for secession and only 16 against. All anti-secession votes come from the village of Portersville, where a few native Northerners are known to reside.

218

Chronology

1862

*January 27: The county's first artillery company is organized at Covington by H.J. Maley. It will soon take its place as Company C of the 1st Tennessee Heavy Artillery Regiment.

*July 15: Under Commander Issac Newton Brown, who spent his childhood in Covington, the ram *Arkansas* single-handedly scores a victory above Vicksburg over the combined Federal fleets of Farragut and Davis.

*September 25: The town of Randolph is burned by Federal troops in retaliation for an attack there two days before on the packet *Eugene* by a small band of Confederate irregulars.

September 30: Captain Lafayette Hill, being home on sick leave, is surprised and captured near Covington by Federal troops who are on an expedition from Columbus, Kentucky. While talking to one of his captors, he is shot and seriously wounded by an irate private who claims Hill pointed a gun at him before surrendering.

November 30: The *New Moon*, a Hatchie steamer owned and captained by John Dearing of Tipton County, is captured and burned in Mississippi's Tallahatchie River by a detachment of the 1st Indiana Cavalry. Besides his boat, Dearing loses several bales of cotton, which have been given him by Confederate authorities as payment for his services.

1863

*Jo Bragg, a well-known citizen of the county who has been supervising a number of newly freed blacks on his uncle's farm near Covington, is murdered by a gang of outlaws headed by a young Covington man named Lou Davis.

*February: County residents are paying exorbitant prices for most goods. Shoes are selling for $80 a pair and cotton thread $3 a spool.

*February 27: Colonel R.V. Richardson's 1st Tennessee Partisan Ranger camp at Bloomington is attacked by two hundred men of the 2nd Illinois Cavalry from Fort Pillow. Finding a guard of only eight men there, whom they capture, the Federals completely destroy the camp.

*March 9: Federal Colonel Benjamin H. Grierson, in command of the 6th and 7th Illinois Cavalry and a six-gun battery, attacks the 1st Tennessee Partisans in the Lemmon Woods near Covington. After two hours of hard fighting, the outnumbered Confederates, finding themselves about to be outflanked, retire from the field.

Chronology

Federal gunboats passing Randolph on their way to Memphis prior to the former town's destruction by Federal troops. *Harper's Weekly.*

The *New Moon* in the early days of the war—probably at Randolph. A close inspection of the men on the upper deck shows them to be uniformed Confederate soldiers.

***March 10:** A detachment of men from the 7th Kansas and 4th Illinois Cavalry, under the command of Lieutenant Colonel Martin Wallace, runs into Richardson's command in East Beaver Dam Creek bottom on the Randolph Road. The Federal advance drives the outnumbered Partisans rapidly along the road until they reach the edge of the bottom. At this point Richardson leaves the road and turns south into the swamp. Wallace soon loses track of the Confederates and gives up the chase.

*August 13: Cadmus M. Wilcox, who left Covington to attend the University of Nashville and shortly thereafter (in 1842) received an appointment to the United States Military Academy, is promoted to the rank of major general, CSA.

Chronology

Brigadier General William Read Scurry. *Generals in Gray*.

1864

*April 30: Brigadier General William R. Scurry of the Confederate Army, once a resident of Tipton County, is mortally wounded in the battle of Jenkin's Ferry in Arkansas.

*October 27: The steamer *Belle Saint Louis* is attacked by about forty Confederates when it makes a midnight landing at Randolph to take on a few bales of cotton. The *Belle* escapes capture when the alert captain has the boat backed quickly away from the bank.

1865

*April 16: The cotton steamer *St. Paul*, having been boarded by guerrillas at Brownsville Landing on April 10, is burned at Morgan's Landing.

*April 19: The 3rd U.S. Colored Cavalry disembarks at Randolph and rides through Covington toward Brownsville in search of the guerrillas operating on the Hatchie.

*April 22: The leader of the guerrillas responsible for burning the *St. Paul*, having been captured by the 3rd U.S. Colored Cavalry, is tried and convicted by a drumhead court-martial at Randolph. At 6:30 p.m. he is hanged from a cottonwood tree.

*May 9: A band of guerrillas intending to raid Covington is ambushed on the square at 11:00 p.m. by forewarned townsmen. Three of the guerrillas are killed, one is critically wounded and the rest are driven off.

Entrance to the old powder magazine at Randolph as it looked in the 1930s. The magazine, a part of Confederate Fort Wright, once held ammunition for the big guns on the bluff.

***May 15:** A mass meeting of Tipton County citizens is held in the courthouse at Covington for the purpose of restoring civil government to the county as a means of suppressing guerrilla terrorism.

May 18: Colonel John U. Green, with a small detachment of men from the 12th Tennessee Cavalry Regiment, surrenders to the commander of a Union vessel lying off Randolph.

June 12: Crewmen of the USS *Siren* remove 170 eight-inch shells from a magazine at Randolph. The ammunition had been left there by the Confederates when they evacuated the place in 1862.

1867

*August: William Sanford and Morrison Munford establish the *Tipton Weekly Record* at Covington. Both young businessmen are Confederate veterans.

1868

The town of Mason is incorporated, and William McCloy is elected mayor.

1870

The court purchases a one-hundred-acre farm in the fourth district and buildings for the poor are erected.
June 12: The Memphis Immigration Company receives another cargo of Norwegian immigrants. These large, powerful men are settling near Mason.

1871

The Tipton County Industrial and Mechanical Association is organized in Covington. Suitable buildings are erected east of town for the purpose of holding annual fairs.

1872

Atoka, a post village and station on the Memphis and Paducah Railroad, is established on land that was formerly the property of Hugh Thompson.

1873

The legislature again reduces the size of Tipton County by cutting off Island 34 and adding it to Lauderdale County.

The first dwelling in Atoka is built by David Bowen, and the first store is erected by John McLaughlin. The post office, which has been at nearby Portersville since 1832, is removed to Atoka, and William H. Thompson is appointed postmaster.

Brighton, a station on the Memphis and Paducah Railroad, is established on a tract of five acres donated to the railroad by Augustus W. Smith. A nice depot is built with funds contributed by the citizens of the immediate vicinity.

John McClerkin erects the first dwelling in Brighton and Moses Vaughn the first business house (a grocery store). A post office is also established, and Robert B. Dewes is appointed the first postmaster.
July 4: The Memphis and Paducah Railroad sends its first train over the newly built tracks from Memphis to Covington.
July 15: William Bates Bowen becomes the first white child born in the village of Atoka.

Chronology

1874

Garland, a small town seven miles west of Covington, is established and named for Dr. John C. Garland, the first physician of the place. Francis A. Archer is appointed postmaster.

1875

*The *West Tennessee Clarion*, founded during the drought of 1874 by M. Wood and George Hunt, succumbs to hard times and is purchased by the *Tipton Record*.

Atoka is incorporated, and John McLaughlin becomes the first mayor.

May 27: Covington is the scene of a big fire that burns the entire east side of the square. The north side escapes only because things are still wet from a recent rain.

September: General Nathan Bedford Forrest visits Covington and contracts with the chairman of the county court for the services of criminals sentenced to the workhouse.

1876

March 7: The Mississippi River cuts a new channel east of the Devil's Elbow. The distance of the cut is about two miles, and the water comes with such force that it will flow upstream for two days. The new channel places Island 37 to its west, and several acres between the main river and McKenzie Chute become an island that will be named Centennial Island in honor of the one-hundredth anniversary of the Declaration of Independence.

September 22: Covington plays host to a reunion of the 7th Tennessee Cavalry. More than one hundred veterans of that regiment, along with a number of veterans from other commands, march from the square to the fairgrounds to hear an address by General Nathan Bedford Forrest.

1878

Drs. J.B. Witherington and Walter Barret of Atoka and Munford, respectively, treat yellow fever victims from Memphis and vicinity who have somehow eluded guards and managed to cross the county

Chronology

line in a vain effort to escape the plague. The cases, which were contracted in and around Memphis where an epidemic rages, but which did not develop until the victims reached Tipton County, are being cared for in tents set up between Atoka and Munford. Many are dying there.

*November: Charles Bryson Simonton becomes Tipton County's first representative in the United States Congress with his win in the general election. The forty-year-old Democrat will represent the Ninth Congressional District of Tennessee.

1879

*L.D. Hamner establishes the *Mason Call* at Mason. This is Hamner's first experience in the newspaper business.

   *An annual Confederate reunion is originated by veterans of Company C, 9th Tennessee Infantry.

1880

*J.W. Boyd, who served as a magistrate form District Nine on the county court from 1878 to 1879, becomes one of the first blacks elected to the Tennessee House of Representatives.

*January 8: It is announced that Tipton authorities have contracted the labor of county convicts to Mrs. Mary A. Forrest, widow of General N.B. Forrest, for the next three years.

October 28: "Mason has only eleven saloons," writes the *Mason Call*. "She needs two or three more."

1881

January 13: An announcement is made concerning the formation of a military company at Mason known as the Mason National Guards. Some suggest that there is a hidden motive behind this organization—"to secure swords and spears and then beat them into plow shares and pruning hooks."

*March 11: the first legal hanging since Civil War days takes place when Andre Saunders, found guilty in January of first-degree murder, is hanged from a gallows on the courthouse lawn.

J.W. Boyd.

*November: L.D. Hamner moves his newspaper operation from Mason to Covington. The paper's publication is continued under the name of the *Covington Call*.

1882

*April 7: The telegraph line from Memphis to Covington is completed. Covington, at last, has telegraphic communication with the world.
*December 7: With a stiff wind blowing out of the north, a fire begins in a small frame two-story house on the west side of the square in Covington. Both the west and north sides of the square burn as do a number of structures on South Main Street from the square to Church Street.

1883

March 17: A Memphis newspaper announces that steamboats are once again landing at Randolph, something they have not been able to do for the past ten years. The current has changed and is cutting Hatchie Island away. If the island is washed away, Randolph will be on the river once more.

This faded old photograph, made about 1867, shows the Shelton House, *right*, one of the buildings on the south side of the square to burn in the fire of 1882.

1884

*The *Covington Call* is absorbed by the *Tipton Record*.
November: Zachary Taylor, the Covington postmaster, is elected to the Forty-ninth U.S. Congress as a Republican from the Tenth Congressional District of Tennessee.

1885

March 9: Augustus Hill Garland, native of Tipton County and son of one of its early settlers, resigns his seat as United States senator from Arkansas to become attorney general in the cabinet of President Grover Cleveland.
July 4: Covington's first organized baseball team, the Covington Favorites, plays its first game against the Seaside Socials of Memphis. Covington wins the game by a score of 28 to 14.

1886

Licenses are issued by the county court clerk to George D. Holmes, insurance agent, and to C.N. McFadden for the operation of a livery stable in Covington. The first pool room, operated by Paine Brothers, is also licensed, as is F.D. Crunk, Covington's first licensed photographer.
October: L.D. Hamner, having temporarily retired from the publishing business, returns to found the *Covington Leader*.

Employees pose in front of the Farmers & Merchants Bank of Covington. Pictured from left to right are John T. Garner, cashier; Edna Locke, bookkeeper; John R. Sloan; and Jim Garner.

1887

June 13: The Farmers & Merchants Bank, Tipton County's first bank, is organized in Covington with a capital stock of $10,000. John A. Crofford is president.

1888

The county's second bank is established in Covington under the name of Farmer's Union Bank. John M. Tipton is president.

The county's first compress, the Covington Compress Co., opens for business.

1889

June 14: Dr. G.B. Gillespie of Covington sails for Europe for study abroad. His itinerary includes study in Berlin, Vienna, Edinburgh and London. In the latter city he will serve as clinical assistant to famed physician Lord Joseph Lister.
*July 6: W.F. Boone & Son of Clinton, Kentucky, signs a contract with the county court to tear down the old courthouse for $500 and to build a new one at a cost of $24,500.
*September 23: The cornerstone of the new courthouse is laid during ceremonies at which C.B. Simonton is principal speaker. Bedded in the stone are several mementoes of the Civil War.

Dr. G.B. Gillespie in 1936, when, at the age of ninety-two, he was the oldest practicing physician in the state of Tennessee.

1890

*May: The new courthouse is complete and formally received by the county. It is judged to be a handsome building with an abundance of room.
*June: Edwin Stoddard, alias Henry B. Davis, is found guilty in circuit court of forging and passing counterfeit checks and is sentenced to a total of six years in the state penitentiary. He boasts, as he is being taken to jail after the trial, that the penitentiary will not hold him long. He will soon make good his boast by forging his way out of prison.
*October: The west side of the square in Covington, having been rebuilt since the fire of '82, burns again.
*October 15: Paine's Opera House, erected by Ebenezer Paine and sons, William and John, is formally dedicated. The imposing red brick building, located on the north side of the square in Covington, has a seating capacity of seven hundred.

1891

June: A log wagon, drawn by six mules and carrying a cannon taken from Fort Pillow, arrives on the square in Covington. Plans call for the old gun to rest beside a monument to be built in honor of the county's Confederate dead.

The "first Fort Pillow cannon," mounted beside the Confederate monument, is pictured here in a 1904 view. A similar gun from Fort Pillow was later mounted on the other side of the monument.

1892

*L.D. Hamner, retired from active newspaper management since 1888, returns to Mason, where his career began, and establishes the *True Light*.

1894

*James E. Caldwell of Nashville, president of the Cumberland telephone Company, appoints Cecil McFadden manager of the county's first telephone exchange.

Covington gets electric lights when, with the blessings of the city fathers, John Craig constructs a light plant on the Memphis and Paducah Railroad on the west side of town.

1895

May 29: A monument dedicated to the memory of the Confederate soldiers of Tipton County is unveiled on the south lawn of the courthouse

Lieutenant George L. Shelton, *right*, poses with a fellow officer of the 2nd Tennessee Volunteers at Camp Meade. September 29, 1898.

in Covington. A crowd estimated at between thirty-five hundred and five thousand people attend the ceremony.

1896

January 11: Route 1, Atoka, Tennessee, is established. It is one of only three such routes in the United States which the Postal Service has set up for the purpose of experimenting with a new system—rural free delivery.

1898

April 30: Company I, 2nd Tennessee Infantry, raised in Covington for service in the war with Spain, entrains in Memphis for Camp Meade, Pennsylvania. Major M.A. Walker of Covington is company commander; Captain James E. Walker, second in command; Frank J. Krodel and George L. Shelton, lieutenants; and John Russell, C.B. McClelland, Pat Murphy and William D. Gee, sergeants.

*June: Shirley Fisher, who came to Tipton County as a slave in 1823, dies at his home in Covington at an age believed to be near the century mark.

Pat Haynis's Barroom, shown in 1900, was one of ten saloons closed in Covington in 1903 by the senate bill repealing the charter of Covington. Pictured here, *left to right*, are D.H. Lauderdale, J.R. McCall, Henry Hewitt, Dick Frazier and Jud Warmath.

1903

March 19: In a legal move to abolish all old, outdated laws and remove them from the city records of Covington, the state senate passes a bill repealing the charter of Covington and all acts passed by the mayor and board of aldermen. Another bill is then passed to reincorporate the town.
April 15: The senate bills passed on March 19 to rid Covington of outdated laws go into effect. Nothing is changed except that old, unwanted ordinances are no longer in effect. No longer is it a crime, carrying the same penalty as that for operating a house of ill fame, for a person to play cards or billiards on Sunday.

1904

The Covington Milling Company, Inc. begins operations in a new building with new equipment. B.B. Boyd is in charge of the facility, located on a railroad side track on East Pleasant Street.

View, looking west, of the Covington Milling Company.

1905

April 14: Munford, named for R.H. Munford, a prominent citizen of the county and one of its early settlers, is incorporated. Its first mayor is S.H. Bass. Other municipal officers include J.C. Harris, recorder and treasurer; D.F. Crigger, marshal; and J.S. Dickason, magistrate.

*October 10: Despite the tireless efforts of his attorneys to gain him clemency, convicted murderer John Hill is hanged in the yard of the county jail, thus becoming the last person to be legally hanged in Tipton County.

1906

*February: The old hand-drawn cart of the Covington Fire Department is replaced by a one-horse fire wagon.

1908

The Tipton County Bank, formed in 1904, is merged with the Farmers & Merchants Bank. The new organization will carry the former's name.

William Green Hill, the central figure in Frances Boyd Calhoun's novel.

1909

*February 6: Frances Boyd Calhoun's novel, *Miss Minerva and William Green Hill*, is published by Reilly & Britton Co. of Chicago.
February 22: The courthouse tower is blown down by a tornado that strikes Covington during the night.

1913

January: The Farmers Union Bank and the Tipton County Bank are merged under the name Tipton County Farmers Union Bank. The new institution is under the management of John T. Garner, president.
March 19: Randolph is reincorporated, though many insist that there is nothing left to incorporate but a hope.
September 17: Brighton is incorporated as a town in a private act passed by the 58th General Assembly of Tennessee.

Chronology

The courthouse tower lies shattered on the lawn as curious onlookers survey the damage done by the twister, which visited Covington on Washington's birthday.

1914

William Jennings Bryan makes a speech in the courthouse yard championing the candidacy for Tom C. Rye for governor.

*August 5: After nearly twenty years, Glenn Springs is formally opened again by Dr. A.B. Blaydes of Atoka. The forty-year-old physician and spa enthusiast hopes to revive interest in the once thriving resort.

*November: The Mason Telephone Exchange begins operation with G.W. Marsh, the former postmaster, in charge.

1916

*June 19: The 1st Tennessee National Guard Regiment, whose ranks include a number of Tipton Countians, is called up to participate in General John J. Pershing's attempt to capture the Mexican rebel Pancho Villa.

Randolph at the time of its reincorporation in 1913.

1917

June 22: The town of Mason enjoys for the first time the convenience of an electrically lighted city. W.E. Frawley, one of Mason's leading citizens, is owner of the light plant.

*June 29: R.H. Green, owner of the *Tipton Record*, announces the sale of that paper to the *Covington Leader*. Green, having been appointed Covington postmaster, feels that the duties of that job will prevent him from giving the time necessary to continue the successful publication of the newspaper.

*September: The first of Tipton County's registrants to be called into active service under the new Selective Service Act leave for Camp Gordon near Atlanta.

*December: Thomas Lauderdale, Tipton County's last surviving Mexican War veteran, dies at the age of eighty-nine.

1918

*January 12: The Mississippi River at Randolph is frozen so solidly that people are able to walk across the ice to the Arkansas shore and as far down the river as Richardson's Landing, where a large ice gorge has formed.

*February 27: Second Lieutenant Paul C. Calhoun dies suddenly while drilling troops at Camp Wheeler, Macon, Georgia. He is the first Tipton County soldier to lose his life during World War I.

Chronology

*March: A twenty-five-acre field one mile north of Covington is secured as a permanent landing site for student pilots making their first cross-country flights from Park Field near Millington.
*September 29: Sergeant Joseph B. Adkison of Atoka earns the Congressional Medal of Honor with his quick decision and gallantry in action near Bellicourt, France.

1921

February 2: The state legislature abolishes the charter of Randolph, and the once proud little town, which dominated early West Tennessee from its position on the second Chickasaw Bluff, passes into history.
May 25: A fire that threatens the destruction of the entire business section of Mason occurs when an oil stove in H.H. Sanders's barbershop ignites and flames sweep across four brick buildings, leaving them in ashes.

1922

March 24: At a special session of the Covington Board of Mayor and Aldermen, it is decided to have the square paved. The estimated cost of the project is $27,500.
August 16: Ed and John, the horses of the fire department that have galloped to the rescue of so many burning buildings in Covington before the arrival of the town's first fire engine, are themselves burned to death in a fire that destroys the city barn.

1925

The Munford Savings Bank & Trust Co., established in 1904, is merged with the Citizens Bank & Trust Co., established in 1918. The institution is now called the Munford Union Bank.
June 22: The Knights of the Ku Klux Klan of Covington stage a dress parade through the streets of the city, presenting for the first time such a demonstration in Tipton County. Dressed in white robes and carrying flaming torches, the silent marchers present quite a spectacle to the hundreds of onlookers who line the streets through which the demonstration is staged.

The paving of the square in Covington in 1922.

1926

Having first been elected in 1918, William A. Owen is reelected judge of the Court of Appeals of the State of Tennessee.

1927

March: A new town is springing up at the Munford-Atoka crossroads. Filling stations are already being erected on two of the choice corner lots. Just what the new town is to be named has not yet been determined, but the people of the neighborhood seem to prefer to call it Crosstown.

1928

January 23: A resolution is introduced before the county court that authorizes the court to appoint a committee to have the tower of the courthouse torn away and other necessary improvements made to the top

Judge William A. Owen.

of the building to fill the resulting hole. It is pointed out that the tower is dangerous, having caused cracks in the wall over the judge's bench. After much discussion, a vote on the matter is called, and the resolution passes by a vote of twenty-four to eleven.

*April 21: A tornado enters the county in the neighborhood of Tipton and travels in a northeasterly direction through Atoka. The entire business district of the little town is leveled by the twister. In just four minutes, the work of thirty years is undone.

1929

*April 1: Covington's first talking picture, *The Barker*, makes its debut at a newly decorated Palace Theatre.

*April 16: The new Jeff Davis Highway bridge over the Obion River is named in honor of congressional Medal of Honor winner, Joseph B. Adkison of Atoka.

*June 30: Harvey "Gink" Hendrick of Covington, first baseman for the Brooklyn Dodgers, is leading the National League in hitting with a .410 average.

October 1: the Tipton County Department of Health is organized from funds made available by the Tipton County Court and the State Department of Public Health. The staff consists of Dr. A.J. Butler, medical director; Bessie Morse, public health nurse; W.B. Holmes Jr., sanitary officer; and Elise Portis, clerk.

1930

March 26: L.E. Gwinn, Covington attorney, issues a formal announcement of his candidacy for the Democratic gubernatorial nomination. He will oppose Governor Henry H. Horton in the August primary.

June 27: A crowd fills the circuit courtroom of the courthouse to hear an old-time Democratic speech by Cordell Hull, candidate for the United States Senate. Hull is introduced in a brief but fitting speech by a comrade of the Spanish-American War, Major M.A. Walker.

August 7: L.E. Gwinn loses in his bid for the Democratic gubernatorial nomination. He does, however, best Governor Horton in Tipon County by garnering 3,282 votes to Horton's 349.

1933

February 1: Dr. Ulys R. Webb of Covington, who entered the navy as an assistant surgeon on October 11, 1901, is promoted to rear admiral, MC, USN.
*May 7: Following a period of almost midnight darkness, a cloud bank forms over the central part of the county, and out of it comes one of the deadliest twisters the county has ever seen. After touching down just south of Brighton, the rapidly revolving funnel cuts a fifteen-mile-long swath through the heart of the county to the vicinity of Charleston, where the greatest damage and loss of life is recorded.
*September 25: George "Machine Gun" Kelly visits Covington. The FBI's most wanted criminal stops in his flight from the law long enough to drink a few beers at a local restaurant.

1936

*July: The luxurious Ruffin Theatre opens in Covington. It occupies the site of the old Palace Theatre, which burned to the ground on January 29.
*August: The annual Confederate reunion, held each year at Brighton, is canceled, despite elaborate plans, because of a polio outbreak in the county.

1937

*May: The Ruffin Amusement Company, with headquarters in Covington, enlarges its chain of movie theatres with the purchase of the Chickasaw Amusement Company, a concern operating theatres at Humbolt and Milan.

1938

*August 11: The Confederate reunion at Brighton is revived. New attractions include a movie and a softball game.
*November 4: Leonidas Polk Marshall, the county's lone surviving Confederate veteran, dies at the age of ninety-five.

Major M.A. Walker at the time of the Spanish-American War.

*November 11: A poignant touch is added to the Armistice Day Parade in Covington—a riderless black horse, decorated with Confederate banners and bearing a Confederate sword, is led in memory of Leonidas P. Marshall, who was a regular participant in the annual parades.

1939

*March 18: Covington's new dial telephone system is inaugurated in simple ceremonies held in the new telephone office on Washington Avenue.

1940

July 11: The Pure Oil Company begins the drilling of a test well on the Rob Roy McGregor farm three and a half miles north of Covington on

L.P. Marshall, the horseman on the left, is pictured here as a participant in the 1926 Armistice Day Parade.

the Flatiron Road. Several oil companies are leasing land from Tipton County north to Reelfoot Lake. Predictions by state geologists are that West Tennessee may become one of the major oil-producing areas of the United States.

July 25: The *Covington Leader* reports that "Tipton County's oil bubble has burst into more pieces than a boardinghouse pie." Whatever the Pure Oil Company wanted to know, it has found out in record time. Drilling operations have stopped, and the drilling crews have returned to Illinois.

*August 8: The Confederate reunion at Brighton is held for the last time. The reason for its demise, lack of interest, no doubt is caused by the passing from the scene of all the county's Confederate veterans.

1941

*Henry Theis, a fisherman, discovers the charred remains of a steamboat that has washed out beneath the bluff at Randolph. The remains are probably that of the *Mississippi*, which sank in 1846 under very unusual circumstances.

Chronology

1942

*February 28: Sanford Farris Ray becomes Tipton County's first casualty of World War II when he goes down with one hundred officers and men aboard the destroyer *Jacob Jones*, torpedoed off Cape May, New Jersey.
*November: Richard B. Baptist, who has been elected and reelected judge of the 16th Judicial Circuit of Tennessee without opposition since 1918, is appointed judge of the Court of Appeals of the State of Tennessee.

1943

August 16: Private First Class Elbert Keel of Atoka fires a shot in Sicily that makes headlines around the world. He has the distinction of firing the first American shell at Italy proper following the fall of Sicily to Allied forces.
*October 10: The USS *Cates*, a navy destroyer escort built by the Tampa Shipbuilding Company, is christened in honor of Seaman William F. Cates, who died at his gun aboard the cruiser *San Francisco* in battle off the Solomon Islands in November, 1942. The twenty-three-year-old Drummonds native has been cited posthumously by President Roosevelt for his "extraordinary courage" in the engagement.

1944

*February: The navy launches the USS *Naifeh* at Orange, Texas. The destroyer escort vessel is named in honor of Lieutenant Alfred Naifeh, a Covington native who gallantly died in line of duty on October 16, 1942.

1945

May 8: With all Covington business houses closed in celebration of VE Day, the Reverend Paul E. Sloan conducts a thanksgiving prayer service on court square. The program is well attended as is another later that morning at the First Presbyterian Church. The latter, under the auspices of the Covington Pastor's Association, is presided over by the Reverend E.F. McDaniel.
September 5: A broken rail on the southbound Illinois Central Railroad track at Rialto causes the derailment of thirty-three freight cars. In the

center of the wreck, cars are piled three deep with some turned crossways of the track. About half of the cars are damaged beyond repair.

1946

*June 27: The War Department releases the first consolidated listing of army dead and missing in World War II. It shows that forty-nine Tipton Countians have died while wearing the uniform of the army of the United States.
October 19: The City Bus Company of Covington owned and operated by Exum and Charlie Fisher and F.R. Fisher Jr. begins service. The bus makes three routes every hour from 7:00 a.m. until 11:00 p.m. Fares are ten cents for adults and five cents for children.
December 31: The Fisher brothers announce the termination of their bus service in Covington. The town is not able to support the high costs of operating the line.

1947

*June 26: Recently released figures by the Navy Department are made public and show that Tipton Countians serving in navy, marine corps or coast guard operations during World War II suffered a total of eighteen casualties. The figure represents six killed, eleven wounded and one captured and later released.
August 4: Company M, Tennessee National Guard, Tipton County, takes an initial step toward reality with the signing of the first enlisted man in the unit, Roy Arthur of Munford. Alvin Byars will be the commanding officer of the unit with the rank of captain, and William Bibb will be the executive officer with the rank of first lieutenant. Company M will be the first guard unit in the county since 1897.

1953

August 20: It is learned that Major Edward L. Lindsey of Munford was one of the army officers who helped prepare papers for the Korean truce negotiations.
September 4: Late television and radio newscasts announce the release by the communists of Master Sergeant Edward A. Pickard of Munford, the

only man of Tipton County origin listed as a Korean prisoner of war. News of Pickard's release comes following the next-to-last exchange of prisoners in "Operation Big Switch."

1954

July 1: Representative Pat Sutton gains the distinction of being the first man ever to land a helicopter in the city limits of Covington. Campaigning for the senate seat held by Senator Estes Kefauver, Sutton sets down in his flying machine behind the Hotel Lindo after making an unsuccessful pass at the square.

1955

*January: Leigh Snowden of Covington is signed to a long-term movie contract by Universal International Studios. She will get to work immediately on her first movie, *All that Heaven Allows*.
March 3: The *Covington Leader* reports that Jack Sallee, a twenty-three-year-old Covington songwriter, has hit the big time with his first publication. The song, "You're a Heartbreaker," which was recorded by Elvis Presley at Sun Recording Co. in Memphis, is near the top of the record charts.
*October 30: Ina Poindexter is presented to the nation on television's *Variety Hour* as one of the thirteen most promising Hollywood starlets for 1956. Her selection by screen producers and directors gives her an inside track in the race for movie stardom.

1958

June 6: In celebration of the centennial of St. Matthew's Episcopal Church in Covington, the cornerstone, which bears the date 1858, is opened. It produces a Bible, a prayer book, an almanac, a bundle of papers and four coins—a penny, a three-cent piece, a half dime and a dime.

1960

April 18: Edith Cockrill, a native of Covington, becomes the first woman ever to serve as a hearing examiner for the Federal Interstate

Chronology

Left: Rear Admiral Langdon C. Newman.
Right: Dr. Thomas High Price as he looked at the start of his medical career.

Commerce Commission. She is a former Juvenile Court judge for the District of Columbia, having served in that capacity from August 1949 to May 1957.

August 9: Captain Langdon C. Newman, MC, USN, commanding officer of the Naval School of Aviation Medicine, is approved by President Eisenhower for promotion to the rank of rear admiral. The Covington native has been in the navy since 1931.

1962

*John Cullum Wilson of Covington is elected executive vice-president of the American Red Cross by the Board of Directors with responsibility for the operation of the total organization.

December 8: Dr. Thomas High Price, who has been the only black physician in the county for most of his sixty years of practice, dies at the age of eighty-nine. Price Terrace, a federal housing project in Covington, was named in his honor in 1960.

1965

*The *Covington Leader*, whose ownership has remained in local hands since its founding in 1886, is sold to a new corporation, the Covington Publishing Co.

1967

July 1: Mark A. Walker, who has served since August 1, 1946, as circuit judge, 16th Judicial Circuit of Tennessee, is appointed judge of the Court of Criminal Appeals of the State of Tennessee.

1971

*July 1: William F. Bringle, a native of Covington who attained the rank of rear admiral in the navy on January 1, 1964, and the rank of vice admiral on November 6, 1967, is promoted to admiral.

1972

April 10: Covington-born Issac Hayes wins the Academy Award in Hollywood for the best original song for a film for 1971—the theme for the movie *Shaft*.

Notes

THE EARLY YEARS

1. F.D. Robertson, Paper from Tennessee Historical Collection, 2 June 1857, Box R2 No. 138R, Tennessee State Archives, Nashville.
2. Ibid.
3. Ibid.
4. *Randolph Recorder*, December 4, 1835.
5. Ibid., June 10, 1836.

COMMUNICATIONS

6. *Randolph Recorder*, June 21, 1834.
7. *Randolph Whig*, April 7, 1838.
8. Ibid.
9. *Tipton Weekly Record*, December 17, 1875.
10. *Tipton Record*, June 29, 1917.

THE MEXICAN FOE

11. *Tipton Record*, May 16, 1888.
12. Ibid.
13. E.G. Littlejohn, *Texas History Stories* (Richmond, VA: B.F. Johnson Pub. Co., 1901), 207.

14. Thos. H. Bell, *A Narrative of the Capture and Subsequent Sufferings of the Mier Prisoners in Mexico, Captured in the Cause of Texas, Dec. 26th, 1842 and Liberated Sept. 16th, 1844* (Waco, TX: Reproduced by Texian Press, 1964), 39. Bell was one of the captives.

The Civil War

15. R.H. Munford, *Historical Sketch of Tipton County, Tenn.*, 1876, Tennessee Historical Collection, Mis. MSS. File, Box T2: No. 67, Tennessee State Archives, Nashville.

16. T.J. Walker, "Reminiscences of the Civil War," 1905, MS, University of Tennessee at Martin.

17. Ibid.

18. *Covington Leader*, June 15, 1895.

19. *Tipton Weekly Record*, June 4, 1875.

20. *Covington Leader*, June 8, 1895.

21. Walker, "Reminiscences."

22. *Covington Leader*, June 15, 1895.

23. Walker, "Reminiscences."

24. *West Tennessee Whig*, June 7, 1861.

25. *Covington Leader*, June 22, 1895.

26. Ibid.

27. Ibid.

28. Munford, *Historical Sketch*.

29. *The War of the Rebellion: A Compilation of the Official Records of the Union and Confederate Armies*, Series I, Vol. 17, Part I, 145. (This compilation is hereafter cited as O.R.).

30. Ibid., Part II, 236.

31. Ibid.

32. Ibid., Series I, Vol. 17, Part I, 145.

33. Ibid., Series II, Vol. 5, 821.

34. Ibid., Series I, Vol. 17, Part I, 797.

35. Ibid., Vol. 24, Part I, 424.

36. Ibid., 426.

37. Ibid., Series I, Vol. 39, 815.

38. Walker, "Reminiscences."

39. Ibid.

40. James Alexander Moore papers, December 23, 1920, MS.

41. *Covington Leader*, October 20, 1938.

42. Ibid.

43. *Tipton County Minute Book F* (Nashville, TN: Works Progress Administration, 1937–1941), 343.
44. Ibid.
45. *Covington Leader*, February 17, 1927.
46. Ibid.
47. Ibid.
48. Ibid.
49. Ibid.
50. Ibid.
51. Munford, *Historical Sketch*.
52. *Washington Post*, December 3, 1890.

Days of Desperate Men

53. *Memphis Bulletin*, April 19, 1865.
54. U.S. Navy Department, *Official Records of the Union and Confederate Navies in the War of the Rebellion*, Series I, Vol. 27, 148.
55. *O.R.*, Series I, Vol. 49, Part I, 406.
56. Ibid.
57. Ibid., 442.
58. *Covington Leader*, February 17, 1927.
59. *Memphis Bulletin*, May 12, 1865.
60. *Memphis Argus*, May 19, 1865.

Reunion and Dedication

61. *Tipton Weekly Record*, October 6, 1876.
62. *Memphis Public Ledger*, September 23, 1876.
63. Ibid.
64. *Covington Leader*, August 5, 1892.
65. *Memphis Commercial Appeal*, July 30, 1896.
66. From the poem "Heroes in Gray" written for the dedication of the Confederate monument in Covington, May 29, 1895, by Vivian Poindexter and read by her at the ceremony.
67. *Covington Leader*, May 31, 1895.
68. Ibid.

Amusements

69. *Munford Times*, September 1, 1906.
70. Ibid.

71. *Covington Leader*, May 15, 1947.
72. Ibid., June 21, 1934.
73. Ibid., April 15, 1937.
74. Ibid., May 28, 1942.

The Courthouse and the Courts

75. C.B. Simonton Papers.
76. *Covington Leader*, May 9, 1890.
77. Ibid.
78. C.B. Simonton Papers.
79. Ibid.
80. Judge W.A. Owen, "Do You Remember?" *Covington Leader*, September 17, 1931.

The World Wars

81. *Memphis Commercial Appeal*, November 11, 1951.
82. *Covington Leader*, July 1, 1965.
83. Ibid.
84. *Covington Leader*, October 5, 1944.
85. *Liberty Magazine*, June 26, 1943.

Disaster Years

86. *Tipton Weekly Record*, May 28, 1875.
87. *Covington Leader*, September 27, 1923.
88. *Randolph Recorder*, April 10, 1835.
89. *Covington Leader*, May 11, 1933.

Tipton County's Own

90. *Covington Leader*, June 30, 1911.
91. Ibid.
92. Ibid., July 2, 1931.
93. Ibid.
94. Pamphlet, "The Publisher's Story of Miss Minerva and William Green Hill" (Chicago, IL: Reilly & Britton Co., 1909).
95. *Covington Leader*, October 27, 1932.
96. Pamphlet, "The Publisher's Story."
97. Ibid.

98. Ibid.
99. *Covington Leader*, March 21, 1924.
100. *Atlanta Journal*, July 6, 1926.
101. *Covington Leader*, Sept. 7, 1944.
102. Navy Office of Information, Biographies Branch (01-0111), Washington, D.C.

About the Author

Gaylon N. Beasley holds a master of arts degree from Memphis State University. A native of Covington, Tennessee, he now lives and teaches in Memphis. *True Tales of Tipton* is Mr. Beasley's first book.

Please visit us at
www.historypress.net